UNDERTOW:

SURVIVING THE PREDATORY PSYCHIATRIST

A Memoir

by

Trudy Seagraves

Library of Congress Cataloging-in-Publication Data
Seagraves, Trudy
Undertow: Surviving the Predatory Psychiatrist, a Memoir
by Trudy Seagraves
Covers designed by branchartstudios@yahoo.com
LCCN 2013910367

ISBN-10 1489568018
ISBN-13 9781489568014
CreateSpace Independent Publishing Platform
North Charleston, South Carolina

Author's note: This book includes references and bibliography but in no way endorses the resources herein. To protect family, friends, coworkers, former therapists and physicians, and other patients of Harry Brown, names have been changed, except those of well-known persons, Arms Acres, Cliggott Publishing, my attorneys, teachers, and the dogs.

Dedication

To all victims of abuse, and their often confused and distressed loved ones, I humbly offer my story. Perhaps it will bring clarity, comfort, and the assurance that full recovery is possible. With immense gratitude, I thank Connie Janssen, Devera Black, and Joanna Rosen. My heartfelt gratitude, also, to the many writing friends who critically read my manuscript in its many iterations: Diana Holdsworth, Posey Armistead, Yuko Iida Frost, John Edel, Geordie Edel, Nancy Burger, Bob Tedeschi, Sheila Kohler, Lennie Levine, Hewitt Schlereth, Beth Bruno, Rasma Belte.

We cannot direct the wind, but we can adjust the sails.
—Bertha Calloway

Table of Contents

Chapter 1—Nightmares

ALARMED AT FINDING HERSELF ALONE ON A DARK street in a bad neighborhood, she rushes, head down, strangely oblivious to the man stalking her, even now only steps away.

From afar, I see what's bound to happen and yell, "Run!" but she ignores me, and worse, swings into a dim alley.

"Don't!" I scream.

Helplessly, I watch a thin young man with fair skin and black hair creep over her, as if a huge spider. Why doesn't she scream? *Why*?

Silently and ritualistically—for he is in no hurry now—he positions her for what he must do. They move in tandem, in known ways, and it seems to me a dance: he, the leader; she, plastic and obedient. Her face, ghostly in the moonlight, is carefully composed to reveal nothing of fear.

Finished—the rape takes only minutes—the man swipes the back of his hand across his mouth. "I have to get home to my wife. There's a problem there." He smiles. "I'd like to see you again."

She looks away, ashamed.

⸻

I am the paralyzed dreamer floating above, until the alarm jolts me from sleep. I hurry through my shower and pull on sweats. Still savaged by the dream, I hang my office clothes in the car and am soon speeding north on the Merritt Parkway for an early appointment with my psychiatrist.

It's a cold, clear March morning, 1985. The hills of southeastern Connecticut are pocked with snow, denuded trees stiff and sparse as an old man's beard. I pray Harry James Brown, MD, has the key to unlock these night terrors and free me. Too much to ask? Maybe. I'm fifty-three and, over the years, have been in therapy far too often. Yes, I've gained self-knowledge and some wisdom, but no relief from my nightmares.

For five months, I've been seeing Harry once a week, and the dreams are more intense, worse when I fall asleep on my back. Then, I'm overrun by phantasms of men breaking into my bedroom to rape and kill. I try to see this exacerbation as progress, to appreciate that the intensity of the work, especially now that Harry has me doing hypnotherapy, is bringing my issues to the surface. And isn't that what I want, what I tell him I want?

Despite the nocturnal stigmata pointing homeward, every therapist I ever saw over many years insisted that my father did not try to kill much less rape me.

Besides, I know the worst about my father and have never dodged it. Hateful, yes, and violent, a man who shot our neighbor's cat, skinned it, fashioned a hat out of it, and wore it tail down for years—for fun. If one's most evil deed—and I doubt that was his—defines one, Hal Seagraves is an awful man.

Tired of laying all my problems at my father's feet, I'm also impatient with revisiting the early years with a distracted mother and contentious elder sister. With four emancipated children, it's embarrassing to still need therapy, to never have mastered the anxieties that spook my days and the terrors that sear my nights.

I'm not bringing resistance. It's too late for that. I have no untold stories, past or current, no secrets, not anymore, except…that's not entirely true. There's one secret I keep from Harry. It concerns his wife.

The therapist I'd been seeing, the one who referred me to Harry Brown, proved unable to help my husband of a year and me with our marriage, describing it as a two-step dance: when one of us moved closer, the other backed away. For Eileen, that pattern suggested that something deeper blocked my progress.

"If anyone can access it, Harry Brown can," she said. "He's a therapist's therapist. We all go to him. Take it as a compliment if he's willing to fit you in."

I'd heard his name. When you've lived, as I have, nearly all your life in southern Fairfield County, it can be a small community. The New Age had hit Westport hard, and Harry Brown was known for enthusiastic championing of esoteric spiritual systems, eager to share information on psychic surgeries, past-life regressions, the teachings of Gurdjieff, and the like. A friend to many local traditional and nontraditional therapists, Harry spread the word on the values of high colonics, channeling, reading auras, shiatsu massage, MariEL and Reiki healing, tantric sex.

We were pilgrims rushing to buy *The Aquarian Conspiracy*, hoping to learn where we'd been and where we ought to go. I knew of more than one person booking trips to the Himalayas. I knew of others signing up for a month or six at Kripalu, a yoga institute in Massachusetts, where guests wear white cotton socks instead of shoes, eat vegetarian meals in silence, and study at the feet of the guru, Amrit Desai. I'd been to Kripalu. Twice. Had it been magical thinking to hope the isolation tank or foot reflexology or rebirthing or walking meditations at dawn would set me right?

I thanked Eileen for his number and moved to leave. She put a hand on my arm and impulsively confided that Harry's wife had suffered breast cancer, now metastasized to the brain.

"I don't imagine there's much hope," she said, "but they're doing everything, even traveling to Germany for new treatments. She's so young! And she's beautiful and a beautiful singer, like you."

At work the next day, I looked him up in the library of the medical publishing house in which I am a senior editor. Board certified as an emergency room physician, he was also board-certified in psychiatry and neurology, later specializing in Bioenergetics. He sat on the board of a local school for nontraditional psychotherapy.

As it happens, I'd read much about Bioenergetics, principally through the works of its founder, Alexander Lowen, and his predecessor, Wilhelm Reich.

Driving home after work that evening, I realized I knew Pat Brown and had sung in a few recitals in which she also performed. I recalled finding her beautiful—but on the heels of that, fear washed in, great gobs of it. As soon as I could, I exited the Merritt Parkway and pulled to the side, trembling. Why? Was it that Harry wouldn't have time for me? No. I'd find someone else. Then what? Oh—of course. I swallowed hard and tried not to cry.

Bedridden, bald, and going blind after surgical treatments for "something" in the brain, my mother had died at forty-nine. The loss of her, great as it was—I was only twenty-two—had paled in comparison to the horror of being left with only one parent, *him*.

Eileen meant no harm with her empathic confidence. The result, though, is that every time I run in the side door to Harry's home office, I'm painfully aware that his wife lies suffering in another part of the house, just as my mother lay hobbled and hollow eyed, waiting for me to get home from school and help her bathe, dress, make dinner.

In terms of transference, I know perfectly well that Harry represents my father. It's the wife-mother dying in the other room that devastates me. For some reason, I'm unable or unwilling to tell Harry what I know.

———◦∞◦———

Weaving north on the parkway, I'm thankful Harry understands my issues with men and still astounded at how skillfully he helped me untie the knot of a brief second marriage. Within three months, he'd led me to a comfortable realization that it could never work. Walter, too, was relieved, which allowed us to stop battening on each other like angry wasps. After Christmas we painlessly divided our few mutual possessions and promised to get a divorce…sometime.

Together, we moved his possessions from my condo in Norwalk to the cozy cottage he'd rented on the Sound in nearby Fairfield. When January bled into March, and I was frequently shattered by the hell of hypnotherapy, I turned more and more often to Walter for comfort. Soon we were spending most weekends together.

———◦∞◦———

I park in Harry's driveway and run through the side door into his rangy colonial, then up two steps into his large office over the garage. When his door stands ajar, as it does today, I'm to go in and wait. I kick off my sneakers and sink bare feet into thick lavender carpet, then tuck myself into a small but deep overstuffed chair facing his, by a large window. The sill, I see, is still cluttered with quartz crystals and small gift boxes that have been there since Christmas.

The glass-topped table between my chair and Harry's is strewn this morning with paper scraps, a personal check face up, three audiocassettes, two mugs of half-finished tea, a bottle of nutrients (C with selenium, this week), and tissues. His ledger checkbook from Westport Bank and Trust is open on the floor, amid a tumble of New Age books and magazines. I often borrow a book or two, still looking for magic through New Age and Eastern philosophies.

Scattered about are pillows of every size. A cluster of chrome and leather chairs occupies the center of the room, and a few have been pushed against one wall. I assume the larger pillows and the chairs are for the classes in Bioenergetics Harry runs for as many as seventeen local psychotherapists.

Under the back window is a double bed occupying a third or a fourth of the width of this generous space. Bioenergetics requires a firm place for patients to flop and kick heels and pound fists, to scream and weep. Some therapists employ a twin mattress on the floor or a sturdy cot. Yes, I'm unnerved by the implications of a real bed, its homely, patterned sheets, pillows, blankets. Yet…it's practical.

I look around the room, aware, as always, of the unboundedness of it all. In the past I'd have fled a therapist with a double bed and crystals, personal effects strewn helter-skelter. But this is *Harry's* room, and I'm beginning to see everything about him through a lens of acceptance and admiration.

And then I notice *Tales of the Sexy Snake*, a new paperback by Jan Kennedy. I borrowed her first book, also on shamanism. She does more than enter altered states: she becomes an animal. She started life as a real-estate agent and sounds eminently sane. All this—the New Age books and crystals—are not only familiar; Harry says they're necessary adjuncts to expanding my life.

I've been admitted to a select group—a family, as it were—of patients privileged to learn from this talented, unconventional human being, a man on a spiritual quest of such high order that ordinary boundaries are unnecessary. If I recognize a name on a check or a scrap of paper, what's the big deal? I have the integrity to protect that patient's anonymity. Harry's inner sanctum is built on trust, his and ours, and I willingly carry this sacred burden. In a peculiar way, I'm glad Harry risks exposure in the sense that he does not hide behind his craft. He speaks freely about himself and others.

I've come to appreciate lying on the bed and kicking hard, pounding fists and screaming, and have availed myself of all Harry's expressive tools. When I end on my back on the floor crying, as I sometimes do, Harry drops down and gathers me in. He'll pull me across his lap, whisper tender ministrations, and tuck my head into his shoulder. Comforted by the sheer bulk of him, for he's more than six feet and heavyset, I'm grateful for solid arms; warm, meaty hands; the silky caress of his gray beard; and especially for those large, brown eyes glistening with empathy and love.

He smells of soap.

When I occasionally question his right to hold me, he counters with outrage. "I train seventeen therapists a week, most of them women, some you *know!*"

And it's true, I do. I also know some of his patients now, and it's reassuring to see him through their shining eyes. These connections started a few months ago, when he suggested I call his patient "B.," a young, unmarried woman having nightmares of early molestation. Who was it? Her father? The male baby-sitter?

"Call her," he said, scribbling her name on a paper scrap. "She's willing to talk to you. I asked her. She's seeing something—I'm not sure—her issues are similar—" He'd waved a hand over to me. "You can help her. You're older and further along. She's pretty frightened. She lives with her father, and I don't think he—" He shook his head. "Let me know what you pick up. You have good instincts."

Networking, he calls it. I gather that Harry believes one gets better faster in community, that sharing similar issues helps alleviate shame and guilt.

When I called patient B. that evening, she was home alone and frightened. I drove to her house and stayed with her. We talked a long time. She wants to be a writer.

As I make new friends with whom I can share my own terrors and never feel ashamed, the standard proscription against connecting one patient with another seems irrelevant, if not foolish. And so, when Harry says, "Just call so-and-so; you have a lot in common," I eagerly follow the rainbow, knowing how much he values my observations.

—∞—

I look up, then, from where I sit waiting in his office, and catch sight of him hurrying across the grass to the front door. He must have run one of his three teenagers to school. I know what it is to rear teenagers without a spouse, and he might as well be doing just that. Soon enough, from the kitchen, I hear the kettle whistling, and smile. He's making tea for us.

While waiting, I turn back to Jan Kennedy's book, but it's a sea of meaningless words. I can't concentrate. As Harry has taught me, I close my eyes and tune in to my body to locate the source. My stomach's fluttery. And, yes, it's fear. Why now? I close my eyes and without willing or wishing instantly see a replay from a few months earlier when Harry wore a midnight blue lounging outfit to my session. Suddenly my cheeks are hot with shame at remembering the difficulty I had in looking elsewhere but at his penis and testicles in bas-relief behind thin velour. Afterward, I did everything in my power to dismiss the incident as a misguided effort to dress casually, comfortably.

He hasn't worn that again, but I must have been worried that he will. If so, don't I have *some* control? I don't have to look. Or maybe he knows full well what thin fabric reveals. Of course, maybe it was a test. Was he stimulating a more intense transference? If so, it's working.

I'm deeply in love.

Chapter 2—Tunneling Into the Past

SOCK FOOTED—NEVER SHOES IN THIS ROOM—AND CLAD IN blue jeans and a red-plaid shirt, Harry swings into the office, brown eyes loving as a mother bear's. He flings the door closed with one hand and with the other holds aloft two steaming cups of Long Life tea.

Although mustached and gray bearded, his face is alive with light. He's beaming. As always, there's a narrow red ribbon around his throat. It looks like frayed seam binding, but I haven't yet got up nerve to ask what it's warding off.

I talk about my week and share the dream that awakened me, while he stares at me with large, limpid eyes. The idea that he isn't listening finally silences me.

He reaches for his tea. "What does the dream remind you of?"

"It's obvious. We were all afraid of my father. I mean, it takes place in Flushing. We lived in an apartment."

"Who else had access to you when you were little?"

"I had constant nightmares as a kid, but I wasn't afraid of anyone except my dad."

"What kind of nightmares?"

"Oh, that's easy." I laugh and tuck bare feet under my hips, hands warm around my mug. "Always the same dream. Not a man, but a car. My father's black Franklin. I'd be playing in the street, and the car would try to run me down. Well, not only the car. I'd see his face through the windshield. I'd wake up screaming and throw up."

He nods and stands. "Let's go there." Padding sock footed to the back of the room, he points to the bed. I lie on my back. He pulls up a chair.

"Imagine you're breathing into my hand." He means the hand stroking my waist.

Breathing deeply, eyes closed, works magic. As he's taught me to do, my conscious mind, my intention, directs me to fall as deeply as possible into the unconscious. I want to *see* the dream, get inside it. At first I'm in a dark tunnel. For weeks, now, I've seen my father, a shadow lurking in shadow. When I try to see what he's doing, I tremble so violently that my mind shuts down and the vision vanishes. Today, as I breathe from the belly, I hear myself whimper involuntarily. I'm afraid of the swirling tunnel: I know who awaits me.

"Breathe," Harry commands.

One really deep exhalation flings me into a dim room. "He's there!" I grab Harry's arm. My head flies back and I choke, lips splitting open.

Harry murmurs soothingly and wipes my tears.

"I'm *sick*."

"I know. Breathe into my hand." The hand on my abdomen.

I draw my knees up, but my father still lurks in shadow. A thin, young voice—my child voice—speaks into the tunnel. "Daddy, why did you come into me?"

Horrified, I shake my head, as if that will negate what I just blurted. Eyes open, I prop myself on an elbow. "I'm gagging, so oral sex, Harry, and I get it, believe me. But I know he would never do that. Never."

My father is a prude—oral sex with a child?—an attorney whose portrait in oil hung in the most prestigious patent-law firm in the world. This one-time trial lawyer, if present, would be outraged at my accusations and could discredit me in seconds.

And then, unbidden, a shocking recollection, long buried. "Harry, I know who it is! And it's not my father. A long time ago—oh, I must have been four or five—a man did something awful to me. *That's* the man in the shadows triggering the gagging."

To remember most clearly, I lie back and close my eyes. "When I was little, maybe five, I found myself led by the hand of a strange man into a basement. It has to have been the apartment house in Flushing, because it was a janitor. I don't know how I got away from my mother or why I was in the cellar of this big apartment building. It's weird.

"Suddenly it goes dark and I'm scared. Obviously, he hit the light switch. Next I know he's wrapping my fingers around his penis, and it's sticking straight out. I don't understand sex or erections, or any of that, of course, but I'm terrified. We're right in front of the furnace, flames licking the grill. When the lights go on, his pants are zipped, like nothing happened. I almost can't believe anything did happen—until he grips my neck and shoves my face up to furnace. I can still see the round door. It's plenty big enough to shove me in. He opens it, and the heat blasts out, but I don't dare make a sound."

Now, my heart is pounding. I'm sick to my stomach.

"Don't stop."

"Shit, Harry. All right. He—he grabs my arm. 'Ya see the flames?' That's what he says, all friendly, like he only wants to show me how furnaces work. I get the message. I see his face perfectly. His eyes are black and crafty. He has this dead-white skin and thin, black hair. Oh, my God. Oh, *no*. It *is* my father."

My head flies back, lips stretch taut, and fluid floods my throat. Blindly, I reach for Harry to keep me from plunging deeper into the hole in time gaping beneath me.

He takes me in his arms. "Sing ah," he whispers.

When I can stop sobbing, I join him in exhaling deep-toned ahs. Gradually my head, neck, and shoulders soften, and my breasts, warm against his chest, fill with comfort.

When he moves back to his chair, I open my eyes.

"Look at me, Trudy."

I can't. I turn away. The furnace in our first house had a round door. It wasn't our apartment in Flushing. There was no basement; the heat was piped in from Manhattan. It wasn't any janitor. I was five the year we moved to Manhasset.

"Trudy, look at me. He's not here."

I can't. I ache for my mother and her arms around me, her soft breasts. I want my mother, not Harry. Where is she? Where *was* she?

As fast as possible I want to rid myself of the man in the shadows, walk out of Harry's office dressed for work, and regain the feeling of a competent editor ready for whatever the day brings.

I try to grin, as if to say, *Let's seal this up, bury it, or I can't get through the day.* I sit. I rub my arms to bring feeling into them. Finally I stand and grab my sneakers. I'm in a hurry to get out of here.

At the door, he gathers me into his broad chest and full, soft body and tenderly pats my head into his shoulder.

***

An hour later I dump my briefcase in my office and duck into the ladies' room to load on rouge and eyeliner. I must look as bad as I feel. But, no—I look the way I always do. How can that be? And yet haven't I taken pride in presenting a serene face to the world? Or is it a mask?

"Not bad for fifty-three," I tell the fair-skinned, slender woman in the mirror, glad to have inherited naturally curly auburn hair, green-blue eyes, and unlined English skin from my mother. It always amazes me that I'm still pretty. When I was growing up, women my age were plump, gray, and dowdy. That I am not, that the shameful wounds of a hidden life don't show, will help carry me through the day.

I pick up a manuscript scheduled for publication in one of the monthly medical journals my company circulates and don't stop pencil editing until I realize I'm starving. It's only eleven. I stretch, get up, and go looking for Michelle. "How about it? Anyone going out?"

"Not I, said the little red hen."

We chuckle. "You brought your lunch, you fink."

"I did, I did, indeed, but Sheila's going to town. She's picking up new eyeglasses." Town, or the main street of Greenwich, is a few miles from our building. Sheila's favorite restaurant is a patisserie serving elegant meats and cheeses on croissants. I can just about taste the imported ham, the creamy brie.

Michelle and Sheila are two of our senior editors with whom I've worked many years. We're close, content with one another. I head for Sheila's office, but my boss, Sarah, stops me in the hall.

"I was just coming over. Dick wants us in the conference room at noon. He's ordered—" she says, and stops. We smile knowingly. Our beneficent president orders in generously, very generously. This will be an impromptu lunch meeting for the senior staff.

Too hungry to last another hour, I head for the managing editor's office, pause to make sure he isn't on the phone, and load my palms from his candy bowl. "Oh, the candy man, the candy man. See you at noon. Anything special you want me to bring?"

"I'd like you to bring the pictures you want for Photo Clinic the next four months. Harlan got a call from Greenblatt wanting to know why we haven't published him lately. See if you can do that."

"Gotcha," I say, heading back to my room. It's only then I think to check my desk calendar, and sure enough, I've booked lunch. Twelve o'clock, Dan's birthday. I give my old friend and former lover a call to reschedule, and wish him a happy birthday.

For a moment, then, I stall out. When I'm away from totally engaging work—the editing—or chitchat with coworkers and bosses, I begin to obsess about Harry and the bed, my flashbacks and intuition. I grab my watering can and head for the kitchen. Monday is take-care-of-my-plants day. It's also the day we editors are meant to peruse the many current medical journals circulating through our inboxes. We're challenged to keep abreast of the latest developments. Feeling the way I do, there's no chance I can concentrate on such as the *New England Journal of Medicine* or *JAMA*.

As I feed and soak my peace lily, two jade plants, an African violet, and a pink begonia, and spritz a flourishing fern hanging midwindow above the wide sill, my thoughts turn to Dan. Fine, pale hair frames a long, pale face with a big, straight nose and full, sensual lips. Aegean-blue eyes are ringed with fine laugh lines. This bright, handsome fellow, an artist, is devoted to humor and sex. Since my marriage to Walter, three years earlier, I've hardly seen Dan except around town.

When I scheduled lunch, was I was exploring more than friendship? When I fell in love with Dan, years earlier, I knew he was a womanizer. In fact, he and I long ago acknowledged, even laughed about it, that his behavior suited me and mine, his. It guaranteed a way out of commitment.

Dan's involved now with a woman from his church. If he is the Dan I know, he also sleeps around, including lunchtimes. I used to have nooners with him. If I fan those flames, I'll be the other woman, but I won't be the only other woman, and it's 1985. The sexual freedom of the seventies is gone.

Later in the day, as I drive home to Darien, my thoughts turn again to Dan. What is it I'm really looking for? Beside, Walter and I are still making love...Oh, well, fodder for Harry.

Before I head up to bed, I must check the furnace room behind the garage. All clear. The wooden bar securing the glass slider is in place. After a sweep through three floors, cautiously inspecting every place a man can hide, I fasten my bedroom door with the brass deadbolt my sons installed and check the window nearest the bed to make sure it isn't locked. If I hear someone on the stairs, my plan is to drop to the second-floor deck. I might break an ankle or a leg, but "he" won't get me. Even injured, I can drop another twelve feet to the ground and run and hide, and I'll scream. And scream.

I don't always leave lights glaring in the bathroom, but I know what I'm in for after putting Dan off. Yes, I am better. I separated peacefully from Walter and have the comfort of his sweet nature and safe sex. I'm able to live alone without the Chow Chow I had or a pistol beside my bed, all six cylinders loaded, cocked, and ready to fire (as I had to do in the Darien house after the children left and our old dog died). I'm able to live without a boat siren rigged to my bedroom door, without all the house lights on.

Sometimes I sleep through the night, but only since I turned fifty and moved into this condominium, built like a fortress. I feel safer here than in the Darien house—an abject colonial with flimsy outside doors, a cavern-ous basement with a recalcitrant furnace and ground-floor windows.

Afraid, yes, but improving, I tell myself as I slip into bed. No, wait a minute: all the fear has come up tonight *because* I decided not to pursue sex with Dan, to not give Dan what he wants.

Chapter 3—Ambushed

MARCH IN CONNECTICUT MAY BE BALMY ONE DAY, trees tipsy from sap and ripe with promise, or as chilling as an evil premonition. It's a Sunday late in the month when I head out into a bitter morning that smells faintly metallic; it's near freezing, low, gray clouds drooping like wet velvet draperies. In mittens and a down jacket, I drive to my favorite diner. Cheered by the sweet smell of pancakes and sausage, I drop into a booth and order extravagantly.

Breakfasts were Mother's specialty. That diffident, soft-spoken, tender lady not only fed me well; she rarely sent me on to school if I didn't want to go.

Still in our nightwear, we waited for the Dugan bread man to pound up to the door with his basket of temptations. Pushing the breakfast dishes aside, we feasted, again, on sweet cakes and honeyed tea. My younger brother, Teddy, not a sweet eater, lay spread-eagled on the rug in his Dr. Dentons, quietly brooding over private wars as he pushed trucks and fire engines around.

Mildred June Burnard was born eighth of ten to a capable mother and a gentle Welshman employed by the railroad. With seven elder sisters, I suspect baby Mildred was petted, then ignored when adolescence hit. Regardless, her life changed abruptly when she married my father and they moved from Tacoma to New York City. In his thirties, Hal was the golden man. This slender, handsome, wealthy contender, dashing in English knickers and creamy leather jackets, was an engineer who excelled at golf and wrestling, aced the stock market (before the Crash of '29), and bought a new car every year. In 1900, there were only four hundred gasoline cars. That only twenty-seven years later my father owned a new Tin Lizzy meant he stood high above the crowd.

The joys of Mother's family were making music and being together. They never denied a past without electricity or running water, for there was always enough food and fabric to feed and clothe a family of twelve. Whether hiking Mount Rainier with a picnic or clustered around their upright piano, being in the Burnard clan *was* the party.

With seven elder sisters, perhaps my mother learned joy, but she never learned independence.

Because of her sumptuous voice, she sang church solos from girlhood until the year before she died. My father, an ardent devotee of classical music, uncritically adored her voluptuous mezzo-soprano. After Ann and I came along, nineteen months apart, he bought a concert grand for the three of us.

By the time we were five and six, he started acquiring the first of a half dozen violins, from quarter-sized to full, as we grew, and over the years paid thousands for lessons for all three of us. He took us to countless New York concerts and recitals, bought records by the dozen and all the sheet music and bound editions we ever wanted, cheerfully carrying them home from Schirmer's New York store. How I loved to see that distinctive tan paper bag under my father's arm as he strode into the house.

My sister Ann never blew off practicing our assigned half hours on violin and piano. She never missed school and even skipped a grade. I was the slacker. So was Teddy. Careless and adventuresome—always looking for something to do that was not quite safe—we eagerly broke my father's rules. Although regularly whipped, not terribly hard, with a razor strop or a leather belt, not always for an offense, we kept right on pushing the limits of our world: exploring houses under construction, stealing our neighbor's grapes, holding peeing contests behind Whittlesey's garage (girls against the boys), climbing telephone poles, running along the railroad tracks on the board barely covering the third rail.

Once on a summer's day, Ann and I made sheet tents in the driveway, to play house in, but were careful to put everything away before my father got home—except we forgot an old down pillow. And sure enough, it rained. He found the soggy pillow and ran bellowing through the house, Ann and I screaming denial, never thinking he'd whip the innocent Teddy, crouched under the piano, with the coil of electrical wire he had in hand. Teddy was five.

Those raw, red welts became another bond between my brother and me, for I held him later, while he cried, and comforted him with stolen marshmallows until he slept.

Much later, after we moved to seven acres in Wilton, and I was in sixth grade, our bond led us to cut school and hide in the sheep house of our small farm, smoking corn silk. We hid in the huge sewer pipes under the road to smoke cigarettes, ran around in the dark to peek in neighbors' windows, and three times set deliberate fire to the dry fields between our house and Perkins', next door.

Ann and I played together, but rarely, as time went on. As if Satan throwing spells, my father split us apart from birth, declaring I was bad and she was good. Perhaps our very natures contributed to the rift. I do know

I taunted and she tattled. I rebelled and she dared not. A terminal distrust, finally, rotted the occasional rope one of us threw out to the other.

The good cheer I seek in a syrupy breakfast this chilly Sunday morning is beginning to sicken me. I'm lonely. Walter moved to Fairfield eight or ten weeks ago, and although I see and talk to him often, we haven't made plans for this weekend. Now I miss his knack for unabashedly mothering me. I dash to my car just as the clouds empty and ice water scrims the windshield. Revisiting the past and not ever being able to escape it is doing me in. And I'm furious. I want justice. Revenge.

"Die, you bastard," I howl, as I drive. "You goddamn son of a bitch!" I pound the armrest, the only effigy of my father within reach. Mr. Innocent, natty and confident in his condominium forty miles away, is oblivious to what he did to me, to all of us, his concern only for the sky to clear for golf. His passion. That and the stock market. Mr. Multimillionaire. Not that I'd seen any of the old man's money.

Rage ebbing, and more sad than I remember being, I park in the garage under my living room and trudge slowly upstairs, seeking the consolation of my home, with its graceful Queen Ann furnishings, English chintz, and familiar spicy scent. As I gain the top step and walk into the living room, I suddenly topple over, throwing a hand on the wall. My knees collapse under me, and I slump to the carpeting, plummeting into the tunnel. Darkness falls around me, sucking me down, down, as the demon of my past looms over me and a searing pain rips into my vagina, as if a knife.

Curling around myself, I scream for Harry. And scream.

The act so long denied has ambushed me.

Calling on every reserve, I crawl to the kitchen telephone. I must reach Harry. I leave a message and stumble back to the living room, seeking the rug. I'm five, on all fours. Or a baby. Or eight. Or ten, drowning in the depths of a childhood I do not want to know I had.

Minutes pass, or an hour. I force myself to stand, walk, leave another message. This time, after I hang up, I hear again the clear, young voice: "Why did you come into me?" Afraid of what I might hear next, afraid I'll tumble into a fiery hell from which I cannot ever climb out, I know I can't wait for Harry.

"Walter," I blurt, when he answers the phone. "I'm remembering something my father did, except it's happening in me and all over me. I'm being raped now, *now*, and it's my father." I wipe saliva and tears from my chin. "*He's* doing it, and I can't bear it, and I can't stop it. I can't go on. It's happening now!"

"I hear you, honey. Oh, Lord. What can I do? Tell me!"

"Can you come? Now? *Right* now?"

"I'm on my way!" he shouts. When I move to hang up, I hear him say, as if to himself, "Jesus. I always knew it."

The next week, Harry does not lead me to the bed to address what I'd told him when he finally called me. I think he's afraid. I know I am. And so we drink tea and talk of other things. I've been praying for a warm April, for sun, for anything that signals new life.

Determined to use the hour profitably, I decide to process what's been happening with my best friend, a woman who is far too often arrogant and dismissive toward me. I want to understand what keeps me stuck in wounding and shaming friendships, for she's not the only woman who treats me with disdain.

I pick my way through my last conversation with her, relating it faithfully. Am I off base or is she? Do I take offense too easily? I'm sick of second-guessing relationships. He listens meditatively. His fixed stare unnerves me. Finally, embarrassed, I grow silent. I wait. And wait.

I jump when he throws out his arms. "Do you realize you spent ten minutes talking about this woman? Blow by blow?" He slaps hands on his knees. "And there's all this work to be done."

I drop my eyes. What have I done wrong?

"Trudy, no, look. Look up. Look into my eyes."

Slowly, I obey, as he rolls his chair forward within reach of my fingertips. Eyes and fingers locked, we begin breathing synchronistically. We've done this before. The goal is to clear our chakras by exchanging energies, allowing them to rise to higher levels.

"We have three levels: asleep, awake, or ascended," he often says. "I'm in the awake level. I'm not ascended, but there are moments I reach it."

I was asleep, certainly to whatever is in the tunnel. I'm trying to wake up—to everything. Otherwise, I wouldn't be here. Higher levels? Well, God and Christ, of course. And the Buddha. Whom would Harry pick? His guru, Shyam, the occultist Gurdjieff, and others I have probably never heard of?

Still connected by eyes and fingertips, he starts chanting what sounds like deep vowels and signals me to join him. When he finally stops, he's smiling, obviously pleased with me. I leave, skipping down the steps and over to my car, glad he's not angry at my rant on my shaming friend.

Flattered by the intensity of his attention and alarmed by the sexual feelings it keeps at a pitch, I arrive the following week furious, jaded, and jealous. *What's going on here?*

There's Eileen—beautiful, bright Eileen, who referred me to Harry. If he locks eyes with her, touches her, hugs her, and leans over her on the bed the way he does me, what's to stop them from making love? They're not exactly doctor-patient, are they? They're colleagues. He'd have sex with her if he could.

To lead into the subject, I inject a sly remark insinuating they're sexually involved. Or were.

He stiffens. His eyes narrow and flick away as he begins a story about a trip to a remote island with his wife and children. I dig bare toes into the carpet and push my chair back. I can never understand his stories, but I know this: he's very angry.

"There was only one place to eat on the island," he begins, "and dinner was at six. The line formed outside the dining room, but the maître d' kept us standing—and standing. We could see the buffet was ready. It was crazy making. We got mad. And he got mad."

I push my chair farther back and wrap my arms around my midsection, a heavy pulse ramping up in my chest.

"But here's what I did: I didn't react. Not me. I saw it as a challenge. Each night, I stood at the head of the line so I could draw him out. We became friends." He laughs, amazed and delighted with himself.

"But the others, they went nuts! They said, 'What the fuck is this?'"

I cross my legs and pull my feet under me and scrunch down.

"'What the fuck's going on here?' they said. 'Why is this person jerking us around? What the *fuck* is this?'"

My mind shuts off, and I'm hot with shame. I can't hear. When I dare look, he's stopped talking but is staring me down. And then the rebel in me takes over. Why not ask me why I said it? I'd tell him, I would! If you're so intimate, confiding, and seductive with me, what keeps you from going all the way with others, especially the pretty ones like Eileen?

Or perhaps he isn't seductive with her. She's married.

Grudgingly, I decide he was right not to answer my sly charges. He was using an Ericksonian technique. Milton Erickson was well-known in the fifties for talking in oblique ways to patients, who then responded by dealing positively with unconscious blocks. As Harry explained it, by addressing a patient's unconscious issues vaguely or indirectly, the patient does not defend against change. I don't know anything more about it, except to suspect that Harry's strange tales are intended to teach me lessons. But what lessons?

I leave brooding and full of regret, obsessed with solving the confusion around me. To that end, I find myself rehashing our sessions while driving, in bed, and first thing in the morning—anywhere, anytime I have a moment to myself. Determined to divine what he wants me to do, how he wants me to be, and what he wants me to say or not say, I review every word exchanged and sometimes write them down verbatim, for I must decode the hidden messages. I must figure this out.

How can I ask why he continually invites me to meet him at weekend workshops, when part of me is hungry for attention? Often, he gazes at me as if I were a dreamy scene replete with information only he can decipher. My need to understand him is edging out my interest in other men. Certain that he sees auras in full color, I worry that my body throws off a pulsing red flame more telling of love than anything I dare say.

⁓

The day is soon coming when I'm to attend a five-day workshop I signed up for back in December. Then, I hoped an intense Bioenergetic group experience, under the aegis of Alexander Lowen, world-renowned psychiatrist, author, and founder of Bioenergetics, would move my therapy along by months, if not years. The experiential sessions are for therapists, but others are welcome. The treatment level, to use Harry's favorite, all-purpose word, will be very high.

I had been looking forward to it, for it's taking place the first week in April. Finally spring is here, the earth in thaw. Primrose and daffodils are breaking ground in a tablecloth of soil at my front door. I've noticed mourning doves fashioning a nest on the crossbeam under my back deck, a birthing room safe from hawks. But I don't feel safe, not anywhere, and certainly not safe enough to drive up into New York State to this conference.

I'm too vulnerable now, too uncertain of what may surface. I want Harry to give me permission not to go. When I signed up, I did not know about my father. I bring it up at the top of the hour.

"It's next week. I'm scared," I tell him.

"Why? You've taken Lowen's classes for years."

"Sure, *exercise* classes." Al's wife and sometime coauthor, Leslie, holds the classes. I used to go once a week, as with yoga and Ta'i Chi Chu'an in the past. Harry believes exercising twice will speed our work, and so I go now faithfully to the Lowens' house in New Canaan. Occasionally I see Al there. He and Leslie know I'm Harry's patient. The Bioenergetic world is small. Besides, Al trained Harry. With their wives, the foursome traveled the world introducing Bioenergetic techniques. (Harry, being Harry, has confided more about this unusually gifted and generous couple than I ought to know.)

"Oh, go!" he says. "You don't have to participate. Give it three or four days, get a sense of which leader's safe for you."

"But I'm really scared." Since the episode on my living room floor, I'm terrified of letting a strange therapist get at me.

"I led those workshops all over the world. I was on the international circuit." And then softly, sadly, head drooping, he adds, "I doubt I ever will again."

His wife's terminal cancer, for I know that hospice is there, is affecting his freedom. I sympathize, but I want to talk about *my* fear. I see the stigmata of incest hanging in rotten shreds all over me and still can't believe it happened. I can't. I cling to any competing memory to absolve me. Absolve my own father! Jesus! Everything I have ever known votes against it.

The teeter-totter of knowing–not knowing is almost more destabilizing than if I'd crashed into irrefutable evidence of rape. Do I want to open myself further so far from home? But Harry has no desire to talk through my issues this morning. Yes, I'm mesmerized by frequent tales of his weekends with psychics and healers, flattered he urges me to do the same, indeed invites me to meet him at holistic centers such as Omega, in Rhinebeck, or the Open Center, in Manhattan. I ought to look into nonsurgical surgeries, Eckankar, sweat lodges, high colonics. Any and all spirit-world adventures promise to accelerate our work, deepen me spiritually, and bring me joy.

I want to believe him. I wait for him to tell me not to go. And wait.

Two days before the workshop, Harry astounds me by leading me to the bed. Like a dumb animal, I submit. Within moments, I'm adrift in the tunnel. This time, a child cries, "I'm bleeding!"

No more! Not today. I open my eyes and surface. I try to sit.

Harry commands, "Stay with that!" I pull angrily away. He's not pleased. He's disgusted. I flee, remembering the child's words and hating myself for not staying with the images.

That evening, after inspecting the house and locking my bedroom door, I sit up in bed and write to Harry. He has to know how I feel. I don't think he does.

April 10, 1986

Dear Harry,

Although I know better, today I had the feeling you didn't want to work with me, that you were bored and impatient, because you thought I was exaggerating and hysterical.

I know it's nuts, but I can't stop imagining you have a deal with my father that this information is not to come out, and, if it does, you will simply discredit it, that you believe I'm defective but he isn't. What the hell, even I can't believe I'm saying these things about him. Or about me. It's like finding out I had been adopted.

I can't mail it. It's too crazy. To soothe myself, I mentally spin Harry's therapeutic wheel, praying the spokes—kicking and screaming, hugging and chanting, Ericksonian tales, Bioenergetic workshops—will propel me out of confusion and incest, and into joy.

Chapter 4—Into Madness

I LOVE TO DRIVE. MOVING FAST RELEASES TEARS or joy and either way often leads to song, sometimes entire arias. A phrase from Yum Yum in *The Mikado* runs through my head. I roll it out full voice: "*The sun whose rays are all ablaze with every living glory...*" I climb to the high G, relishing the power of producing a huge and still beautiful sound. As I sing the reprise— "*She don't exclaim, I blush for shame, the moon's celestial highness*"—I open the car windows, glad the power of the sun is behind me, backing me up. More songs, these from *Pinafore*, as anxiety gives way to excitement. I'm lifted, too, by the majesty of undulating hills and valleys greening Route 9 north, in the Empire State, along the Hudson.

People are expanded either by mountains or the sea. For Walter, it's the sea. For me, it's rising ground, whether Mount Rainier or where I live atop a small promontory from which I can see miles across the valley. I call it Hawk Mountain for the brown-tails that chase the crows and turkey buzzards, then dip by my home-office windows on the third floor, urging me to take wing.

An hour later I'm in a conference center/motel in Pauling. Al Lowen opens the workshop. Natty in tweeds and fine leather shoes, he perches on a folding chair, one arm casually draped across the back, one leg crossed daintily over the other. He's surrounded at a cautious distance by a seated semicircle of twenty-six therapists and me—moons to his sun. By volunteering as guinea pigs, these psychotherapists hope to learn how best to incorporate Bioenergetics into their own standard psychotherapy practices. Calling for volunteers, Al selects a woman from many raised hands.

And then, a shock.

I watch in horror as she strips to underpants and bra. No one is surprised. Al asks for comments, tentative diagnoses—and then I understand. If personality blocks are firmly embedded in muscle and sinew, we must be able to see them.

Which type is she? Masochist? Psychopath? Rigid type? Those of us who've read Al's books, and perhaps all of us have, hazard guesses, if only privately. And then he goes to work, giving twenty minutes with each of three guinea pigs. All I take away is the rapidity of his lancing powers, as he deftly exposes deep fear, fury, or grief, issues these volunteers may have been unaware of, whether rage at a father, grief over a molesting older brother, or the genesis of a crippling social anxiety.

Al can be kind, but I will never let him work on me. He's merciless.

Promising to return Thursday to conclude the workshop, he leaves, as do a few others who came only to watch the master work that day. Our remaining group will be led by two licensed Bioenergetic trainers, Jack and Perdita. Divided into two groups, we settle into a routine of morning and afternoon sessions. After two days and many hours slipping in and out of the two classrooms, I gravitate to Jack. He reminds me of Harry.

Tuesday morning I'm ready. Stripping to panties and bra, I stumble to the middle of the room, face red with shame at exposing sturdy legs mottled from varicose veins. I stand facing ten therapists on folding chairs, the exercise mats at my feet—nothing else but a chair for Jack and a box of tissues for me. Now shoulder to shoulder, he takes my hand and looks kindly into my face. He's stocky with clear, blue eyes, white hair, and ruddy cheeks. I pray he will not ask me to do anything I shouldn't.

Members of the class comment on my body. To my surprise, I'm deemed not a masochist (my private worry) but what Lowen terms the rigid type: forced to draw in to survive. My shoulders are broad and rib cage narrow, not a "fit" with my heavier hips and thighs. Energetically, the group decides, a connection was severed at the waist, where I'm narrower, a signal I don't want to know my lower half.

To stop trembling, I unlock my knees, allow my abdomen to soften, and drop my shoulders. When I can speak, I say, "I'm a medical editor, but I'm not here for my journal. I'm here for myself. I'm in therapy with Harry Brown."

He nods, and others do, too. Harry is well-known.

"Something's surfaced in the last couple weeks. I think my father did something to me." My chest collapses as I struggle to breathe. I think immediately of a woman Jack worked with yesterday, Hilda, sexually abused by both parents. He playacted grabbing her arm while she struggled to get away, yelling, "Leave me alone!" Each time, he let her win.

"What makes you think something happened?"

"I don't know, but I feel it in my body. I feel terror at night. It's happening all the time." Coarse spasms wrack my slender frame; my teeth chatter uncontrollably, lips trembling around the words: "I don't know whether he did it or not. I want to know."

"Why do you want to see it?"

"To get *rid* of it! I can't get rid of it if I don't know it's there."

"Look." He points to the floor. "Grind your feet."

Rising on the balls of my feet, I grind them into the linoleum, and soon heat streams into my calves and up into my thighs. I set my tremulous jaw and grind deeply, flooded by a fountain of anger at *someone.*

"Goddamn you!"

Jack kicks the mats together. "Kneel! Pound the mats!"

I drop, lean on a hand, and pound with all my might. "Goddamn you to fucking hell, you bastard, you know-it-all."

"Who?"

"Goddamn him to fucking hell."

"Why?"

I'm in the crib. Ann and I get to giggling, and Daddy storms in and smacks me, only me.

Still pounding, I'm dimly aware Jack addresses the group. "What's missing?"

I never hear the answers. I'm swept into a sea of fury at what Dad did. *And what was that?* I freeze. I sit on my heels; I scan the faces in my group. Will they believe me if I say he raped me, or think I'm exaggerating? My brother will not want to believe me. Ann won't want to. Maybe my sister Sherry. If no one does, I'll be locked in that crazy place, taking it in.

I sink to all fours.

A hand presses lightly on my waist. Jack's. My mood shifts, lifts; I'm encouraged, and with that, the knowledge that my father can't destroy me no matter what I tell. I sit up and laugh, and the others laugh with me.

Jack reaches for my hands and pulls me to my feet. "What does Harry do to get anger out?"

"Don't know. Oh, yeah, I grab my father in my bare hands and tear him to pieces."

"Then do it!"

I try to lift my arms—and let them fall. What's the use?

Jack hands me a tissue. "Tell me more about yourself, besides the medical editing."

I blow my nose and wipe my eyes. "Well, I'm a singer."

"Then sing!"

I pick a B natural out of the air and allow breath, perfect pitch, and twelve years of voice training to deliver the beginning phrase of "I Know That My Redeemer Liveth." When I stop, fairly quickly, I'm OK. I can breathe. I'm grounded.

From the back of the room, I hear, "Her moods *change* so."

Shamed by that, I stumble to my chair. I'm worse than the others, far worse. I start to dress. There's something I didn't get to. What was it? I don't know. Frightened, I look for Hilda. Only someone with her wounds—abused by both parents—will want to have anything to do with me. She hurries over and, kneeling, slides her arms gently around me, murmuring, "You did great! You're fine. This'll help you, you'll see."

"I wanted Jack to help me get to it, but he won't. I know it's there, but I can't believe it, that he would do that. I feel sick and dirty. I'm not like the others. I'm crazy."

Taking my face in her hands, she speaks as if to a child. "That's the way you feel when you first begin to know. It's all right. You'll get clear. At first, you'll see flashing images, you'll have body memories, and you won't be able to believe them. But I know it happened. I knew it when I first saw you."

I believe her, but I don't know why I do. Can she also understand that if my family won't accept it, it can't have happened?

⸺⸺

I slip out of Jack's afternoon class to observe Perdita with her group. Petite Perdita is dressed in a bat-winged top, garish slacks, and spike heels, her long, brown hair swooped up around the sides and top of her head like a wig designed to shade her eyes. I like this frail-looking, thin-legged thera-pist. Outward appearances and high heels to the contrary, she is grounded and dependable. I feel it.

After dinner, Perdita calls us together to take questions and clarify tech-niques. When the meeting breaks up, I move quickly toward the door, anxious to be alone. She rushes after me and lays a hand on my arm. "Are you all right?"

"No." I tell her of my work with Jack, my struggle with the now-I-know-it/now-I-don't teeter-totter.

She positions me in front of a footstool padded across the top with a rolled blanket strapped in place. "Stand here," she says. This ersatz Lowen stool is, like the wood-and-leather Lowen ones I'm very familiar with, for opening the chest literally and the heart figuratively.

"Lean back," she says. I wait for the last person to leave the room and close the door. Arching my upper back over the stool until my head hangs loose is frightening; the ghost of him looms over me. Nausea floods my throat. "He's pinning my hands down!"

Perdita lightly touches my waist, then above it and below it, as if rear-ranging ghosts in my body. "Now breathe, *breathe.*"

When I tell her my legs burn from blood coursing into them, she's pleased. "Now stand and lean over your toes. That will ground you and keep you in control."

The next breath brings a terrible knowledge. If I take it in—take him in—he won't kill me. "Everything I've built up, Perdita, everything I've done for myself will collapse if I have to know. If he did that, I won't exist. I'll explode and disappear into the universe. What's held me together is believing he never did."

"That may be what has kept you in pieces."

"Do you think he did something?"

"You tell me. Say, 'I know my father raped me.'"

I shake my head. "I only know it in my body."

"Yes."

What does "yes" mean? "Perdita, what did you see in my face that you offered to work with me? You must be exhausted."

"Fear. And energy blocked here." She points to my waist.

"Blocked? How can that be? My life's full. I've been married. I've had lovers."

"You're afraid of being raped, so you take it in out of desperation, not for pleasure and release."

"But I do get release! I love sex!" Instantly, as if my mind is intent on making me a liar, I recall an interaction on Sunday. "That man, the gynecologist who left early—"

"I remember."

"He liked me, I mean as a friend, a date. He wants to see me and asked for my phone number. I couldn't say no. I wanted to. I will, when he calls, but face to face, I couldn't."

"You acquiesce not to be killed."

———⚬⚬⚬———

Before bed, I open my journal to record the day, verbatim where it concerns me; otherwise I cannot stay with the knowledge. When I put the notebook away, a memory floats in. I'm in my late forties, seven years ago.

My father calls to say he's stopping by Darien, in a day or so, to take me to dinner—not my children; he has zero interest in them. I immediately call my Episcopal priest. In a private healing session, I tell him what I remember, that my father felt my breasts when I was a teenager and "accidentally" fumbled them after my children were born, and that he's a rageaholic. What is wrong with me that I can't let it go? I ask Father Mullin. I want to forgive, so I'm not terrified to see him, and I don't know how. I'm *way* overreacting, I say.

"You're not overreacting," Father Mullin says. "And forget forgiveness, for now. I'm going to help you, prepare you to confront him. It's high time."

Full of new courage and determination, I drive home. It's summer, and all four children are living there, not yet off to their colleges, marriages, and careers. They know my fear of Dad and are more than happy to disappear before he arrives, so I can have it out with him. They're not afraid, but they don't like him.

When I hear his car in the driveway, I step outside. As always, I've put on a thickly padded bra and more than one shirt. He pecks me on the cheek with wet lips, then waves a hand dismissively toward the used, four-door Plymouth I bought because it was only $1,800. The sight of it has made him furious. "Goddamn gas guzzler! Why'd you buy a thing like that? Don't you know you're polluting the atmosphere?" I hear the independent clause: *you goddamn fool.*

Familiar theme. Natural resources and machines are far more important than people. It never occurs to him there are five of us here needing a car, and a big dog, that I struggle financially. His brand new oversized four-door Mercedes Benz sits at the curb. German cars are worth buying. I want to throw up. We go into the living room. The house is spooky quiet. We sit.

I begin without preamble. "Do you want to know why I haven't seen you in years, why I avoid you?" My heart is beating so hard it's moving my shirt. "Remember that Thanksgiving you walked us to the door, Kurt and me and the kids? You managed to slap a hand on my breast. How dare you!"

"*What*? You're crazy!"

Rushing through it, now, I name incidents as far back as my budding teens.

"Dad." I get to my feet. "I don't care what you believe or whether you're aware of what you do. I'm telling you right now, once and for all, it must never happen again."

He frowns, baffled, then talks about how he'd pat Deborah, his second wife, on the breast to show affection. He sets it up that I'm putting a sexual spin on mere affection, that I'm weird. He's persuasive, and I almost believe him. His voice, his logic—is he now my truth?

At dinner, he confides how awful it was to be married to my mother twenty-five years, that she never took responsibility for anything, ran up bills, was careless in the house. On and on. He wanted to divorce her, but he couldn't trust her to rear us properly, responsibly.

If I didn't know better, I'd have comforted him. In fact, I do, a little bit.

Later, safe in my own bed, I sit up to journal, all the lights on, my sweet border collie beside me, a stiff scotch—my third (or fourth?)—on the night table. I'm grateful for strong, brave sons and immensely capable, no-nonsense daughters, all of them in their beds, and only a scream away.

And then, I think, if that's all that happened, his feeling my breasts, why am I always terrified of him? What's wrong with *me*? He's just a father who loves me.

———

Wednesday morning, I slip outside of my room at the motel to walk in the early morning mist, praying long and hard for God to settle my teeter-totter. After breakfast, I huddle in the back of Jack's classroom until he begins work with a therapist in his underpants who's a sociopath. Group decision, confirmed by Jack. I sit up. Despite everything happening to me, I'm fascinated.

Typically these men (*very* few women) have overblown chests with high-borne shoulders and heads, an intense facial expression, and piercing glances. One is always drawn to the intensity of the upper body, especially the eyes. Shoulders lie high because all the energy is in the head. This personality is ruled by the mind, not the heart, and is lawless and aggressive about achieving power, either sex and power or money and power or all three (Saddam Hussein, I think). Such persons are often heads of corporations and nations and have no difficulty substituting their own constructs for reality, which leads to steep profits and more power. They disregard their own lies, if indeed they know they're lying. Lowen says no.

Sociopaths are hardwired. There's no cure. Such a person can't "talk it out," learn to behave "better." Morality as we know it, that soft hurt in the chest when we've injured another, is missing. The buttocks and legs are usually thin in relation to the body. If not, they *seem* thin energetically, even disconnected, as opposed to the relatively sturdy legs of someone like Jack. With the sociopath, one is always drawn to the head and shoulders, where all the energy is.

These sociopathic or psychopathic (Lowen uses the terms somewhat interchangeably) therapists, and there's more than one here, are not serial killers any more than are certain foreign heads of state. Often intensely charismatic and warm, such beloveds are often followed to the ends of the earth. Jim Jones's beloved swallowed cyanide in Jonestown rather than question his promises and lies. Lowen writes that on close contact with another person, a split emerges between the seductive effect and sadistic teasing, enticing words and broken promises. Their lack of concern for truth and the well-being of others is monumental. These men are takers in the community and in the home.

I take copious notes. Is it possible my father's agendas toward me had nothing to do with me?

The masochists here, women and men, carry a visible pad of fat on rounded upper backs and shoulders, nature's response to martyred burdens, an outward manifestation of an inward posture. They weren't born that way, with heads forward of the body. The body has finally adapted to an inability to throw off sainthood and stand up for self-hood.

Oral types are usually ectomorphs, "tall and lean, seeking to caretake as a mask for extreme neediness," Jack explains. "They engage you into thinking they're taking care of you, because they do fuss and fuss, but it's to ensure your devotion to them. Gradually, the dynamic shifts as their needs subsume yours, crush you. They use you up and suck you dry."

"Rigid types draw in." How well I recall Al's pronouncement the previous Saturday morning, when he pointed to a lean, well-formed, serious-looking man in boxer shorts. "Energy is husbanded for survival."

I'm a rigid type, outwardly successful and inwardly defended, heavily defended.

And then it's Julie's turn. Julie is a middle-aged therapist, professor, and dean of women at a university. Crouched on the blue mat in her underwear, knees under her chin, she sobs describing her father's drunken rages. Jack signals a large man to hurry over and sit back to back to physically support her.

Suddenly she stops breathing and her head flies up. I see by her eyes she's slipping into a tunnel of lost memories. The room grows absolutely still.

Anguished, she blurts, "I was always afraid he'd rape me."

Pierced through in my belly, I stumble from the room and hurry down the hall into an empty classroom. Unable to stand, I lean on hands and knees, mouth open, sucking air, drooling on linoleum, telling myself over and over I'll be OK.

I've hung on to believing that all I felt was fear that he would rape me, but I know he did. I know it. But I'll be OK, I will if I keep the energy in my legs and cry from the belly. I can clear it, I can. I know how to be here for myself. I'm strong and powerful.

Nausea stays with me through lunch. I want to work with Jack again, see everything that happened, finally, and accept it. I'm desperate to *know* beyond a shadow of doubt, but I can't raise my hand. Jack doesn't want anything to do with me. Perdita doesn't, either. I must go through this alone. I hurry to my small room, lie on the rug between twin beds, close my eyes, slow my breathing, and let myself drop into darkness. It's not long before memories shift in and out of focus, form shadowy scenes.

We're taking a walk. Dad's holding my hand as I scamper along a path in a densely wooded area. He lifts me to the top of a low stone wall, and I'm King of the Hill!—until I slip. I'm not hurt! Jumping up, I laugh and run ahead, scuffling red and brown dry leaves, inhaling a panoply of molds. My dress is a favorite red-and-green plaid. Mother made me wear a green cardigan against the autumn breezes.

Then, I'm not scampering. I'm lying on a bed of leaves, not laughing, not daring to disobey. He wants to see. I can't speak. He leans over me. He holds me down. He smells of leather, stale tobacco, hair tonic. I scream.

My head flies back as a knife rips into a place I do not know I have. The scene shifts and I'm home. Daddy carries me into the apartment and lays me on my bed, fully dressed. I cannot speak. I'm hurt *down there*, bleeding, burning. He's angry. He tells Mother, "She fell running along the top of a stone wall, fell on a rock. Sharp, like this!" He makes a triangle with thumb and index finger.

Mother cries. Ann hovers, staring and mute, knuckles in her mouth.

I'm on my back on a white table. Mute, I stare into the doctor's eyes.

I'm at our maid's apartment. There are other black women and men milling about. My family does not know where I am, or so I think. It burns to urinate. I'm afraid of what the men have in their pants. They're kind, laugh a lot, and try to make me laugh. Or talk. I don't know how many days I'm there. I cannot speak.

⊶⊷

Our last morning. We drag folding chairs into a semicircle to wait for Al to cap the workshop. Our send-off is watching the master work deeply and at length with one person. While we wait, Jack shares psychiatric rubrics. My favorite: "Most talking is a defense against reality." It's funny when you think of it, and so true.

Al, dapper, wiry, and youthful for seventy-odd years, bursts into the room laden with shopping bags of books and monographs he's written, cheerfully greeting old friends and new.

To keep out of his sight line, I tuck in the bend of the circle behind an enormously fat woman whose thigh spreads onto my chair. Even if he spots me, he won't make me work. He'll ask for a volunteer, a dime a dozen here. Besides, I've been vocal about never wanting to work with him. He reminds me of my father: small, lean, wiry. Penetrating.

Finished distributing books and monographs to those who requested them, he leans far around in his chair and looks directly at me. "I'm going to work with Trudy this morning."

I'm appalled! Jack and Perdita set me up. Jesus! Why? Is it to help me break through? How can I do this?

Al drags his chair to the center of the room alongside the blue exercise mats and sits, one arm over the back of the chair, a leg crossed nattily over the other. He does not consider I might refuse.

I strip to briefs and bra and pile my clothes neatly on my chair. I stand beside him, shaking from head to toe, unable to raise my eyes from the mats, concentrating on softening my knees, keeping my spine flexible, shoulders down, belly soft, all to let energy flow from head to toe. None of that helps.

"How're you feeling?"

"Terrified."

"Why?"

"I never wanted to work with you."

"Yeah?"

"You remind me of my father."

"How's that?"

"You're arrogant and sadistic."

He smiles around the room. "And you're afraid."

"Terrified." I don't care anymore about unsightly veins and drooping breasts. Actually, I feel more myself without clothing.

"What are you afraid of?"

"I'm in therapy at home—" I begin. "Some stuff surfaced. I'm remembering—my father raped me." The words leap out before I can make them conditional. "I don't know when. Something happened when I was five. I saw most of it. Autumn leaves. Outside."

"And this is the first time you remembered? Last week?"

"Last few weeks. And here. And with Harry. I breathe and drop into the tunnel and see my father. I choke. I cry, stuff like that." I shrug my shoulders. "Be sick."

"Where's your father now?"

"He's alive and well. Eighty-nine years old, but totally sharp, just like you." *Bastard.*

My nose runs. Where are the tissues? I look around and spot Jack to my left. I thought he'd gone home. I hurry over to him and grab his hand.

"Harry, you're here!" He's Harry. I don't care what anyone thinks.

"You can sit next to him for a minute." Al points to my face while addressing the therapists. "You see the tension in her jaw?"

He waves me over. "Look here, Trudy, stick your jaw out. If you're afraid of me, don't stand there with your jaw back. Take an attitude of aggression. Be menacing the way an animal bares its teeth."

I bare my teeth and stick out my jaw and glare.

He's delighted. "There, you see? Look how her face changes." He turns to me. "Now you look alive, not like a victim. So tell me what happened."

"One day in hypnotherapy, I hear myself say, 'Why did you come into me?' I don't know why. And home alone, something happened." I suck air.

"What?"

"You know, what I said." I tell him about the janitor who was really my father. "I've always been afraid of furnaces. Now I know why. Even when my small oil burner clicks on or off, I jump."

"What're you working on?"

"This—situation."

"Right."

"With Perdita, I bent over the stool—" I stop, then tell him all of it.

Speaking to the class, Al describes the slight heaviness around my hips, the bluish veins, and the sexual implications of energy blocks around the pelvis and thighs.

I interrupt. "It's not sexual! I've had phlebitis. I've had *four* children! I carried twins to *term*."

"Tell me about your children."

"They're grown, but I protected them. Even when the furnace broke, I didn't make them go down in the middle of the night. The valve would stick and we'd wake up freezing, and I'd have to climb behind the furnace to get it started. Dozens of times."

"You took care of them, didn't you, in ways your mother didn't take care of you."

I start to cry.

"So how do you know he raped you?"

"I know it in my body. And it happened in my room, my room here."

"What happened?"

I tell him of the images of the night before, on the rug between the beds. "I know this isn't rational, but if it didn't happen, I can hold myself together and be safe. It has to *not* have happened."

"OK. Now, I want you on the mat. On your back."

I flop down, glad to get off wobbly legs.

"No. Arch your back and tuck your ass into the mat. Knees flexed, feet flat on the floor. Breathe. Breathe again. Put your head back. Good. Let the vibrations build in your legs."

Heat flows into cold legs as they begin to vibrate coarsely. I've done this exercise many times at Leslie's, enjoying a whoosh of confidence.

I'm still crying.

"Keep your jaw out!" Al leans over me. "Growl."

Jaw out, I growl—and suddenly feel not helpless, but intact. Amazing! And yet, seconds later, my vagina is on fire from pain.

"I'm bleeding!"

"You're bleeding *now*?"

"No, *then*. I'm bleeding *then*."

"Breathe."

Jaw out, I breathe as if life depends on it. When he speaks to the class, I hear only separate, meaningless implosions. And then I notice he's sitting back, relaxed and dapper, one leg swinging confidently across the other. I hate him.

Soon I can't focus. I close my eyes and am lost in my child self, impaled but not comprehending, screaming loose, wild screams.

The second the assault is over, I fling myself away from the spot. Kneeling, I dig both hands into my hipbones, frantically trying to disengage my body at the waist.

"I want Harry!" I yell, cradling my crotch.

"You see? She wants her therapist. He's like a mother, soft and fat."

I'm confused. Fat like Mother? But that thought flees as I find myself crouched on a carpet of multicolored fall leaves. I see a policeman, tall and pear-shaped.

"Ann!" I cry. "Why didn't you come with us?"

Al's voice drones as crib rails form around me. My father stands at the end, holding my feet up by the ankles. He's angry: "It's too hot for underpants. Pull up your nightie. Spread your legs."

I look for Mother…She's taking me to church. She has to sing a solo.

"Don't let a man do anything to you," she whispers.

Al's voice cuts through. "Most therapists stop right here, uncover the incest, and begin work. With Trudy the problems go deeper, to two more levels. Her mother wasn't there for her." He peers at me.

"Trudy, can you work? It will help you, if you can."

I will do anything to stop these invasions, this madness. I nod.

"Did your mother nurse you?"

"Nine months."

He shakes his head sadly. "She was taken off the breast too soon. Have you ever longed for a nipple?"

"Yes."

"Why don't you buy a baby bottle?"

"I tried that. It feels stupid."

Al places a small towel in my hand. I lift it to my mouth, suck, and am swiftly connected to the peace and safety of my mother's breast.

"Trudy, the other level is—" He leans over me, elbows on his knees. "Your parents sent you into madness. If you go back, you'll heal. Are you willing to go to the edge of madness?"

I know only that I cannot long survive in this state. I must believe Lowen has the power and skill to bring me back.

"Yes."

Breathing deeply, listening to his insinuations, connecting only to his eyes, I drift down, down, alternately sticking out my jaw and digging my hips into the mat, hanging onto life with parts of my body, falling to the edge of a gravity-less universe through which at any moment I might disappear forever, held to life only by his voice and eyes fixing me in space, but not in time.

No shape, no words. No place. No self. Eyes. Only his eyes.

I shut mine to block him out and search for Mother. I reach for her and find nothing, falling, falling into a hole in time. Spinning into no place. Nothing for me. Nothing but darkness. A surrender to all but a contract to return.

Eyes. I open mine and find his.

How far will he let me fall without a body?

"Kick!" he commands.

I raise my legs as high and straight as they'll go and kick until I have a body and the core pain is gone. When I falter, he commands, "Kick!" and I pound the mat with my heels.

"Get me that towel!" Al yells, then twists it and shoves it at me. "Bite!"

Biting hard stiffens me, gives me determination. I scramble to my knees, spit the towel out and, holding it down with one hand, stab it over and over with the other fist. Jumping up, I grind the towel under my feet, grunting as I destroy my progenitor.

"The final healing for Trudy will come when she loves another man—if she does the work, and she will." He smiles. "Being with another man will heal that. Heal her."

I crawl to Hilda, wanting to lay my head on her knees. She tries to take my hand, but I pull away and stand. I shake my head and make my way to my seat. I must be alone. I struggle into support stockings and hear the whispers:

"Denial—"

"Denial."

"She's in denial."

Dressed, I turn to Al. "But do you think he raped me?"

Chapter 5—Flashbacks

I DON'T GO HOME. I DRIVE TO WALTER'S. We walk the deserted beach, and walk, kicking sand. He doesn't know what to make of the conference. He's stunned and baffled. He's worried sick about me, the way I look.

I'm proud of having survived. Harry will be proud of me. Despite everything, I don't think about drinking. I quit after we were married a year, one of many changes I made hoping to save our marriage. It's been eighteen months, and the desire is gone.

Walter gives me cigarettes and feeds me. He tucks me in bed with the dog and sits up reading, smoking, drinking. After breakfast, I drag a beach chair to the water's edge and drink coffee and pray and write in my journal. I record everything to do with the conference. If it's written, I believe it.

An old friend, Don Alphonso, stops by from up the cove, where he lives. He's on a medical leave from NBC, recovering from a heart attack. The three of us talk and laugh and, together, prepare an elegant fish chowder. I appreciate the warmth and camaraderie of the Don, as I call him, but my flesh isn't all there. I feel papery, as thin as a fragile rendering of myself, as if about to burst into flames. My eyes are hollow wounds, and the despair in them reflected in the mirror scares me.

When it's time to go home, I'm afraid. I can't be alone. Walter follows in his car. He'll stay at my house as long as I need him.

Saturday, I put on sweats and drive to the Lowens' for Leslie's class. I take the back way from Norwalk to New Canaan, through winding country lanes. Wooded areas flashing by flip me into childhood. I can't see the road, can't turn the scenes off.

He will say nothing happened.

My teeth chatter.

The class is crowded. Al joins us. We stretch, skip, bend. We punch air, screaming, "Fuck you!" We grunt and burp and twist and vibrate knees, and cry. When Leslie leads us into a squat from which we're to kneel toes out, I hesitate. I can't kneel that way. And then I do.

It hits me: that's the position I took in the woods when I tried to disengage my body at the waist. My feet have turned out effortlessly. Revisiting the woods unlocked the arrangement of bone and sinew. Then, something sharp cuts deeply into that place. Always that place. I fold over and wait. When I can stand, I step past the others and slip into the back hall. I close the door and lie on my back on the runner, trying to breathe my way back to myself.

When I have enough control to drive, I let myself out and run into Al in the driveway, carrying a shovel, gardening, it seems. Is he proud of me?

"Thank you." I don't know what else to say.

"What are you thanking me for?"

"You know."

"Yeah."

I look out over his fields.

"Keep doing the exercises, Trudy. They'll ground you."

"I have trouble knowing anything happened."

"Yeah."

"Otherwise, why can't I sit with my feet turned out without crying? That's the position I took after he did something."

He nods.

"And I have sharp—"

"It'll get clear for you, Trudy. Right now there's a lot of rage that has to come out."

I leave the Lowens' and drive an hour, maybe two, and find myself heading south on Ridgefield Road, in Wilton. I pass the old colonial I call the Bigelow house (the owners from whom my father rented it). I see myself on my back in the double bed in the guest room, waiting for my parents to come home. Why did he sometimes make me sleep there, alone, instead of in my twin bed in the room I shared with Ann? I was thirteen.

No. Please, God, not at thirteen.

A mile down the road I spot the driveway to what I know is a crude cedar dwelling my father designed. He disdained architects. He knew more than they. I brake and crane my neck to see the house from the road. I can't. It's hidden at the end of a long, rutted drive. The driveway ends at the kitchen door. There's a front door on the other side of the house, which no one can see or find.

Bastard.

I was eighteen in that house. Will I ever know all of it? Do I want to?

I pull away, then drive up into Elmwood cemetery, across the street from that house. I park in back under the trees near an old well. I pump a tin of cold, fresh water. The water tastes like fresh air. I leave the pump handle up, the bucket full, as one does, and walk to Mother's headstone.

Mildred Burnard Seagraves
1906–1954

Easing onto the flat stone at her feet, I sit and give in to a crushing need for arms, her full, soft body. When I hear a car grind up the hill, I set out briskly across the graveyard into the field beyond, striding through long grass surrounded by clumps of dense underbrush and scrubby trees, antler-rubbed bark. A flock of geese honk and flap heavily away. Stepping through a breech in the overgrowth, I enter a second field, a sun-washed meadow smelling of heat and hay, walled by huge trees. Near the center is one small tree.

I've been here before, bringing a blanket to lie on, spending an hour or two, after my cup of well water and a talk with Mother. Sometimes I've followed a narrow path through a densely overgrown area into a dark grotto, where I stand on an old wooden footbridge and watch the stream tumble over smooth stones. Not today.

I stop at my one small tree and breathe myself into one with the grasses, the sun, the sky. A deer crossing at the far end gives me a long look, flicks its tail, and moves on in search of fresh greens. I'm no threat.

An hour later, I park in the village by the luncheonette where Mother and I often ate bacon sandwiches on white toast. I love coming here for lunch. The Greek ladies who run the place know me and always smile. As I step from the car, a thin young man hurries by pulling a little girl by the hand.

I flee.

Chapter 6—Sisters and Daughters, Brother and Sons

THE END OF APRIL, WALTER STARTED PLANNING A barbecue at his beach house for Sunday, May 9, a combination birthday/Mother's Day in my honor. Walter's kids are away—one in New Haven, one in Hartford—but mine are coming, except my daughter in the Midwest.

The morning before the party, my sister Sherry arrives from New Hampshire, with two baskets, one laden with wine, gourmet cheese, homemade scones, and almond cookies; the other filled with hand lotions, designer soaps, and sachets of lavender and mint from her garden. And that's Sherry, a beautiful, talented, kind, and generous woman with honey-colored skin, cinnamon hair, and our father's dark-brown eyes.

I put the coffee on and the scones in the oven, get out butter and cream, and hug her again, long and hard, inhaling the spicy cologne she wears. While we eat and catch up, I try to think how to frame the only thing I have in mind.

"You're so thin," she says, abruptly tearing. "I felt your bones."

"There's something I haven't told you. If it's difficult for you, stop me. I don't have to talk about it." Although Sherry and I speak often and at length on the phone, and she knows something of my strange therapy, she doesn't know the Dad part.

"If I'd seen your eyes," she says, "I'd have come months ago."

"They look bombed out."

"They do." She leans forward. "I know what it is." And with that she hurries to my side of the table to wrap her arms around me. "I'm sorry he did that to you. I'm *so* sorry."

When we sit facing, again, she says, "Trudy, I know he didn't do anything to me. I'm sure of it. They weren't easy years, but…" She stares through the glass slider into the hills beyond, the hills that hold the house in which she was born when I was fifteen. I can almost fly a kite to it.

She shakes her head, and her coppery hair licks her chin. She tucks it behind her ears. "I'm sure he didn't do to me what he did to you." She says it kindly, firmly. "I'm sure."

And I'm grateful, but I do not trust myself to speak. "Sure" is not in my vocabulary anymore. I step to the sink and look out the window across the valley to Belden Hill. *What happened there?* I wonder. And then, for the first time, I'm aware of the radio in the living room. I hearken: Schubert's Unfinished Symphony. There's hardly a piece of classical music Sherry and I cannot identify, thanks to my father. Thanks to my father, she and I are musicians.

OK, then, it's not possible. He couldn't. He wouldn't. He didn't.

My pulse pounds in my neck, and I'm sweating. I look at Sherry, kind, loving friend. I want to weep with relief at having a sister's total acceptance of whatever I will or will not ultimately claim. Sadly, though, as much as I cherish her, it's the elder's approval I crave. Ann is my imprimatur. She was the family hero, the child who could do no wrong, the one who was perfect. Truth is, she was.

I sit and try to load sweet butter onto a warm, featherlight scone that breaks apart in my hand, and laugh as I lick my palms. We laugh together. We're both mad about food.

"I told Ann," I say, finally. "It didn't go well."

"What happened?"

Ann lives in the Midwest, too. We seldom see one another but have always spoken often and at length on the phone.

"I'll tell you everything, but it means revealing an incident in the woods with Dad. I was five. Are you sure you want to hear it?"

"Yes."

In as flat a voice as possible, I tell Sherry how Dad took me alone to the woods, the pointy rock he said I fell on, Mother's shock and tears, the strange doctor, staying with black people, seeing a pear-shaped policeman.

"So, a few weeks ago—" I swallow hard. "I decided to see if Ann could hear something so bad about Dad. She absolutely stunned me with her response. She validated *all* of it! She remembered my coming back from that walk, wounded in the genitals, bleeding, being taken to the doctor."

As I tell Sherry the rest of it, I'm transported to that first welcome conversation, to how overjoyed I was.

"I remember all of it vividly," Ann had said. "Mother and Dad had such strange looks on their faces. Dad got angry and said you fell on a jagged rock and cut yourself down there, but the atmosphere was *loaded*. Their affect was not consonant with what was going on."

Desperate for more of Ann's memories, I went on to ask, "Do you remember I stayed with black people? Was it a couple days that Mother got me out of the house? Did that happen?"

"Absolutely!" she said. "And that was strange, because we didn't know black people, except the maid. And I didn't go with you. The whole thing was very odd."

If Ann believed me, maybe I could find a way to accept it, live with it. With her help, I could reconstruct some of those years. And with her support, maybe even recover.

Eager for more confirmation, I rushed on, "I never knew why I dropped out of kindergarten. That furnace thing happened right after I started. I couldn't go to school every day. Did you know I never made a full week until tenth grade?"

"Yes."

"Ann, *everything's* beginning to make sense. It's a giant puzzle I'm finally going to complete. Hundreds of nightmares of him running me down in our black Franklin. The terrible nights—"

And she replied, "I was horrified when you told me you kept a loaded gun after your kids left. Now I know why. *Way* too much fear."

"There's choking all the time, too, when I work with Harry. Something oral—"

"*What?*"

"Ann, I wish we'd had this conversation years ago."

She spoke as though resigned. "I kept out of his way. Maybe I sensed something and set you up. I have a lot of guilt—"

"No! Stop it! It's not your fault. Don't feel guilty about stuff *he* did."

"You were always in trouble. Mother made me responsible for you when I was only two." Certainly true because, although nineteen months older, Ann was forced into the role of parent by both of them.

Frustration ramping her voice, she went on, "You'd do things I couldn't control—dash across the street and stand there and taunt me. I wasn't *allowed* to cross."

No wonder she dislikes our mother, no wonder our sisterhood was uneasy—is uneasy—yet we love one another deeply.

"I was thrilled Ann heard me," I tell Sherry, "validated a memory. Now I *knew* I wasn't making things up!"

She has been listening with a hand over her open mouth, until she blurts, "I wonder if she's telling you all she knows."

"If not, Sherry, she never will, 'cause maybe I'm the enemy now. She called first thing the next morning. In her mind, without collusion it never would have happened. I was so mad, hearing that; I screamed, '*Mother* didn't do it!' and hung up on her."

"Her saying it never would have happened tells you something," Sherry observes.

"Well, why is she so angry at Mother? Why does she go on about Mother sending us to birthday parties in wet socks because the wash hadn't been done, or buying dumpy pine furniture and selling the Chippendale. Actually, Dad wanted pine for the Wilton house. He made that furniture. It was for *him*. It's all very confusing. I blame Dad for the setup that Ann was perfect and Mother and I were bad and dirty. Sloppy, irresponsible."

"Did you tell Ann that?"

"No, but she bought into it. They still do. Oh, I know Mother dropped the ball." We are silent awhile, spent from talking truth—if all of it *was* truth—until I say, "You know the worst part of telling you both? It makes it real."

The next day, at Walter's barbecue, I try to laugh and act carefree as I open my gifts. I don't want my kids suspecting I'm full of grief and sickeningly needy. They're respectful, as always, but not likely to miss anything. They know I'm in deep trouble. They know.

When Sherry leaves, a few days later, and I can no longer keep myself afloat, I plunge into a morbid state, safe only by walling myself off from everyone, even Walter.

Still, I attend an exercise class, after work. By this time, I know warm-up stretches bring a knifelike stabbing down there. I'm not the only one who doubles over. Leslie encourages us to express anything released by the strenuous movements she guides us into and out of. It isn't unusual to watch others cycle through wrath, grief, joy. Most of us are in some form of therapy, I suspect, and the atmosphere Leslie creates is supportive and nonjudgmental. But during a second class, that week, I'm unable to stop crying in any reasonable time, and tiptoe over bodies to slip into the back hall leading to Al's office. I shut the door, lie on the rug, and give in. To my surprise, I'm able to return feeling stronger.

The renewed energy lasts only until a series of dreams in which my father looms over me in the bedrooms of two other houses in Wilton. I was a teenager in both. A child is one thing—but adolescence? How can I ever handle this? I must have had *some* control over him or myself. I am filthy with sorrow. Why didn't I stop him? Why didn't I *know*? Are the dreams even real?

Late in May, Ann calls about plans we made in April, for her and her husband, Eugene, to stay with me Memorial Day weekend. Of course, nothing's been settled since I hung up on her, but I'm sure we can visit as sisters, respecting our different experiences with Dad. I am desperate to see her.

As soon as I hear her voice, I know they won't be coming. Still, I plead and bargain: "Ann, you can't go to a motel! And Walter will be here; we'll be a foursome. *Please* come."

"We're staying with Dad."

I can't speak for the pain in my chest.

"He wants us to come," she offers.

"No! Well, at least come for dinner Memorial Day, a cookout, like we planned. Walter will be here, and I've invited others—"

"There isn't time."

"You'd rather be with him."

"You don't understand!"

I start to cry.

"He's expecting us. And also, Eugene is upset."

"Is that why you won't come? *Eugene?*" Rage rattles my teeth. Eugene's a gifted surgeon who fled Hungary. What is there about life he can't understand?

"That's part of it. I told him about you." Ann waits a beat. "He's very upset."

"Ann," I say, giving up. "I understand. I can't grasp it, either. I worry I'm making it up. I guess it's possible. Let's give each other time."

<hr>

As I do on days I'm uncertain of anything, since I can barely trust myself to know truth from fiction, I write out disturbing conversations, mostly those I've had with Harry. Today, the moment I hang up, I grab a pad of lined paper and transcribe our talk word for word. Even as I write, I almost cannot believe she's going to stay with Dad. Writing may be my only means of understanding the painful truth of what just happened, and of forgiving my sister for loving her father.

Actually, I occasionally transcribed conversations a long time ago, when trying to get clear about my marriage to Kurt. Writing—and rereading—forced me to see that our marriage was never going to work, helped me go ahead with divorce, which released us both.

Finished, I drop the pen, stack the pages, and start reading, sad to the bone. Faced with a verbatim record, I hurt everywhere: head, knees, feet. It isn't Ann's fault. We were brainwashed into Dad's cult. I'm sad for both of us. But for me, now, the loss is huge—her husband, their four children, Eugene's relatives—people I love, whom my children love. And the loss for her will be equally devastating.

I want to call her back and force her to look at Dad from a different perspective, ask herself if he's worth honoring. And what about Mother? Yes, she had faults, she sure did, but that poor woman, married to him, no wonder she died, no wonder she wanted to. On the tip of my tongue is "Don't you realize that if not for Mother's friendliness to everyone in the world, and in Wilton, and to Eugene's family, you would never have met your husband?"

Back then, although half-sick most of the time, Mother had rallied enough to start her own real-estate business, after quickly acing both broker and agent exams. She found the perfect house in Wilton, for Eugene's mother and aunt, one large enough for three grown sons to visit occasionally, and then invited the whole Hungarian family to tea. Delighted, they soon reciprocated. Before long, I and Eugene's mother, a brilliant concert pianist, were having weekly Sunday musical sessions. She accompanied and coached me on the Italian arias I was studying with my voice teacher in New York City. And she often played for Mother, too. Although she'd be dead within three years, Mother still delivered Wagnerian arias in a huge, velvety voice, her musicianship impeccable.

Having met the youngest son, a bachelor surgeon living in Massachusetts, Mother engineered the tea party so the Vassar girl and the charming air force major could meet.

Claiming he had too much to do that day, Dad hid in his workshop over the garage, where he often spent nights and weekends making furniture. Not being at the gathering didn't stop him from mimicking everyone after they left. He pranced around pretending to be blind, mocking Eugene's aunt, perhaps one of the most refined and generous women I'd ever met, for wearing Coke-bottle glasses.

And we laughed with him. We egged him on.

Then, "Eugene's a sausage with four toothpicks," he declared, and we all roared at his clever description of the major's pear-shaped body, slender limbs.

Why had I gone along with the derision, when it was never in my personality? My father's tickle was always to check one's body for malformations. Too tall, too short. Hips set too high, shoulders sloping, legs bowed or knock-kneed. Too weak, too fat. The defects spread to race—kike, spic, nigger. Too dark, too black, too dirty. Only Aryans were spared.

All of us children liked to say in defense of Dad that he was fascinating. I had always found other fathers insipid, flat, ordinary, boring. Dad was in the forefront of certain scientific knowledge. Every word he uttered, every pronouncement, was thick with a roiling energy that said, *You better hear this. You better learn. You better remember, you fool!* Spellbound, we sat at his feet, memorizing his reality.

What we didn't realize was that what made him compelling was his sociopathology, our submission to a cult leader. We were but children and could not yet distinguish the sword of truth from the razor of mania. And so we stared, when he spoke, entranced by the range and depth of his perceptions. Sure, we were scared, but only of big dogs and spiders and the dark and thunder and boogiemen. And the Franklin, his car.

How could you fear the captain of your ship, someone who told you his integrity was beyond question?

And look at his astonishing generosity with music and flowers and antiques, fine books galore, and fresh vegetables, the occasional surprise from Abercrombie's: a cashmere sweater or scarf from Scotland, a new three-speed bike, an ice-cream maker, bows and arrows and the target and leather gloves to go with them. His sweetness when bestowing gifts completely exposed a yearning man stripped, for the moment, of his protective overcoat of rage. How often did he warn us: "Don't ever sunbathe. The damage will continue to appear until the day you die, even if you subsequently stay out of the sun. Don't drink fluoridated water. Don't eat refined white flour."

His understanding of the solar system was immense and benign, his love of opera and Shakespeare heavenly. His dinner-table diatribes on politics and world events, although driven by racism and paranoia, opened my eyes to the necessity of reading beyond the front page.

When I was eight, he and I went running along the sidewalk one day, and he took my hand and challenged me to see how fast I could run, if I could keep up with him. I was thrilled—until I fell, backwards, fracturing my skull. He knew enough to forbid X-rays near the throat, knowing radiation could trigger thyroid cancer.

So who is this devil-savior? I don't know. I do know I feel sick destroying his reputation, as if I've called on spooks to ride him out of town in the night.

***

Joseph stops by my house after work one evening to move an old dresser into the garage. My third child, born two years after the twins and two years before his brother, Joseph was born on Christmas morning. Perhaps that's why he's blessed with the clarity, humor, and sweetness of a peacemaker. Sturdy and practical, this solid young man, who has my spicy coloring and his father's lean, strong, well-shaped body, lives to make humor and houses.

We sit at my kitchen table while he cracks open a beer.

"Mom, you're not doing so good, are you?" Head tilted to one side, he grins to soften the words. He looks at me as if I were his child. "What's going on?"

"I'm not sick, I'm not." I laugh. "Is that what you think? I'm going through some difficult stuff, and it has to do with—my father. That's all."

"You're thin. And you're not working, or are you?"

"Oh, yes. Of course."

I can't tell him it's the flashbacks that lay me low. His wife's expecting their first child in six weeks. I don't want him keeping secrets from her, and I don't want her hearing about rape while she carries a child. That also means I can't tell his brother. The boys are close.

When Joseph leaves, I want to tell my girls. I want them close. I need them. What will I say? Will they believe me?

Elizabeth lives nearby and Laura in the Midwest. It's easier to talk about horror from a distance. And so, I pick up the phone. As with Sherry, I back into it cautiously, trying to sense whether Laura can handle it. Her response startles me.

"Mom, I don't know why, but I'm not surprised. Of course he did! It's as if I knew all along, without saying it to myself. I never liked your father. He's a horrible man. I'm sorry, but that's how I feel."

I've never heard Laura call anyone horrible. "How do you know?"

"I can't say exactly, but something was wrong. I sensed it without being able to label it. And it explains some things about you that never added up. You can't imagine how it all fits. Look, it stopped with you. Feel good about that."

It's true, and I do. But I did things I'm not proud of. "Laura, do you remember the time you came to the dinner table wearing a yellow sundress?"

"God, yes. You were off the wall."

"You had a beautiful fifteen-year-old body, and you were wearing the sundress without a bra. There was nothing wrong with that, but, see, the boys were at the table. They were thirteen and eleven, and I couldn't stand to see you so exposed around males. I was alarmed. I didn't know why.

"I made you feel ashamed. I'm sorry. You hadn't done anything wrong. I couldn't handle it. I've never been able to wear anything like that because it makes me feel too vulnerable. Even shorts."

"Forget it. I knew at the time you were unreasonable. I understood."

She reminds me, then, of seeing my father at a large family get-together at my brother's the year before. Dad, dapper in English tweeds, a red-plaid tie on a snow-white shirt, scotch and water in hand, sidled up to her in the kitchen. "And who are *you*?" he said, ready to have this beautiful, soft-spoken woman admire him, flirt with him.

"I'm your granddaughter," she said as she turned on her heel.

He had not attended her wedding, several years earlier. Or Joseph's. I invited him, of course, but grandchildren were never welcome in his life.

That evening, my daughter Elizabeth calls. "Mom, Laura told me. I have to say, I'm not surprised. I'd like to come down and stay with you. May I?"

"Please."

Chapter 7—The Way We Lived

ON MY LUNCH HOUR, I CHECK FIVE BOOKS out of the Greenwich library, all on incest, all written by daughters. That evening, I lock my house, then my room, and sit up in bed to read the first.

On the dust jacket is a black-and-white photograph of an attractive woman of about forty. Hoping for my story, I quickly scan details and descriptions, searching for a blueprint depicting recovery. The seductions by this father went on until the victim was eighteen, a gentle wooing to which she responded with orgasms. Profoundly disturbed by their eroticism, I'm grateful my abuser was selfish and brutal, that sexual love, as I came to know it, was not stained by pleasure with him. Finally, I put the book down to undress for bed. The phone rings. It's after eleven.

"Hello?" I answer cautiously.

"Is Ann at your house?" It's a thin, male voice, peremptory, brusque—and familiar, a man who never says hello.

Why is my father looking here for Ann?

And then I remember it's Memorial weekend. He's expecting her. How have I managed to forget?

"Dad," I say, holding a pillow over my breasts, "I haven't talked to Ann. I don't think she's planning to come here."

I hang up, settle into bed, and catch myself watching the thin strip of light under my bedroom door to see if a shadow crosses it. I hold my breath, listen for footsteps in the night. How long will it take me to get the screen up and drop out the window onto the wooden deck below? Not long. If I hang full-length, I probably won't break an ankle. Surely someone will hear my screams before the man realizes I've got away, before he races to the kitchen to trap me where I've landed.

"Nuts," I say. "Stop it." I've played that scene hundreds of times. Still, I'm glad my sons installed the brass dead bolt on my bedroom door. I'm glad Walter gave me an alarm system; it's hidden under the couch, its beams set to detect the slightest whisper of movement toward the stairs to my room.

Over the next three days, I skim the other four books. None replicate my story. The victims knew all along. Jealous, I long to have lived that way, to have been connected beyond doubt to all of it. But what is all of it?

But I do learn that, to survive, the abused child develops an extraordinary ability to sense every nuance of danger, every signal for what may happen next, not unlike the hyperalert Vietnam vet or concentration-camp victim constantly sniffing the winds of change, so that at any moment he can jettison his will in exchange for life.

Harry tells me that once the survivor's acute ability to see and sense is free to flow toward experiences other than those needed for survival, the hypervigilance can be used to explore new worlds, new careers, new ways of living.

I know that persons charged with sexual wrongdoing deny it when caught red-handed. They split off so completely that they truly do not see it as happening or as having happened. Or it was not their intent, or it was misunderstood, or it was the other person's fault.

For the deniers, it never happened. Or not that way. Or not that much. Or it was my fault. Or Mother's. I was never whipped with his belt or the razor strop; I made that up. It was my "narcissism," my need to "gain attention." I'm hearing through a few relatives that I'm a liar and insane. The word thrown about is "psychotic."

Or maybe I'm not insane, according to them: just sick, bad, and dirty. Nothing new about that.

Although two exercise classes a week aren't helping me stabilize emotionally, I stick with it like a dog tearing at a rag. Driving over back roads to the Lowens' one Tuesday evening after work, I pass stately white colonials riding on crests of perfect lawns. I lived in such houses from ages eleven to eighteen, and not far from where I'm driving, one in New Canaan, two in Wilton.

The Belden Hill house, in Wilton, is only a mile or two across the valley from my condominium here. In winter, I could probably see the roof with a telescope. Dreams are taking me there, lately. Some are benign. In one, I'm sixteen.

I don't want to remember the dream, but I do remember those years. Dinner over, I do the dishes, wash and dress my baby sister, Sherry, for bed. She sleeps in a crib at the foot of my parents' sleigh bed. How I cherish this sweet, compliant one-year-old, her tiny fingers feathering my face, my hair. I grab any chance to hold her, care for her, comfort her. Bending over the crib, I tuck her in and tell her "The Three Bears," and while she understands not a word, she knows I love her.

I think about the years in those big houses. In 1943, when we moved to the New Canaan house, nine bedrooms, five baths, Mother hung organdy curtains. I hated not having shades. The house was as safe from intruders as a locked jail cell, yet I shunned those black windows at night and undressed in my closet. Who did I think was out there, lusting after me?

In the Belden Hill House, in Wilton, after Sherry was born, Mother was asleep by eight o'clock, too ill to endure another minute of any demand. None of us were yet aware she was dying from a rare metabolic disorder. Her physicians saw a constellation of symptoms indicating a syndrome, but which? She suffered night fevers and sweats, aching joints, malignantly high blood pressure, jaundice; and cholesterol deposits were spoiling the unlined English skin around her eyes. Whatever was after her, it was deadly.

She wasn't always sick. She rallied sometimes for weeks, months— started her real-estate business, cleaned the house, cooked so I didn't have to, sang solos at church—then collapsed for many more weeks or months. Mother's doctors had identified diabetes insipidus, stemming from a pituitary malfunction. They believed this was only one aspect of an overall syndrome that still eluded diagnosis.

Diabetes, contrary to common belief, is a general term meaning "excess flow." Diabetes *mellitus* refers to excess flow of *urine*, commonly referred to simply as diabetes. Diabetes *insipidus* is a rare kidney disorder in which the tubules can no longer hold water. My mother had to drink gallons day and night, or die.

Evenings, Dad slouched in an overstuffed chair slipcovered in dull green, reading. I sat nearby on the couch, a stiff, three-cushion Lawson upholstered in a worn brown fabric, homework on my lap. Mother spent most days on that couch in this room we called the library, bed pillows under her head, a huge pitcher of ice water and a glass within easy reach. No one used our huge living room, unless we were at the piano or singing.

Before I turned fifteen and started tenth grade, I was still cutting school one or two days a week. Home on winter days, I made a pot of tea, loaded it with sugar, and pulled a spindly Windsor chair up to a boxed radiator to pass the day reading the likes of de Maupassant or Poe, while Mother read or dozed on the couch nearby. We were cozy together, and sometimes went to downtown Wilton for lunch. As I plowed through our library, I was grateful my father, right after the Depression, had bought hundreds of books by the pound from the newly poor rich folk on Long Island.

Ann went off to college from that house, the Belden Hill house, the autumn I was sixteen. Sherry was nine months. My brother, eleven, kept to his room over the garage, largely ignored, I believe, forgotten by everyone but me—because we still played outside, setting fires, running wild in the dark, letting the goats come in the house when Mother wasn't home.

Now that I was sixteen, in love with a senior boy, and no longer cutting school, I sat on the student council and joined the debating team, where I was elected president. My first task was to write and defend a paper on McCarthyism. I couldn't wait to tell my father of the honor bestowed on me. After dinner, one night, I found him alone in the library.

"They're not really Communists," I began. "See, it's a witch hunt. McCarthy—"

"What's the matter with you, ya goddamn fool? They're *Commies*. Don't ya know that? Goddamn Jew commies." He glared at me from the corners of his eyes, frown deepening, outrage pushing the words. "They're *traitors*. They oughtta be strung up. All of them."

His long, lean face tilted downward, dark-brown eyes peering suspiciously from under stiff, black eyebrows, flaring nostrils packed with black hair, upper lip a thin slice, lower lip full and pouting. Always wet.

His body tightened at my effrontery. And then—undisguised disgust. "Ya don't know anything!" Slouching deep in his chair, pelvis tilted up, he picked at his fly with little jabs of comfort.

"Ya goddamn *fool*. Ya don't know what you're talking about. I know all about that. I'll tell ya what that is—"

Without moving or speaking, chest and heart sick with self-hatred, I listened again to his theories of Jewish conspiracy, how Jews were diabolically committed to undermining our country. They had a network, and McCarthy had the courage and integrity to expose it.

"Now, Westbrook Peglar," my father went on, "*he* has integrity." Peglar, a sports columnist for the *New York Journal-American,* hated the Roosevelts, all Jews, and possibly everyone else but Aryan men.

Hurting like fire in that tender place just below my breastbone, I folded my school papers and put them back in my notebook. I was beginning to recognize that if there were too many days without his searing and humiliating disdain of me, I sought it. Why else bring up McCarthy?

But, as always, gradually his voice softened as he warmed to me, now no threat, for only he existed, and he could relax, free from the assault on any idea not his.

I asked Mr. Demeter, my cheerful, square-faced history teacher, to meet me after school the next day. I often baby-sat for him and his wife, and I felt more comfortable telling him face-to-face that I could not stand up in assembly in front of the whole high school and read a paper my father did not approve of.

"Oh no," Mr. Demeter protested. "You can. You've done the work. You defend your position. It's important you present it."

Because of that generous soul, I read my paper and defended my viewpoint, not my father's. Because of Mr. Demeter's respect, I tucked him into my mind to join the others I kept at hand for solace.

As if a little girl on the floor with paper dolls, I loved the men and women who believed in me: Mr. Kenney, my headmaster; Miss Tacke, my Latin teacher; Mr. Lind, chemistry; Mr. Miller, English; Mr. Worley, music; Mr. Gilbert, from eighth grade, in Georgetown; "Jim" Perkins, Mother's best friend, next door; Mrs. Fuller, a loving neighbor; Mr. Wainright, in the choir, where I, too, sang solos; Reverend Roland, the spirit behind our youth group at church.

Chapter 8—Bare Belly to Bare Belly

"You pick up so much, Trudy. Really, you have a gift. I know! I train seventeen therapists a week. I see them privately, too, some of them. You really oughtta look into it. Get training. Go see this woman at Southern. She's great! She's a friend."

Nervous and flattered, I follow Harry's latest rainbow to the brochure he picks up from a big stack on the floor. It's about the master's program in social work at Southern Connecticut State College. He shoves it at me.

I'm to earn an MSW.

Only days earlier, I called Harry from work, begging him to sign off on a medical leave. "I can't stop the flashbacks, and I can't stop crying, even here."

"Oh, no, no, no," he said. "You're leaking energy from the heart chakra. I want you to call someone who can help you. He's in Greenwich; see him—today."

Certain he was pushing me off on another therapist, I started to cry. And then he added, "It's Shiatsu. He's a safe guy. I know him, his sister, his whole family."

The young masseuse *is* safe; he's gentle and tactful. I make plans to see him again. But my energy continues to drop. I'm still losing weight. My right hip pains all the time. When I tell the masseuse that I'm sure I have cancer, he smiles. "Trudy, you don't have the energy of someone with cancer. Your energy blocks move around. It's when the block is always in the same place you have to worry."

"But thought is not disembodied," I argue. "It's not the cartoonist's bubble floating above the character's head, attached by a thin stream of air. Trauma never floats away. It rots the body."

Now, I interrupt Harry. "I can't do that. I can't even work!" He's not listening. He's still blabbing about Dr. Devon and social work. Jan Kennedy's books on shamanism are gone, and Barbara Devon is the flavor of the week.

Finally, I yell, "You're not listening! I can't *function*."

"Well, but this'll help and give you a focus." He points to the brochure in my hand.

"Stop it!" I say. "I can't. I don't have a college degree."

"Start talking classes. You'll see."

A few days later, after work, the obedient patient, I drive north for two hours, find the fucking school, and locate her office. Her assistant looks up to tell me that because I don't have a college degree, Devon won't see me. In fact, she won't see me ever.

I wander the halls until I find another psychology instructor.

"May I audit your class?" I ask.

"Not unless you complete your undergraduate."

"Before I spend years doing that, can't I just see how it feels as a career change for me?"

"I'm sorry."

But Harry—Harry is undaunted, although I've told him countless times I have never, ever wanted to become a psychotherapist.

Mid-June. Next to May, my favorite month, except I feel cold all the time, everywhere, even in the sun. My mother had a phrase for this state of mind: death warmed over. That's me.

"Sure," I tell Harry, next visit. "Of course I've heard of Omega Institute. It's a New Age conference center in New York State. I've been to Rhinebeck, but not there."

He hands me a catalog from a clump on the floor now crowding out the Barbara Devon effort. "It's holistic, Trudy. I'd like you to go to a weekend conference with me."

With me? I hold my breath and wait.

"My son's going. They have wonderful sacred music." He's staring at me. I must look dumbfounded.

"Well, not in the same car, exactly. Meet me there."

Baffled and alarmed, I shut down as a wave of nausea heads for my throat.

"What's wrong?" he asks.

I shake my head.

"Let's have you on the floor, scream it out."

And I do, until my throat hurts. When I get up to leave, he suggests I start coming twice a week.

A few days later, he calls me at home to see if I'm OK. And a few days later, another call, then another. I'm startled the first few times. It's usually in the early morning. I admit I can't stop crying no matter where I am.

Finally, I take matters into my own hands and ask for a medical leave. I can't wait for Harry.

"Only a month," I tell my boss, certain I'll be better by then. She doesn't ask any questions, doesn't need to see a letter from Harry (which I offer to obtain), and keeps me on full salary. I've been there nine years. Still, I'm astounded at her confidence and generosity, the well wishes of all my dear, dear friends and bosses at Cliggott Publishing.

⊸∞∞⊷

I lie on his bed, eyes closed. Harry wants to know who is taking care of me.

"Well, Walter, but I can't be around him more than two days." The sweetness of short weekends sometimes seduces me into believing my husband and I can have more. When I awaken from bad dreams, he curls around me and wipes my tears. I often end kissing him. As many times as we've kissed, I never fail to respond. His body promises comfort, renewal. With him, I move in known ways to a place of safety, intense pleasure, and finally, peace.

We love going out for big breakfasts. Like children on holiday, we often drive far up into the country, even to southern Massachusetts, stopping along the way for tea and treats, laughing at nothing, feeding scraps to Friskie, our Australian terrier who rides in my arms, ears back, nose out the window.

Three days with Walter is too much, I tell Harry. I go nearly crazy bumping shins on mental constructs I can't or don't wish to follow. I quickly tire of talk of money, money, money—always money and the things it buys, things Walter seems to want or need. We can't pass a Mercedes or a Jaguar without a comment, part envy, part admiration. I don't say, *I don't* care *what it costs or even that it exists! I have no interest in cars!*

"Another reason?" I tell Harry. "I don't drink anymore, don't smoke, or try not to. But—he's sweet and he listens. He doesn't always get it. He wants to. He's very good to me."

"It isn't time yet to look for another relationship. Breathe into that, soften, let go."

Harry motions me to move over on the bed, so he can sit by my hip. He leans over and wraps his arms around me, then lowers himself tenderly across my upper body, heart to heart, I close my eyes, but I also stiffen, ready to spring away. Within that caution, I try very hard to let go.

His beard is silk on my check. I inhale his clean, soapy smell. Moments pass as we breathe, chests moving as one.

"Let go."

"No. I'll feel too sexual."

"What's wrong with that?"

As his large torso melds deeper into my breasts and belly, I'm flooded with heat and intense sexual desire.

"I don't like—" I go rigid.

"You don't think you're the first person's ever sexual in here, do you? People have orgasms in here."

Sure. But I'm not one of them. People leave their bodies, too, float up to the ceiling. I know that now. If I could, I'd leave mine in a heartbeat.

I picture the Magic Wand vibrator lying half under the bed, for weeks now. And that's about all I remember, until I'm in the car driving home. There, alone, I cling to Harry's oft-repeated argument that he touches people in ways that are not sexual. I trust him. I'm safe. I will always be safe with him. He has total confidence in what he's doing.

———— ⚬⚬⚬ ————

"Twenty-five years," I tell him.

"You mean you haven't let anyone see your legs in all that time?"

"You got it, Harry. Well, bathing suits, of course, but no shorts, no short skirts. That's why I wore shorts today. It's warm, almost hot. I'd like to learn to do this without being afraid."

"I compliment you on trying it out here, where it's safe." He looks at my legs. "They've been through a lot."

"Babies, ugly veins, yeah."

"You know, Trudy, I like the way you've opened up. You're very psychic. And you're a natural healer. Maybe you don't want to go the social-work route. There's lots of colleges. They don't all have requirements. My college didn't have a campus."

"Where?" I ask.

"Carnegie Mellon. There was no campus. You could go to California, become a minister. There's a lot of programs, and it doesn't take all that much training."

He leans over to grab a New Age newspaper from a growing clot of brochures, papers, books, and letters strewn on the floor around our chairs. Pointing to classified ads for mail-order ministerial degrees, he shoves it at me. "You could do it."

I know the insult and blush. "No, thanks."

Why is he angry with me?

"Look, there's lots of spiritual groups around, Trudy. Try the one in Pound Ridge. They're very pure people. They meet on Sunday nights. I go quite often, so I can see you there. It'll help you open up."

I don't say this, but I happen to know about that group through a friend in AA, a shy, wealthy woman who'd been a member a long time and left fearing for her life. She's forbidden to speak of anything that went on there. They're a cult that bilked her for thousands of dollars.

I shake my head. What the fuck?

"Here. Try this, then." He lifts a slim folder from another stack and opens it. A brochure of a nationwide spiritual group. "My wife's a minister with them. They're having a three-day workshop down in the city. You ought to go."

I've heard about them, too, soul travel, teaching acolytes to leave their bodies and travel as soul entities anywhere on earth or in the heavens. Devotees speak of slipping in and out of others' homes at night. I wonder if Harry visits me at night.

They sponsor a local chapter, he tells me. I take the brochure, lean down, and stuff it in my purse. Since it's nearby, maybe I should go.

"I'm tired," he says, stretching, yawning. "Let's sit on the floor." He drops cross-legged onto a clear space in the middle of the room. "Sit," he says, and I do. "No. Opposite me. Cross your legs."

"Let's pray," he says, staring at my crotch. "You like to pray."

"Heavenly Father," he begins, and I drive my whole being into a nut behind my ribs, where I'm safe. When he's done praying, I get up. He stands and reaches for my hands, leans over, and pecks me on the lips, then propels me out the door, saying, "See you around the campus."

There is no campus.

It's five days before I can function at all.

The meeting of that nationwide spiritual group is in a shabby narrow colonial on a side street in a middle-class neighborhood of Greenwich. I can hardly sit still or keep my face composed. The leaders are often at Harry's, I learn, seeing his wife through death from brain cancer. I'm frightened of everyone here. I hate myself for coming, for his pushing me to come.

"Why'd you send me there?" I demand at my next session. "The guru is obviously gay, but he's married and hiding it, for God's sake."

"I don't like them. I tolerate them because she loves them. My teacher is Shyam, in New York."

"Is that where you go Wednesday nights?" Somehow, my fury has faded. I want to know where he goes for spiritual fulfillment. Why he sends me on fools' errands.

"After class we go out to eat; then I drive home and lie awake until four, and I'm up at five." So that explains why he appears exhausted on Thursday mornings, my second weekly session. I suggest we change our time. After all, I'm not working. He declines. He says it's the tea that keeps him awake. Only the tea.

I wonder if he'll see patients during her last days, and beyond.

The following Monday, instead of parking in the driveway under the front windows, I leave my car at the windowless side of Harry's house, walk alongside the garage, and slide in the side door. Tucked in my chair, I wait.

A door slams. From the window to my right, I see him rush out the front door with his daughter. He waves to me to indicate he's taking her somewhere. I don't mind. He's trying to hold the family together.

My chair is falling apart. It's covered by an army blanket to hide a deep hole in the upholstery. The blue-patterned sheet and gray army blanket on the bed are rumpled, the pillows askew. The long, blue couch on the wall behind me is heaped with cushions and a rumpled blanket. Earphones and several tapes are nearby on an end table laden with candles, incense, books, a kitchen table knife, and crystals. Also new to that table are oddly rimmed goggles with an electrical cord plugged into a nearby socket. Does he light candles, lie on the couch, don goggles, crank up flashing images, and enter altered states?

A crystal bigger than a baby is leaning against the wall behind me, like a dead oracle. A huge clump of spiky crystals has recently taken residence behind his chair.

"These're from Arizona," he had explained. "You can go with a local group and mine your own. You oughtta do it. Look into it. You'd enjoy it."

Other crystals and semiprecious stones—all sizes—are finding their way into the room. Many end on the sills of the two large windows facing north and south.

One day, after a particularly horrific hypnotherapy session, Harry slipped a small, clear crystal into my hand. "Carry it with you." Shades of the seductive Dr. Sink, I thought on the way home.

Thirty years earlier, when my third child, Joseph, was born, I suffered from postpartum depression. I saw Dr. Sink infrequently over several years, and ended confused and suicidal. Despite abundant evidence of his serious problems, I was emotionally unable to leave and find someone healthier. Instead, I blamed myself as I spiraled down. One winter's day, just before a trip to Saint Thomas with Kurt, Dr. Sink picked up a clear tourmaline from a scattering of semiprecious stones on his desk and handed it to me.

"Carry it with you," he said, "and know that I love you."

For over a year I kept it in my hand, pocket, or purse, or tucked under my mattress near my head when I slept. As much as I clung to this strange psychiatrist for my sanity, I was disgusted, as his barely noticeable stutter became disabling, that he frequently reeked of perspiration. The faster he fell, the more desperate I was for him to do something to help me. Abruptly, one day, he announced he was leaving for a year, that a Dr. Melbourne was taking over. I later learned that Dr. Sink was being sued by the family of a woman patient who'd committed suicide. She took pills and hid in her attic.

Relieved to find myself with an energetic, highly functional, and clean-smelling psychiatrist, I was also glad Dr. Melbourne was as formal as his office, free from semiprecious stones and walls crowded with patients' amateur artwork. One day, after working with Dr. Melbourne only a few weeks, he probed my longing for my mother. I couldn't stop sobbing. Ten minutes went by, then twenty. My time was up. Shaking, I headed for the door, praying for the nerve to take an overdose of the meprobamate I had in the house, because now I had a plan: if I hid in the attic, no one would find me in time.

Suddenly, Dr. Melbourne blocked the door. He stared at me, looking stern. "If you're willing to work, you will get better. That's a promise." He stepped back, then, and let me go.

Afraid to go home and be alone with meprobamate—the children were at the sitter's house—I drove to my church, parked in the deserted lot in back, lay across the front seat, and wept until the need to die leaked away. Thirty years, and that was the last time I had wanted to die, until Harry.

I saw the good Dr. Melbourne weekly for two and a half years before my trust grew strong enough to reveal details of Sink's whacked-out therapy. Afraid Dr. Melbourne would blame me for getting Dr. Sink to tell me he loved me, I was relieved when he validated that the worsening of my symptoms was the result of my therapist's problems. Before long, I was healthy enough, and angry enough at Sink's cat-and-mouse games, to take the tourmaline into the basement and pulverize it with a hammer.

Never again, I vowed, would a wounded healer hook me with a symbol of his love for me, weaken me by contaminating the room with *his* needs, his incompetence.

Harry's different, I tell myself, as I pocket the crystal. His approach is unique. He can do things others cannot. He's gifted. If not, he wouldn't have been able to open the incest. That's why I want to die. Who wouldn't? I will get through this. Harry is trained in many disciplines; he knows how to use sound and energy to heal people. He's spiritually evolved. He's willing to try anything. And I'm desperate enough to allow it.

⸎

As I head into his room to wait, this day, I stifle the litany of complaints crowding my head, run across the room, and crouch behind an overstuffed chair resembling the large, green one I used to hide behind in the apartment, in Flushing. I settle, knees to chest, glad I'm paying attention to this weird impulse. Perhaps acting out that time in my life, my despair over Mother's not seeming to see me or find me, will help heal me.

Harry spies me there, walks over, and stands looking down. I don't know whether to laugh or cry. And then—he unzips his fly. He pushes his jeans down to the pubic hairline, well below a rounded belly. He motions me to stand and push my pants down.

"Trudy, I'm going to do something. I'm not being weird. I'm not being sexual." He points to the floor. "Lie on your back."

I comply.

He drops heavily to the floor to lie sideways across my body, bare belly on bare belly. I stop breathing. He does not move. Finally, half rising, he pulls his pants up, indicating I'm to do the same. He holds his arms out, motioning me to crawl into his lap. I lie encircled across his full, soft body, and sink my head into his shoulder.

"If you were going to take a trip, where'd you want to go?" he whispers into my ear. "What's your favorite place?"

Chapter 9—Bait and Switch

ACCORDING TO THE LAB RESULTS, MY BLADDER INFECTION has cleared. Then why the constant pain? The whole area is on fire, weeks, now. I feel trapped, angry, sad. I can't tell my women friends how I feel about Harry, what he's doing and saying. I try telling my sponsor. She admits she was in love with her therapist. I suspect they had sex; she doesn't quite say. She doesn't seem to find much wrong with that. She's a social worker. She asks me for Harry's number. She might see him sometime. Her marriage is bad. I leave our meeting feeling I've landed in a strange world where all the rules for conduct have changed.

I want a second opinion.

I tell Harry, "I want the name of a social worker."

"I have a list," he says, dryly. "Why?"

"I need to talk to a woman, someone I can trust."

"Why?"

"Seeing you twice a week is too much. I don't want you calling me to see how I'm doing. I feel trapped. I know that's what this bladder business is all about. You're closing in. I can't stand it!"

"You don't need to see anybody. I'll back off. You're not trapped. I'm trying to help you. The work has to be seductive. These are cycles you need to go through, allow yourself to feel connected. You need to learn not to get angry when you get close. You never learned that. If you can do it, you'll open in ways you never *dreamed*."

Two days later, waiting for Harry, I'm too distressed by bladder pain to even browse the toppling pile of books and magazines on the floor next to our chairs. He's still calling me often at seven in the morning. We've talked about hospitalization. I want that.

He kicks the door closed, two mugs in one hand, and trips. I suck air as my hands fly out to protect myself from his landing in my lap. Inches from me, he catches himself and laughs, then sits, but not before I see his fly is unzipped. I point. He fixes it and laughs again. He tripped on purpose. It was all an act. I'm afraid to ask why.

Forty-five minutes later, after a painful session on the bed in the tunnel—more of Daddy doing I'm not sure what, Harry leans way over to gather me in, bury his face in my neck.

After a few long moments, he pulls back. "Look at me. Feel the soft air coming in the window."

I sigh and try to let go.

"You can take me with you," he says, "carry me with you everywhere. Call me frequently. Let's see each other two or three times a day, for a while."

Jesus! I pull away. What is he *saying*?

"I mean, two or three times a *week*."

I get up and shake my head. Even as I fully respond to the mating call, I know it for a bait and switch.

"Please sit over there," I say. "I have to have something out with you." We settle in our chairs.

"You're handling me far, far too much. I feel sexual all the time. And then guilty and ashamed." I can't say, *Your wife's dying in another room while we hold one another on the bed*. He still doesn't know I know.

He doesn't see the problem. "You have to love me on all levels—heart, sexual, mind, spiritual—to free yourself."

"Why the hooks, Harry? The quick invite, then you back off: 'Oh, not exactly *with* me,' you say. It's too seductive!"

"Trudy, the work has to be seductive, or you can't get through these levels."

The door is open; he is not there. I slip into my chair to wait—and sink. The hole in the middle is about to give way entirely. I tuck my feet under me and shake my head at Harry's latest acquisition dominating the room. It's an enormous metal contraption, reminiscent of the monkey bars I swung on in grammar school. Surely, even someone as large as Harry—who's ballooned to possibly well over three hundred pounds, it seems—can hang from it, swing down, or flip over. These imagined feats seem easily supportable by various levers, springs, and bars.

But Harry declines to explain its purpose.

Tossed on the rug are three red *batakas*, overstuffed, red-cloth swords used in the Bioenergetic world as harmless bats or fake penises. One is easily two feet long, eight inches across. Harry uses them as penises. He holds them between his legs when I lie on my back on the bed. He acts out Dad coming at me, and I scream.

I want to tell him none of this is helping. Lately, I've noticed a small copper pyramid under the middle of the bed. When I pointed to it, he explained that it sends healing energy to anyone lying there.

I stare at the bed, wondering what stories it could tell. Its rumpled covers suggest patients writhing in agony, struggling to recover memories, or deny them. Al Lowen doesn't have a double bed. His small therapy room has a simple, white, surgical-looking cot with a clean, white sheet.

From the window, I spot Harry pulling up in front of the house and rushing in the front door, knowing too well what it takes to be mother and father to teenagers. I tried to parent four at the same time. Moments later I hear the kettle whistle; then the door to his part of the house slams shut, and quick footsteps cross the narrow waiting room. He kicks off his shoes and flings the door closed with one hand, balancing two mugs of hot tea in the other.

Embarrassed by the grievous state of his family life, I talk about my week but find it difficult to stay on track.

"Stop," he says. "What're you feeling?"

I close my eyes and breathe deeply. Guilt. And under that, like the flip of a light switch, joy. Joy at being alive. How strange!

"Go back to guilt, stay with the feeling, and let it flow away."

But it's tears that flow. Finally, I rummage through my purse for my latest dream. "I'm on a journey, and I'm stuck on a spit of land with a hook, something like Cape Cod. See?" I show him my drawing and only then realize I've drawn an enormous penis. "I'm stuck at the base of it. I want to travel to the tip and leave. I can't."

"Hmm," Harry says.

"This represents you." I tap the penis with my fingernail. "I'm stuck on a man's penis. It might as well be my father's."

He doesn't see the dream that way. "Besides," he says, "you're not ready for sex. You're still healing from your first husband."

"I left him fifteen years ago!"

"You talked about it last time."

"I don't remember."

"I do. You need to heal before you get involved with a man again. This is not the time."

"Maybe not, but guys are picking up signals. There's three showing interest. Why do I feel guilty? In the past, I was so needy I picked people I couldn't—"

"Let's go over there." He points to the bed.

When I'm settled, he pulls up a chair, leans over me, and places a hand on my waist—except, this time, he slips his fingers beneath my sweats and underpants and lightly strokes my belly.

Tears of helplessness leak into my ears. I long for my mother. As though reading my mind, Harry lifts his hand and lays the fleshy base of his thumb in my mouth. "Suck," he says, and I do, sexually hot to my toes.

He brings both hands up and cradles my cheeks. "Look into my eyes." His thumb teases my chin and upper lip.

"Mother!" I yell, closing my eyes, reaching blindly for her, seeing instead crib rails and a clear image of Dad's penis, his glassy, dark eyes boring into mine.

"Die, you bastard!" I scream, clenching my fists, as Harry springs out of harm's way. I want to beat someone to death—but I can't. I freeze.

I *wanted* it. Him. I must have. Oh, Jesus, it *was* my fault, all of it.

Eyes still closed, I fall back, arms out for Harry, who holds me close until childhood fades. When I hear the tinkle of a tiny bell, I open my eyes. So *this* explains the ornate brass bells of all sizes scattered around the bed.

"Let each bell reverberate where I hold it. It'll bring healing."

I throw my arms over my head and draw my feet up sole to sole. He rings the bells over my body, one at a time. One tone is musical yet tinny, like a harpsichord. Another emits a round mellow *thwang* as he holds it over my heart and midriff. A heavier bell over my genitals goes *thwack*.

"The neck and genitals are vibrationally connected. A holding in one produces a holding in the other. They're Tibetan bells. This one"—he picks up the largest, probably too heavy for me to lift—"will release your stiff lower back." It rumbles over my abdomen.

He drops it on the floor to sit beside me.

I search his face. Have my reactions pleased him?

"I love you," I say. "And I know you love me, no matter what you say. I know you do."

He looks away, then back, unsmiling. "Yes, I do."

Can I stay open yet safe, loving and not needy? Can I trust he's not available to me as a man? Can I love without guilt or shame someone who knows everything about me?

Driving home, I tell myself Harry's going to take me through this, let me go, and I'll be OK. I'll be OK. But so often the phrase "no decent way out of it" echoes through my head like a chant from an ancient scroll.

That night, as I often do, I sit up in bed writing in my journal, admitting *I am needy and scared and vulnerable and sensual, and I want to focus all of it on somebody*, then put it away. I check the strip of light under the door. No moving shadow. I'll be all right.

The next morning, I meet two women friends for breakfast. When I leave, pregnant with secrets, I venture alone to an old Hadassah thrift shop and rummage among musty dresses, longing for Mother.

It seems strange going to Harry's on Mondays at noon. Even before he sits and hands me my tea, he says, "I'd like you to see someone. She's a psychic with a gift for tuning into people. It might help you get clear."

"You mean she can see for *certain* if it really happened? What should I tell her?"

"Whatever you want. She'll know what to do." He lowers his voice: "Trudy, it's a safe place. I work with her myself every Saturday morning. And my wife does. And sometimes my kids join us. When I have sessions alone with her, I get into my eagle and soar." His right hand becomes a swooping eagle.

He's my eagle, I think, and say, "I thought you went away to workshops every weekend."

"We do. After."

At the end of the hour, Harry gets up to rummage through his bookcase, spilling much of its contents onto the floor.

I move to the door and survey the room. The thick, lavender carpeting is littered with cassettes, some around his chair, others scattered near the bed, a few on tabletops. They're recordings of sounds or chanting to enhance healing and the spirit. None are stored in a large wooden cassette-storage box propped against the back window. A wifely effort to contain him, I suspect.

I picture Harry lying on the long, blue couch or the bed listening to music through earphones, his wife in another part of the house. How much time does he spend here alone? Is he angry with her?

When my mother died, I was angry. Long before she was too sick to function, she used illness as an excuse to abandon us—or so I believed. Maybe she *was* too sick to function. Dying people sometimes wield power over those around them as a form of revenge. I can't help wondering if Harry has broken his wife's spirit, that she's dying to set herself free. If he's had sex with patients—well, not *if*, he told me he had—then surely she knows, at least on some level, to use his favorite phrase.

As I come out of my reverie, Harry is standing, handing me a catalog. "I brought you this. They have great summer weekend programs."

I glance at it. "I know. You told me. I sent for one." Rhinebeck, New York, is a two and a half hour drive. I can't even drive to work. I shake my head.

"It'd be good for you, Trudy. I go a lot. The weekend of the twenty-eighth they're having a kinda spiritual concert. Sounds you never dreamed! This guy sings two notes at the same time. It's weird." He laughs and pretends to lose his balance, as if the singing is so amazing it literally bowls him over. He's been doing this lately. I'm embarrassed for him.

According to Harry, only spiritually evolved people can produce a dual sound. Perhaps he forgot he told me this and showed me the tapes he sent for. I can't imagine listening. My idea of music is firmly grounded in rhythm and harmony, Verdi, Mozart, Haydn, Puccini, Bach.

A man will do anything to distract himself if his wife is dying. I shake my head again.

"Just try it," he urges. "Well—go—not exactly in the car with me. My son's going."

I can't handle that! What's wrong with him?

The next morning I awaken at dawn with a pounding headache and bloated stomach. My upper back and arms are stiff and sore. I want to take my fists and smash something. Or someone.

———

At her cottage door, I'm greeted warmly by a pale-skinned, clear-eyed, plump woman. She hugs me, then leads the way to the kitchen for a cup of herb tea. We're on Candlewood Lake, about an hour's drive from my condo in Norwalk. Over tea, she tells me about her work on Saturday mornings with Harry and his wife.

"They're resolving some serious marital problems, and sometimes we bring the kids in."

"He told me they go away, after, to workshops."

She nods. "Omega, usually. Have you been there?"

"No." It doesn't occur to her I don't want to hang out with my psychiatrist and his dying wife, his three kids. I take a deep breath and exhale the thought, hoping it will disappear completely. How much does she pick up?

"He was all set to come up tonight and do energy work, get in his eagle and soar, but his wife called to cancel. It's their twenty-first wedding anniversary. She wants him to take her to dinner. She's lovely! They have a *neat* relationship."

Right. It's their last anniversary, and he made plans to fly solo with a psychic.

"Why don't you come over Saturday mornings; then you don't have to drive up here to Danbury? I'll work on you in their basement. Harry won't mind."

"No," I say, keeping my face bland as I lower myself onto an Indian blanket on the floor.

She kneels over me and places semiprecious stones on the soft parts of my trunk, arms, legs. Can she see inside me, read my heart; will she tell Harry I'm hopelessly in love with him? I lie spread-eagled, wishing for a lead shield.

Soon, though, I forget him and drift away behind my eyes as scenes form and dissolve, clear as gentle jump cuts in old black-and-white movies, before the talkies. I'm a Roman nobleman in a white toga, then a Dutch girl in wooden shoes playing by the side of the dyke; my older sister pushes me in. Why won't she love me?

I'm an old wise woman living in New England, gathering herbs from my garden. I'm the village healer; the townsmen want to kill me.

Then, I'm little and it's this life.

I beg this sweet woman bending over me, tending me: "Can you see what he did?" The phrase from a song, *Can you see what I see?* floats through my head.

She can't.

I leave trembling and in tears, knowing that because Harry wants me to, I'll return again and again, spending money I can ill afford. At home, because of her encouragement, I spend hours in prayer and meditation, sending Harry healing energy.

———

The door is open; I kick off my sandals and stand stiff with anger. Instead of waiting in my chair, I flop on the bed and kick straight-legged and beat the mattress with my fists—and it works. When I get up, I'm energized and no longer furious. I see Harry placing hot mugs on the glass-topped table. He turns and opens his arms, happy to see me. We hug. Still not speaking, we settle in our chairs. The windows are open, the air gentle. It's July. As I try to settle myself, I'm aware something's under my skin. An irritant.

"Maybe I'm driving myself too hard," I say, "what with all my reading, going to various meetings, planning a trip to Vancouver for another Bioenergetic workshop with Lowen, and then, when I quit my job, you know, I plan to sell the house and go back to school, maybe write a book. Now you want me to see another psychic, in Naugatuck. And you want me to find a spiritual group."

What began as a run-through of how my life is now ends in frustration at his sending me here, there, and the next place.

He sits squared-off, hands on his thighs, and stares at me.

Fuck. I spring up and head for the bed. "Let's go over there so I can lie down. I want you to take care of me." I perch on the edge of the mattress.

"You'll abandon me." I have blurted that, having no idea I would.

He pulls up a chair. We're knee to knee. "Why?"

"Because I'm too much, too sexy, too heady, too many activities—"

"Go back to the first."

"You're threatened by me."

"I haven't been threatened in a long time." He laughs heartily. "My hands are warm. See? Do your number. I can handle it."

I give up trying to express what I'm feeling, collapse onto the bed, reach for his hand, and place it on my waist. He slides warm fingers under the waistband of my sweats and underpants, and gently strokes to my pubis. I shiver. I hold my breath, then exhale the mantras he's taught me. He's offering healing. It's OK. He's a doctor. He knows how to touch in ways that are not sexual.

Only a few weeks ago, walking me to the door, he told me how, when on the international Bioenergetic training circuit, it shocked him to watch the French therapists. "They can't touch nonsexually. They freak out the women! I tried to tell 'em, you're *seductive*. Maybe it's cultural," he concluded, seeming to fall and catch himself a couple of times, that little off-balance stumbling act he's been doing.

OK, he is *not* being seductive. But still, I'm glad my skin is butter soft and fragrant from peach lotion. And then, a trembling starts, deep inside me.

I plead with him: "All I want is to be your friend, don't you understand? For my father, I was irresistibly sexy at three, four, and five, even two! You know what he did in the crib. It was my fault he couldn't control himself. If I get close to a man, I'm too threatening. I'll be abandoned."

My ears and hair are wet from tears. What I meant to say was, don't abandon me *within the relationship*.

"That's over, Trudy. I'm here. Look at me."

I turn my face away. He turns it back, a hand on my cheek.

"Trudy, look at me."

I shut my eyes, surprised to hear myself call frantically for my children. "Elizabeth! Joseph!"

"They aren't here. *I'm* here."

I toss my head violently. If I love him, he'll turn on me.

"You had no safe place to be. Your father hurt you, and your mother wasn't there for you. She let him do that to you."

I turn and look him in the eye. "She tried to protect me! She couldn't help it."

His hand gestures me to slide over. He sits on the bed. "I'm Harry and I'm here." He slides his arms underneath me and gathers me in. "I'm not threatened. I'm not going to abandon you. I'm not going to let you down. Those are images, Trudy, your children, your father. They're not here. You live too much in your imagination." He scrubs his warm face down into my shoulder.

"*You* brought me into the tunnel."

He raises his head, mouth inches from mine. "Yes, but those are memories. It's not happening now."

"What are you talking about! It's happening all the time."

"Trudy, I'm going to do something. I'm not being weird. I'm not being sexual." He crawls slowly onto the bed so he can kneel over me, pressing his full body down snugly onto mine, chest to chest, belly to belly, his thighs warm and tight against my outstretched legs.

"Stroke my face," he says.

As heat courses through my body, I close my eyes, helpless and bereft as an infant. I reach for his face, wanting it to be Mother's. I feel his beard.

Instantly, I make a pact with myself. *I'll call my doctor, two doctors, if I have to, to get enough Valium, and if he can't keep his distance today, I'll take my pills and go to sleep in the attic.*

I don't dare move. I wait. He doesn't move. I realize he isn't going to do anything more. Gradually energy prickles my soles and moves slowly up to my hips.

"Let go," he says as he climbs off me and the bed to sit in his chair. "You need to relax your muscles so you can feel touch."

"I try all the time."

And then I dare say it. "What if I love you? How will you handle it? Will you want me as a woman; will you abandon me?"

"You already love me," he says quietly, reasonably.

"Yes, but I'm in a terrible bind."

"I won't abandon you."

"I have no way to know that."

"Do you trust me?"

I nod. And that's a lie.

"Then all you can do is trust. I won't abandon you. I love you."

"Why?"

"Because you're an exciting woman. You have a beautiful mind and spirit and a beautiful body. I like your energy. I like to watch you move."

"If I accept that you love me, it'll blow me apart. I'll explode and disappear into the universe."

I see it happening. It happened before. I don't know how I know that, but I do.

Chapter 10—Mothers and Fathers

WALTER AND I, LIVING APART NOW FOR MORE than half a year, have settled into an easy routine. He comes to my house on weekends and helps me shop and cook, happy to be needed now that he's no longer working. At his beach house, we do the same. His kids are both away at school. Besides Friskie and a few cats, he now has his old Portuguese water dog back from his former wife. When the weather allows, we take low chairs out onto the sand to sit at the water's edge and throw sticks and flotsam for Friskie, not Sconnie, who's nine and likes to snooze on the couch inside.

One day, alone on the beach, water lapping at my feet, busy writing in my journal, I look up to see Walter hurrying from the house. "I just got off the phone with Kurt."

"What on earth does my ex want with you?"

"Don't you remember the day I told him about that parcel of land?"

I did remember. Walter and I had stopped by my sons' construction site, where they were putting up what proved to be prizewinning condominiums. And then Kurt appeared. He hadn't seen me in ages and commented on how thin I was.

Here was a perfect opportunity to tell him about my father and take ownership of why I hadn't been the wife Kurt had hoped for, my part in why our marriage failed. And so I suggested we three walk over to HoJo's for coffee. "Let's let the boys get back to work. I have something I want to tell you."

With Walter by my side, I explained what I knew about my father so far, as best I could, and with no show of surprise, Kurt said, "I always thought that might have happened."

It was then that Walter told my ex about a parcel of land for sale, thinking Kurt might help the boys purchase and develop it, and he could earn a finder's fee. But that was weeks ago. We assumed he wasn't interested.

Walter folds himself down into the low beach chair and lights a cigarette. "We just might have a deal on that land, Trudy. Maybe I'll get a fee after all. But here's the thing. Kurt wanted to talk about you. He said, 'I'm having trouble with the fact that she's suddenly aware of this incident with her father.'

"'Hell,' he said, 'if something like that happened to you or me, Walter, we'd sure as hell know it a week later, a month later, and fifty years later. It's not something you forget until you're fifty-four. Her family's funny, though, and as far as the old man's concerned, he's hostile as hell.'"

"I kept him talking," Walter went on, "because I wanted to know what he thought of your mother. He said she was gracious. He liked her."

My eyes are closed, but I feel Walter take my hand.

"Honey, do you remember when we first met? You hated her. But you'd tell me how she took you to a special stream in Wilton, to pick watercress. How she kept you home from school just to be with you, took you to lunch at nice places, and shopping. She bought you a hope chest and filled it with linen and lacey nightgowns. She taught you to sing—in German! It blew me away that she showed you how to darn socks the proper way, with one of those wooden eggs."

Oh, Christ, I think, dropping my head back to watch the occasional cloud hurrying east. Maybe I can dissociate here, ask myself why our weather always come from the west.

But it's true. I told him all that, and more. The only reason I recounted those memories was because Walter still missed *his* mother. He seemed comforted hearing what I could dredge up about mine. Despite Walter, she was my mother and the sum of all her parts, not just a few, and she totally let me down.

But he was back to socks. "Do you know how many women can darn on one of those egg things?"

"No. But I've done it, many times."

"Good God, Trudy, don't you *listen* to yourself? You look so happy when you tell me about her."

"So you're saying, if I hate her so much, why do I feast on her memories?"

"Yes! You treasure them, only you don't seem to know it."

I doubt I know much of anything anymore.

"Kurt thinks maybe you swung into the latest psychological fad. The media's been harping on child abuse the last two or three years."

"I can't blame Kurt for not getting it. I have trouble, even now."

I pull my hand away from his and hold up two fingers for a cigarette. I need time, space. I need to breathe.

He cups his hands around a fresh cigarette. "How come I get it?"

"I don't know. Most people don't."

"I told him, 'Kurt, what she feels is real, and I'm doing everything I can to support her.'"

We sit quietly for a while, absorbed by the ebbing tide.

"Forgive me, Trudy, if I betrayed you in asking about your mother. I had a golden opportunity to talk to someone who knew her. I wish I'd known her. My mother died when I was seventeen. Those homely parts of your mother—I'd have liked her. Not that she didn't let you down. Christ, Trudy, I *know*. But all of what you are, so much of what you are—what I love about you—is her."

"Well, I do know one thing: without my mother, I'd never have learned pleasure or generosity. Never. I'd never have learned how to play. I still play in lots of ways, even feeling as bad as I do. Did I ever tell you she let me take percale sheets and down pillows outside to make tents in the driveway? Ann and I invented a game called Arabian Nights. Dad would have killed us.

"She hid everything fun from my father. The hope chest, too, my trousseau, kept secret. Once a month, he went to the patent office in DC, for a couple days, and let me tell you, we played! Creamed eggs on toast for dinner, fudge for dessert, dress-ups all over the living room. She let us listen to the mysteries on the radio, *The Shadow* and *Bulldog Drummond*. He forbade everything but classical music, as if that were a punishment. But when he was away, we'd sit on the rug in the dining room next to the radio eating homemade candy out of the pan, happy as truants.

"You know why I polish my fingernails? Mother painted mine with her best manicure set, best polish, *Chen Yu*, all the rage in the forties. Once, she got hold of a rare collection of nineteenth-century taffeta dresses with bustles and beads, and she let us play with them until they were rags. He didn't approve of dress-up, makeup. Red nails meant you were cheap.

"I wanted long hair, but he cropped it. You know what she did? She saved to get me a permanent wave. I was eleven. He would never have paid for it."

"Keep talking. You're giving me back my own mother."

I see tears in his eyes, and go on. "She had this way, when she powdered her face, of wetting a finger and wiping flakes off her nostrils. That's the trick, so you don't look powdered. I still do that.

"Oh, and chocolates! She never went to town, which in our house meant Manhattan, without bringing home a box of Fannie Farmer's, and she didn't care if I put the yucky green ones back, bite side down. She didn't care if you made a mistake, and she didn't punish, not for anything."

Another memory burbles up, the day she told me masturbation was perfectly normal. I tell Walter, "I can still see her laughing, head back, letting me know it's too silly to worry about. 'Everyone does it,' she said."

Walter laughs, then sits up to finish a coughing fit and lights another cigarette. "Do you remember telling me that after your kids had confirmation and had to start going to confession, you told them not to confess masturbation, that it was normal, and the Catholic's ideas about that were nonsense?"

"I did tell them not to do it in public, you know."

But he doesn't laugh. "You need to own your mother, in yourself."

"I guess. Maybe. I used to credit my father with everything, teaching me to do cartwheels, which I did with my kids, even in my thirties. He taught me how, but it's Mother who allowed me to play."

"You took them camping after you divorced."

"Oh, that was purely selfish. I loved the silence and the woods, and they loved it."

Needing something, craving something, and not knowing what, I jump up and head for the house. "Maybe I hated the wrong parent."

<hr />

That night, at home, I spend hours rummaging through old photographs, searching for negatives of the photos of Mother I destroyed in the twenty years I despised her. There, to my relief, is a large studio portrait of her before she married. She's beautiful. Serene.

I'll get it enlarged and take it to my painting class and begin her portrait in oil. The photo is in black and white, but I know her skin, her darkening hair, green eyes.

The next morning, feeling as though I've stumbled into a new land, I call Ann. I speak quickly, wanting to share my discovery, get out all the reasons we failed to credit Mother with anything. I wish I could hold my mother in my arms and tell her I forgive her everything, and I love her, but I would never share all that.

Ann is not hearing me. I bring up Deborah, the woman Dad married a year after Mother died.

"But Ann, why did we end up hating—not hating, so much—disdaining Deborah, especially the last fifteen years before she died?" Deborah had been an ideal, even perfect, stepmother for twenty-five years.

My sister is not so sure.

"But, Ann, she was never unkind. She gave me her sewing machine when mine died, and fabric and dressmaking tools to make clothes. She gave me her silver coffee-and-tea service, silver flatware, crystal, things I cherish to this day.

"She helped me move and paint my house when I got divorced. She made dresses for the twins—hand smocked. When that huge maple fell in my backyard and I had no money, she brought a chain saw and gasoline, for Christ's sake, and she and the boys cut it up. Good God, Ann, why did we hate her?"

But I know why I did, the same reason maybe Ann does. Loyalty to Dad. When Deborah was talking, he'd often wink and grin at us, making fun of what she was saying. We *had* to take sides. Now, desperate for someone to recognize Mother's creative and loving traits, I call my brother.

It doesn't go well. In his defense, I think my mother drew a line around herself to keep my brother out when he was born. I have trouble believing she loved him. Maybe a second male in the house was one too many.

━━∞━━

I go to sleep, my cheek on my pillow, imagining I'm a baby at my mother's breast. I awaken with a solid awareness—perhaps from a dream—that Harry is in a powerful struggle with his own mother, that his conflicting feelings about her contaminate his professional relationship with me.

Although she's long dead, he told me he still regrets her overinvolvement with him. At times she acted the little girl and displayed a sensitive, caring nature, easily wounded. But when her controlling, almost paranoid, sadistic nature triggered his anger, she hit him with a nightstick, shutting him down hard, blocking his outrage. Other feelings were permitted, but never anger.

Oddly, he told me, she was the parent with whom he had a deep soul connection. She placed him on a pedestal. His schoolwork and musical studies were sacrosanct. Unlike his siblings, he was exempt from housework and ordinary rules.

He tried in vain to get his father to let him help with something, anything. He believes the man loved him, but they had nothing to say to each other. And it's like that with his wife, he told me.

<hr />

Burdened and disturbed by Harry's history and sorrows, I arrive at my next session on the point of exploding.

Before he even sits, I say, "I'm angry."

His lips are hidden by a much fuller mustache and beard, but I know he isn't smiling.

"Well?" I prod.

No response.

"You get too close!"

"Too close?" His voice is flat.

"You swallow me up, take everything. Dad took everything, the choicest food, all the intellectuality, sexuality, anger. We had no air."

He stares at me. "Umm."

He isn't going to return my tennis balls. Clearly, he disapproves of what I'm saying. I search for another topic.

"Why do I wake up with headaches?"

"When did they start?"

"Ten years ago. Why?"

"Maybe you felt no one would ever take care of you again."

"I lived so differently before I took the editing job at Cliggott. Oh, sure, I had temp jobs, but I was at Sarah Lawrence working on my degree, singing opera roles off Broadway, solos at church. Maybe I wasn't sleeping, but I had a wonderful life."

No flicker of response. I wait, then go on.

"And I was active in NOW," I say, "a consciousness-raising group, and going to workshops on writing, other things. I sang in little concerts with friends: Vivaldi's *Gloria*, *Pinafore* with a local Gilbert and Sullivan group. I was forever hamming it up around the piano at parties. And dating."

Is he angry because I'm bragging? I'm afraid to continue, afraid not to. Am I egocentric? Does he hate me?

I stumble on: "I worried sick how I'd ever have a productive work life when my child support ran out. Did I ever tell you scouts from network television wanted to do a Friday-night special on me, a woman who'd survived a midlife crisis? About eight years ago. I couldn't do it because they wanted to focus so much on my divorce, and the kids'd be hurt if I revealed too much. Anyway, that was my excuse. And then I got that job as an editor, so I had to give up my dream of finishing college. I drank a lot that fall."

He's turned to stone. I talk on, hoping I'll find myself.

"I took one more course at Sarah Lawrence, but it was too difficult working full time and raising the kids. I couldn't sing as often, and I missed being with my women friends. The job took nearly everything. That's when the headaches started. The tension in the neck and shoulders. Still, those were good years. Even though I worked hard, I sang, I was active in church, traveled abroad, gave parties."

Somehow, the hour ends.

"This is your father speaking," intones my answering machine. "I'm back on the ranch."

The cryptic message means he's back at his condominium in Southbury, Connecticut, having driven north from his winter home, Jekyll Island, Georgia.

I wait for evening, for Walter to come, before returning the call. As my father's phone rings, I reach across the kitchen table for my husband's hand.

"If it seems I'm avoiding you," I tell Dad, "I've been going through something."

"I know! I'm worried about you." His concern seems genuine. He sounds as though he loves me. We chat as if old friends. My father doesn't pry into why I'm too ill to work, but then he rarely questions anything in my life.

As we talk, I keep my eyes on Walter, and he never takes his off mine, even as he sips vodka and tonic and smokes a cigarette. I'm glad we made plans to go out for Italian food after this.

Abruptly, my father shifts into the distant past, when Ann and I were babies. Astonished at this new direction, I sit up. He mentions a black woman who was our maid. Marveling at the coincidence of his gift of memory, after I've about given up hoping for clarification from Teddy or Ann, I blurt out, "Then we *did* know a black family."

"Well, yes," he admits, almost absently, as though I've interrupted a reverie. "Mid had a black woman help her when she had the miscarriages."

Mid is short for Mildred. I have gooseflesh hearing the word from his lips.

"Dad, it's odd you bring that up. I remember staying with a black family when I was little. Why would I have done that?"

"Oh?" His voice fades as he adds, "That's the past, and the past is prologue. Do you know where that's from?"

I do, thanks to him—and end the conversation before he suggests we get together.

His eyes are a muddy brown this morning, and that healthy glow from around his cheekbones has vanished. Harry is gray, if not distraught.

"I'm sorry," I tell him.

He raises his eyebrows.

"I see sadness in your face," I say.

"Yes, I'm very sad."

"I thought about you briefly Saturday night. I had the feeling you were crying." Burdened and embarrassed by his bereavement, I twist in my seat. "I sent you love and pictured you surrounded by golden light."

Actually, I had been speeding home on a train from Pennsylvania, where I'd spent a few days with a close woman friend. The gentle rocking kept all my erotic energy focused on Harry. Hours went by during which I was unable to read or think of anything but wanting him. Yet, every time I pictured him moving about or in session, I'd see tears coursing down his cheeks.

"Thank you." He slides his chair close enough to take my hands in his, rub his sock feet over my bare ones. "I'll take all the love I can get."

"Go away," I whisper, not moving.

Harry waits for me to look up, then stares into my eyes until I flush to my toes.

He's taught me to breathe synchronistically with him and imagine a rush of energy coming in the top of his head, coursing down through his body to his sexual organs, flowing across to mine, up my spine, and out the top of my head, then circling back to his.

"Suck my energy," he'll say, to keep the imaginary wheel in motion.

I'm to take him in on all levels. "Levels" is his word for the chakras—small vortexes of energy swirling in the head, third eye, throat, heart, belly, sexual organs. "Levels" is also his word for depth of feeling, one's ability to peel back layers of psychological trauma.

"Let's look at those levels," he'll say. Or, complimenting me for letting him get close, "Only a few patients are willing to work to these levels." Or "Bring it up from the sexual to the heart, to the head; move it through those levels."

Now, Harry pushes gently against my feet, sliding his chair back a few inches, enough to disconnect our fingers and toes, while continuing to hold my eyes for what seems ten or fifteen minutes. He's careful not to contaminate the meditation work with touch, I think, or trigger strong sexual feelings.

It's impossible not to.

Finally, he shifts, smiling easily to signal the end of communion. "That flow—if you can take in that love, you'll also be able to take it in from other people. That's what it's all about."

I'm afraid to ask directly about his wife, but I need to dispel anxiety about her coming death, how that will effect him and, ultimately, my treatment.

"I pick up things I have no business knowing," I say.

"I pick up things, too," he says softly, head dropping to one side. He looks, suddenly, very young, vulnerable.

For some reason I'm reminded of Emily, one of Harry's patients whom I know through Walter. The day before, she told me gaily she was going to see Harry for hypnosis to get over her latest love affair, lose weight, and stop smoking. She sees him infrequently but "adores" him. When he holds her in his arms on the bed, she flies right out of her body, she brags.

I try to imagine doing that and wish I could.

I tell him of my conversation with Emily, rather than asking him what about me he picks up. "That's her ten-dollar cure," I say. "One visit and everything's taken care of. Wouldn't that be nice? I saw her at Walter's yesterday. She's preparing a script for TV, and he's trying to connect her with producers he used to work with. She's a talented lady. Trouble is, she always stops by when she knows I'm not there. He tells me there's a lot of stooping to pet the dogs in low-cut dresses. You know Walter. Cheap thrills are not his style."

"Yeah, that's Emily. Maybe her father—He bails her out financially. Some sort of sticky side there." He swirls his fingers in a miniwhirlpool. "Not actually incest, maybe, but incestuous. Something."

I can't help wondering what Harry does with her on the bed. She'd never stop him.

<hr />

A week later, his eyes are ashen holes. I tell him I'm deeply concerned.

He says, "You pick up so much, if I denied I'm sad, it'd be crazy making. Most the others don't notice."

"Want to talk about it?" I ask, needing to.

"Not now."

I eye him carefully. Can I tell him what I have on my mind? I back into it. "Things are going well at work. I've been back a few days, and I know I'm going to make it this time." It's the end of August. I was out almost two months. "But that isn't what I want to talk about. I'm angry."

He does not move or respond.

"I'm sick of your getting too close, throwing out suggestions for going somewhere, doing something together. Suggesting I see you at church, like you did last week. Or a workshop. It's all bullshit. You spring the invitations on me when I'm on my way out the door."

I'm afraid to add that after he holds me close and asks me to go to whatever event he's planning to attend, alone, I stew about what to do, afraid I'll see him, afraid I won't. Is he wooing me as a woman? I'm as terrified of unbounded closeness, as I am obsessed by wanting it.

"I'm sick of it, Harry. You throw out a line like bait. And even so, you're not clear. It's very seductive."

"Yes, very."

"But you're standing well back of the line. It's like a fishhook in the heart, only you're on shore. I get hurt. You rip the hook out, and I bleed, because you don't want to see me or meet me to start with. That's what you say, after you invite me. It leaves me naked, exposed."

Even as I blame him, I doubt myself. His repeated warning rings in my ears: "Let it happen with me or you'll never get close to anyone." In his mind, that's what it takes to get me over Daddy.

"I don't work this way when I do workshops," he says.

I assume he means intimately.

"I love to travel, and I love my work. It satisfied my ego to combine the two." Since his wife became ill, he no longer gives workshops.

Although he's shifted my agenda out of sight, I'm relieved at venting, and I let my demands go, sure he's heard me, hoping he has my best interests at heart. I must learn not to attack him. My task is not to overreact but to become desensitized "on those levels."

Later, on the bed, eyes closed, breathing deeply, I forget everything as I acknowledge the coming of fall, leaves turning gold, then red, and finally brown. I grieve for the little girl lying on a bed of autumn leaves in the woods, and also for the woman still helpless to heal from something that already happened. Every fall of my life, I have become ill with one disorder or another, establishing so familiar a pattern that I call it the fall sickness.

"You won't heal this fall sickness by being angry and driving yourself," Harry points out gently, "but by softening, taking love in, and letting it flow."

I try to turn away as he strokes my forehead, nestles his head into my shoulder, whispers an incantation too low for me to catch the words.

"It's easier to look at how I've been betrayed," I tell him, "than to look at how I betray myself." I wait for a response that does not come. His beard caresses my cheek, his full lips warm on my neck. "If I believe in soul continuity and, and—God, then why am I still afraid?"

His fingers are on my face, stroking it. "Because you're here in your personality."

"Harry, is doing therapy a burden for you?"

"I have something to give and I give it."

Suddenly, I'm aware my fists are clenched, hands like ice. "I'm not going to die. I promise you."

She will, his wife will, but I won't.

"What has kept you going, Trudy, is your joy."

"I love you very much."

<hr />

That night, I dream I'm looking out my window. Harry is standing by a lamppost, crying. A policeman offers comfort. The policeman is me.

When I read Harry the dream, at our next session, I tell him that it reminds me of how my father had stood by the lamppost in our driveway the day I left for college. Unable to say good-bye, he'd picked up a stone and thrown it into the woods, face coming loose with sadness.

My only thought as I drove away to college was guilt for abandoning him.

Chapter 11—In the Wake of the Wake

"I KNOW WHAT'S GOING ON IN HERE," I say, as soon as he hands me my tea.

"*What?*"

"I know your wife is sick."

"I told you that."

Embarrassed at bungling the secret I'm finally letting out of the bag, I say, "No, you didn't, but I know the extent of it."

He sighs heavily. "We tried everything—Her breast cancer metastasized to the brain. I tell you things because it's crazy making not to. This bonding work—" His voice trails off. "It's OK for us to share things with each other, as long as we keep clear." "Clear," like "levels," is another slippery construct I struggle to grasp.

As he talks on about the support he's putting in place for her through music and friends, I tune out and picture, instead, the compartments he's laid out for me. Our love for one another in one place, our work in another, his wife in yet another.

Just the fact that I know a beautiful, talented woman is dying and leaving three teenagers is enough to keep her in my thoughts and prayers. And of course, I'm sodden with guilt when her husband lies over me on the bed, strokes my hair, face, chest, arms, belly, fingers almost reaching the wettest, warmest place.

Sweat breaks out above my lips and around my neck.

He asks, "Do you have any classical-music cassettes I can borrow for her?"

I nod but stubbornly return the conversation to myself. "It's not men I want; it's my mother. Men are poor substitutes."

When Harry gives no sign of having heard, I apologize for not being more loving toward him and say, "I wish I could disagree lovingly."

"Trudy, we may go through these cycles two or three more times, as you learn."

<hr />

Dawn. I step out of the shower, surprised to find a message on my answering machine. Should I listen? I'm in hurry to get to work.

It's Harry. His wife died very early this morning, September 25. I'm numb, the way you are when that first sharp in-breath carries you up and away. I stay like that the rest of the day, in a dream state.

He telephones the next day. "Calling hours are Sunday seven to nine. I'd like you to come."

"I'll be there."

He speaks of the emptiness, the relief her suffering has ended. My tears spill onto the mouthpiece. I know what it was like when Kurt left and how deeply comforting to have my children with me, and so that is my first concern. Will he be alone?

"Will your children be home this year, or away at school?"

"Home."

Thank God.

The next evening, churning over how to manage the wake without panic, I pace the kitchen, stopping from time to time to look out over the valley to the hill where I lived so long ago. And then, I do what I've been taught in AA and dial a familiar number.

"Amanda? Harry asked me to come to the wake. I don't want to. I'm scared."

"Wow," says my new sponsor. "I hear it in your voice. Do you want me to come with you?" It would mean her leaving her four boys at dinnertime.

"No, I'll be OK." Besides, how to explain her presence in the funeral parlor?

"Call me if you change your mind. By the way, Deena G. started seeing Harry."

Deena, a social worker, was my first sponsor; she learned about Harry from me.

"But you know what?" Amanda says. "He saw her the day his wife died. He saw patients that day. And it was her first visit. What's the matter with this guy?"

I'm dimly aware, after I hang up, that if my new sponsor, a bright, caring woman, knew of all my thoughts and feelings about Harry and his bizarre treatments, she'd intervene. Maybe what stops me from telling anyone is that I'd have to admit I'm obsessed with him. Actually, I did tell someone. I spilled everything to my friend in Pennsylvania.

Her advice was that he's abusing me, and to leave—immediately.

Being tall, Harry's easy to spot in a crowd. Grinning, he signals me to join him in the back of one of the hushed, upholstered rooms in the funeral parlor. I give the open casket a wide berth, look up, and am stunned by Harry's commanding appearance. No unkempt hair and raggedy beard. He's trim and handsome, corporate looking in a well-tailored suit and patterned shirt with white collar, rep tie. I wonder if the ever-present red strip of cloth circles his throat this evening, if he donned it to ward off untoward spirits.

Taking both my cold hands in his, he pulls me close and kisses me on the lips. "You're here."

Keenly aware of people to my left lining up to kneel before the casket, I shift to keep my back to the remains of the woman I fantasize replacing.

He talks for a few minutes—I have no idea what's said—then excuses himself to speak into the ear of a young man I recognize as his elder son. Harry whispers, nods toward me, and whispers again. The boy, thin and sagging at the knees, as if on heroin, I think, is clearly wasted from drugs. Harry has occasionally touted this boy's extraordinary psychic endowment. There's nothing in my heart I want that boy to divine, so I turn my back and slip through the crowd. I spot Harry's fifteen-year-old daughter, a beautiful girl with thick, silky chestnut hair, and hate myself for my slimy, tangential relationship to her parents.

With relief, I spot my extremely tall Shiatsu masseuse, also a patient, and before I can utter a greeting, a slim, attractive young woman elbows me out of the way and without preamble puts a hand on his arm to say, "I got awfully tired of hearing her yell at him."

Outraged at her disrespect, I say, "Where on earth do you live that you hear their private conversations?"

"From the waiting room!" she says, as though I'm stupid.

Although the family room is next to the waiting room, I never heard anything but the teakettle whistle, and I've been seeing him for a year.

She turns to face me: "All she ever did was attack him. I don't know how he stood it."

I have to get out. Right now. But first, Harry. Fortunately, he's only steps away. Before I can speak, he says, "It's OK to go. See you Thursday."

"Thursday?" *He isn't taking time off. Good God almighty!*

"Thursday *week*. I'm going home to Baltimore."

Speechless, I turn and walk out into the night.

Who are these people from the inner circle, I ask myself, thankful when I reach the security of my car, parked in the dark in back, grateful for a private place to weep into that ancient well where being alone is too often the only safe place. Finally, I lift my face and pound the armrest. He *will* be there for me. It's unthinkable to love a man so deeply, on every level of my soul and being, and walk away empty.

It's mid-October, but warm. I dress carefully in peach linen, sheer hose, and taupe high-heeled shoes, the ones I bought for my wedding with Walter.

When I step into the church for the memorial service, Harry jumps up as if wired. Reaching for my fingertips, he pulls me toward him and kisses me on the lips. Speechless, I move to a seat in the back, deeply ashamed for having come.

I do not belong here.

That was Sunday, and the following Thursday, during my session, he urges me to read *The Tibetan Book of the Dead*. He says it helped him and his wife prepare for her death.

"We were with her when she died. We kept saying, 'Go toward the light!' Souls can get lost in the astral plane, hanging around people, if they don't know they have to leave."

I have an image of her hovering behind him and to his right, watching us, uncertain whether she's in this world or set free for the next.

From what he says about the book, it's very much a spiritual preparation for life, and yes, I believe that all of life is a preparation for death. But I will not buy it. I do not want it in my home.

As I head for the door, he pulls me close and holds me tight. When I pull back, he asks, "Do you still go to that odd spiritualistic church in Greenwich?"

"Sometimes." I look near the door for my sneakers and bend to put them on.

"I'm gonna go Sunday. I want to experience it with you. Tell me how to get there." As I explain the turn under the highway into Old Greenwich, he laughs, hugs me again, and standing too close says, "Tell me again."

Breathless from intense sexual longing, I try to calmly trace the route in the air. He's so giddy and happy, he has trouble following. He laughs helplessly. I laugh. He grabs my hands and pulls me into his arms a third time.

I have no idea how to respond, and don't.

⤬

I select a camel-colored wool crepe suit and a cream-colored satin blouse, the best colors to set off my reddish-brown hair, fair skin, and green-blue eyes. Over my shoulder I sling a superbly crafted Italian leather handbag. Inside, is a love poem for Harry, one I stayed up half the night composing.

My heart pounds as I take a seat in back of the church and rigidly face forward for one hour. After the service, I find him outside with his two sons and a single woman he's described as his best friend. She's tall and rawboned, with a thyroid disorder, if the bulging eyes and goitered neck are any indication. Marilyn seems about fifty, spaced-out, and extremely ill at ease—homely, horsey, unnatural, seemingly not connected to her womanhood. Because she's a foot reflexologist, he's been wanting me to consult her. I know she often drives with him to Shyam's spiritual classes in New York.

He can't be in love with Marilyn. She doesn't look complete.

He hugs me, kisses me on the mouth, and after introducing me, says, "I'm so happy to see you. You look wonderful."

We visit for a few moments, but he's anxious to get away. There's no time to slip him the love poem. I drive home all dressed for nothing, full of longing, afraid for myself, afraid for him, afraid of the future, and afraid of what this meeting means. Most of all, I'm afraid he'll reject me or abandon me. Not that he'll stop seeing me, but that he'll abandon me within the relationship, always my fear with men.

Dad did not abandon me by leaving but by not leaving me alone.

⚬⚬⚬

I haven't seen him in months, and I don't want to, ever again. Guilt ridden from family pressure—mainly my brother and sister-in-law—I finally agree to join her and Teddy and Dad for dinner.

Happy because I'll be seeing my father, Greta sets the date for the following Saturday night. I like Greta. I love her, actually. I love my brother dearly. I haven't said a word to them. I suppose I don't have to go. But like the girl in the dream raped by spider man, I am nothing if not pliant and obedient.

The night before the get-together, I go to bed nauseated and restless, soon awakened by a nightmare of being in the Ridgefield Road house watching a little girl of four dash into the road, while I search frantically for a phone to call Walter. Someone has torn it off the wall, leaving huge holes in the side of the house where anyone can get in. When I finally go back to sleep, I dream my daughter Laura comes running, yelling, "Don't go!" so loud I wake up.

I turn on all the bedroom lights, make sure the door is bolted, and sit up in bed. I cannot share a meal with my father. I must choose. Once my decision is made, I sleep peacefully, but in the morning, after I call to cancel, I pace the house, full of shame and misery.

❧

Where is the promised healing? I've been seeing Harry weekly for a year. I'm obsessed, especially sexually, and confused. Hoping for clarity, I begin to record what transpires during sessions. If I read the pages back later in the week, I'll know what's going on. My habit of keeping journals and recording conversations verbatim has saved me in the past.

I had no other way to know I wasn't the sick, bad, and dirty girl my father imagined.

On October 22, I write:

> *It's late evening. Today Harry gave me two crystals to hold. I closed my eyes, breathed deeply, and flew into anguish.*
>
> *"Transfer those feelings to me," he said, sliding a right hand under the waistband of my sweatpants, under my underpants, a familiar touch now.*
>
> *"There's a large block there," I said, feeling violated by that hand, so close to my genitals, but not daring to bring it up.*
>
> *"Breathe into it and let the chakras open."*
>
> *And then I knew. "If I love I'll die."*
>
> *"So that's it."*
>
> *"Well, start with you. If I love you—I don't want you to play games with me. Why do you tell me about places to go meet you? I'm trying to keep professional boundaries. Why do we have to bring it outside?"*
>
> *I glared at him.*

He moved back and withdrew his hand into his lap. "If I'm manipulative, call me on it. You've worked with therapists on various aspects of yourself, but you've never put it all together. You're afraid to let someone in. Look—you loved your father on all levels. You love me on many levels. Let that love flow."

As I write this, the fear starts, and I listen for sounds of someone breaking in. My heart is pounding, and I think, I must keep control because he can't.

I told Harry, "I can't go through life depending on others not to harm me. It has to come from me." Is this what he wants me to do? I am ashamed for feeling so helpless.

I was happy until I was fifty. I never wanted to die. Was it because there was no man in my life? I warned Harry, "As a child, I lived with a man I loved very much, and I had to hate him because he got too close."

Harry said nothing, as usual.

I feel confused, lost, and deeply afraid of being swallowed. Safe only in shutting Harry out of my life. And yet he says the opposite: "Transfer to me the feelings you would like to have had for him." Who is him?

Canceling dinner with Dad has left me both relieved and guilt ridden. For many years, he has done me no harm. He's a lonely old man facing the winter holidays without a daughter he loves. How to have at least one holiday visit and feel safe? Walter suggests we go together to Dad's right before the holiday and call that my Thanksgiving visit.

We drive to Southbury, and then I'm home, by magic.

I have little recollection of that visit; I don't know whether we met in a restaurant or at Dad's house for tea. Nor do I know what we talked about. All I know is that I was able to look at him a few times and stay with the clear knowledge of who this man is and all he has done. That is victory.

Within days the night terrors ramp up full force, not only because things are unresolved with my father—I have no proof of what I believe he did to me—and I've never confronted him. Worrisome, too, is that Harry's closing in: he's more affectionate, solicitous, loving. Night after night, I lie awake watching the strip of light under the bedroom door to see if the man is lurking, ready to break down the door. Quickly, obsessively, I review my escape out the window to the deck below, where I'll hang full-length before dropping, then sprinting to safety.

The night terrors make it difficult to get up and go to work. Nothing is better in my life. And then I get a call from the Rape Crisis Center. They're starting another ten-week group-therapy session in January. Against Harry's wishes, I signed up months ago.

Do I belong? Or will I be the only one shamed by a ghost long denied?

⚬⚬⚬

We're all victims of incest, all ages. Why have I persisted in believing that women who seek a rape crisis center are only those attacked by strangers? There are such, of course, but clearly the counselors assemble groups based on the crimes.

G., nineteen, was raped repeatedly by her father, from age eight or nine until her late teens. He is rich, successful, and now remarried with a much younger daughter. It never happened, he says, but G.'s suing him anyway. She isn't happy with her therapist.

"You need a heart surgeon," I tell her, giving her Harry's name. "You can trust him."

P. is seventeen with a similar history, but it never happened according to her father. She's inpatient at a local psychiatric hospital, her tender flesh covered with self-inflicted cigarette burns. She's planning to fly to the Midwest to attend a large family get-together for her grandmother's birthday. Her father will be there. Can she handle seeing him? And who will support her? She's an embarrassment to her family because of her stories about him. They count on her to keep quiet.

M. is in her twenties and just remembering she'd been raped a number of times, starting at age eight, by her maternal uncle when she visited him holidays and summers. At the time, her mother shrugged off her daughter's complaints and still refuses to deal with them.

W. is in her late forties and remembers all of it. He was her stepfather and had been gentle and seductive. She was relieved when he died. She's twice failed at marriage and doesn't relate well to men.

I've never spoken with women so like myself. They mirror me in ways that are exhilarating and overwhelming because their stories connect me irrevocably to mine. I become ill with bladder symptoms and feel as if I have the flu.

Because of validation, I also feel more authentic and integrated than ever. Other times, horror sweeps me into a ball, and I hide under my dining room table.

I'm not seeing all of it.

Urged to take better care of myself, I set out to explore the causes of a pounding heart and migrating abdominal pains. My internist, a gastroenterologist, is annoyed by nervous complaints and changes the subject when I tell him I'm suffering flashbacks of incest. I decide to consult another physician.

Dr. Singh, a homeopath, treats me with astonishing respect. Emotional and physical illnesses are one; thus he wants to know subtle details of my ways of living to see how they dovetail with physical disturbances. Finally, my main diagnosis: humiliation.

"We'll start with Pulsatilla." He taps the correct number of grains into an envelope, pours them into a dark bottle of distilled water, and shakes it. "Two drops under the tongue three times a day."

Within twenty-four hours, the heavily pounding heartbeat and irregular thuds that have disturbed my sleep for months have stopped completely. I want to confide in him, too, of my growing doubts about Harry as a physician. I promise myself I will tell the good doctor everything the next time I see him. He will listen.

However, I happen to mention Dr. Singh to Harry, who says, "Oh, I know him well, and so did my wife."

I sink in my chair. Whom doesn't this man know? "Do you go to him?"

"No."

Despite that, I continue to see Dr. Singh often. I tell him, "I'm having intense flashbacks of scenes that are growing like malignancies in my gut."

When I tell my group members the same thing, and that Harry has not lately taken me into hypnotherapy, they encourage me to ask for it and get rid of the images. And so, at the end of January, I tell Harry, "There's more. Would you consider hypnotherapy again?"

I start the hour feeling more like my old self, more real, less concerned about how I appear to Harry, and, for once, unconcerned about his penis. Always before, that obtrusive knowledge: take care.

Dad never takes his hands off his organs. As far back as I remember, he sits on his spine, pelvis tilted forward, hands busy adjusting penis and testicles, idly touching, not in specific, sexual ways but as if to reassure himself everything is still there.

Harry leads me to the bed and stands at my feet.

"Bend your knees," he says, pressing his hands on them, lightly shaking the legs to open and close them.

"I'm numb. I must have done that with Dad—left my body."

"Breathe, Trudy."

I suck air, and instantly Dad shadows in from the left. I know I'm whimpering. I can't stop.

"Say, 'I don't want you to do that!'"

I give up. *Let him do what he wants.*

"Kick me away!" Harry grabs a thick pillow to hold in front of his pelvis. I open my eyes and kick.

"Get on the floor!" he orders, standing with a large red *bataka* sticking straight out between his legs.

On my back at his feet, I'm suddenly five, maybe six.

"I have a stomachache," I wail. I want Mother to call the doctor.

The adult in me knows that although I said "stomach," it's the lower right quadrant. When I was a child, that area often seemed inflamed. Mother usually called the doctor, both of them worried about appendicitis. A scene drops behind my eyes: I'm in bed with ice or heat. Dr. Larson is coming after office hours, at seven. At six, my father dashes upstairs, tosses a shopping bag on my bed, and ducks away. I pull out a new red dress!

Blood money, I think, now.

Towering over me, Harry growls, face menacing, still shaking his huge red penis.

I scream. He throws the *bataka*, steps to my right, and drops to his knees to hold me. He's Good Daddy now. But when he's at my feet or approaching from the left, he's Bad Daddy.

"Imagine I'm your father, only kind," he says, laying a warm hand on my abdomen.

I turn away. "I don't trust you."

"I know. Let's go back and forth between Menacing Dad and Kind Dad." He rises and steps to the left. I close my eyes, but the years fall away and I am once again helpless.

"Don't make me go to school!" I cry. Mother says, beware of strange men on your way to school.

Let me stay home.

The following week, we reverse roles. "You be your father," Harry says, "and I'll be Trudy." He grabs a blanket and flops on the floor, pulling a pillow under his head.

I tuck the blanket around him. With his eyes closed, he is vulnerable and exposed. He trusts me not to injure his tender parts. His penis.

"Harry, don't worry," I whisper. "I may *appear* to grab you, but I won't. I won't touch you."

I turn away, close my eyes, evoke my father's image clearly, and drop his personality over me like a black cape.

In that dream state, I turn and pick up a fat red *bataka* and stick it like a sword between my legs. Turgid with intention, I creep into little Trudy's bedroom, lift the bed covers, kneel on one knee between her legs, plant my other foot firmly outside her leg, and plunge into her, pumping mindlessly, relishing borrowed power.

Mesmerized by a passion for punishment, I stay with it, grunting, until the act is complete.

Dazed, I sit on my heels. "My God, Harry, where does that come from? Am I making it up?"

"It doesn't matter. It's your perception of what happened. Don't judge it."

We switch roles, but I whimper. "I don't want you to do that. My stomach hurts."

Harry backs away, and I open my eyes.

"Harry, what difference does it make whether he did it or not?"

"Because you couldn't develop normally with that going on."

And suddenly I see all too clearly how often I am intensely relieved when a relationship with a man ends.

As I head out the door, I realize I forgot to tell him I've ended something almost as difficult.

Early in January, I gave notice to resign in February, on my tenth anniversary with Cliggott. There are many coworkers here I love, even cherish. And all my bosses are good to me, beyond good, beyond what I deserve. It's that I no longer have the emotional resilience to work anywhere. Fortunately, I've always saved money, and I probably have enough to get me through a year.

When my final day comes, my bosses host a champagne party and give me a pair of gold earrings and pewter candlesticks. My closest coworkers, some eighteen or twenty editors, copy editors, graphic artists, and secretaries, take me to lunch. They know me so well that they know something has gone horribly wrong with my life. They know I don't have a job to go to. I'm presented with original poems and drawings, and books on painting portraits from the Metropolitan Museum of Art.

I cannot imagine nor have I ever heard of a group of coworkers so open, loving, and friendly, or of bosses so kind, generous, and caring as mine at Cliggott Publishing.

Chapter 12—Dad's Genital-Sterilizing Gun

HIS NINETIETH IS THE NINTH OF FEBRUARY. FOR me, dinner at my brother's is a command performance. My son Matt offers to drive. I've shared everything with my kids. What makes it easy is that he is no loss. They never liked or respected him. He chose not to attend their weddings. Even when my brother's daughter was killed at thirteen by a drunk driver, my father, despite perfect health and great wealth, did not find a way to visit while she lay ten days in a coma. He was "too upset."

Sipping ginger ale, I move about the living room avoiding the guest of honor. My children circle me like lifeboats. Dad is hurt by my gift: a box of pastels and a pad of pastel paper. But I'm pleased I didn't betray myself further buying an elaborate gift I can ill afford. Still, there's a rill of shame for treating a helpless old man shabbily. My card offends him more: "Happy birthday to a man who has no enemies. You've outlived them all." You'll outlive me, I think.

Ann, who has sent ahead a dozen long-stemmed roses and a magnum of champagne, calls to speak to each of us in turn.

The music is strong and rhythmic. One relative who adores Dad and is warmed by a drink or two sings along and bounces sensuously on the couch next to him, as he leans over her with archly flirtatious affect. Once upon a time, that scene would have looked dead right to me. Didn't we all adore the captain of our ship? I'd have joined in the singing, if only to please him, have him love me. Would I have been nervous? Yes. Afraid? Oh, yes. Terrified. But that was the way with him. That was our norm.

"Sit next to Dad," Greta urges as we file into the dining room.

I'm very aware she and my brother and Ann are loving, fair-minded, family-minded persons, who want only to have this hideous, stinking, filthy charge fade away and disappear forever. They no more want my father impaled on the cross of my accusations than they wish me to lose the only father I'll ever have.

⁕

I call an old friend I rarely see. It's two days after the party, and I have to tell someone, afraid that if I don't, I'll do it. I can't burden Harry, not with what he's going through.

We meet in Greenwich at the diner. We talk for an hour, and I promise to call him before I stockpile pills or borrow my younger son's pistol. Driving home, I'm relieved because I don't have to keep any promises anymore. The money I saved working at Cliggott is just enough to complete my life, leave my kids the paid-for condo and no debt.

It's 4:00 a.m. I turn on the light to record a dream: My foot is bandaged with strips torn from a man's jockey underpants. Underneath is a score of music. I want to unwrap my wound and sing what I know is written there. I can't. I drift back to sleep, only to wake up minutes later, screaming, "Dr. Deather!" as a shrouded figure comes to take me away.

I get up. I have to. I can't tolerate another nightmare. And then, helplessness gives way to fury, and rage rises up into my back, my arms. I'll kill him, that's what I'll do. Why should I take *my* life?

In a frenzy, I head for the basement storage room, hoping to find something large enough for an effigy. Finally, I settle on an old, king-sized blanket and drag it up into the kitchen. I take a huge knife and drive it into my bundled father, grunting from the effort of slicing wired Dacron. And it's not enough, not nearly enough.

Sweating, I sit back on my heels. Why am I acting like a crazy person at dawn in my own home? Why is *he* OK and I'm not? That's what that fucking birthday party was all about. They all buy into his wonderfulness—not my kids, of course. But why did I give him another pass?

It's barely six o'clock, but I don't care. I stand to dial his number. Let it be *his* problem. Let it kill him. But after two rings, I hang up. Do I *know* what happened? Can I be *sure*?

Collapsing back onto the floor, head in my hands, I see the downward spiral I've created and entered: leaving my job, hanging a wreath of dried flowers over my bed, as if a coffin. I can't eat, or barely.

I trudge upstairs to my bedroom, take my journal, and after letting down the attic stairs climb up there and hide the notebook under the insulation. No one should ever have to read that. Calmer now, I shower and dress. Downstairs, I start the coffee, then get out the vacuum for a thorough cleaning. When it's nine, I call and cancel my three o'clock for Shiatsu. The masseuse loves Harry…

The therapist at the crisis center agrees with Harry's assessment that venerating my father's fanaticism was better than denying his life force, or he'd probably have ended mine. The world understands by now, I imagine, that rape is not a sexual act. The only power act greater than rape is murder, done more in direct proportion to a dread of powerlessness than to hide a crime. I think Dad's constant picking at the zone around his fly is more about castration anxiety and reassurance his organs are still there than pleasure.

But why rape? He had abundant nonsexual means for controlling us: derision, disdain, humiliation, spankings, whippings, scoldings, chores. It was easy to whip Teddy and me; we were not fully human. Ann he saw as perfect. The only child he respected. Or did he?

It's important I tell my group about the good times, that we laughed, made music, played. The summer I was nine, Dad drove the family across the country and back, visiting all the national sights. He once enjoyed tennis, golf, parks, restaurants, parties. I can still see him dressing for a New Year's Eve masquerade in one of Mother's strapless evening gowns, the bodice stuffed with socks, coarse black hair filling the décolletage. Small, hairy feet fit perfectly in Mother's pumps.

He took us camping and to playgrounds, taught us the names of the constellations, the near layers of the earth's composition, and why volcanoes, droughts, and plagues occur. His lectures on world and national politics were informative—to a point. In Manhasset, that point allowed him to applaud the KKK, busy driving Jews out of Long Island. He championed Hitler's "solution."

"If I had one day left to live on earth," he was fond of saying, "I'd line up all the Jews in the world and shoot a cannonball through 'em." Retardates, cripples—anyone he deemed imperfect—exterminate them.

He'd ship the retarded to an island surrounded by alligators. "Survival of the fittest," he'd tell us, laughing.

How it pleased him to hate non-Aryans, all deeply flawed: Spaniards, the French, blacks. But it was his fury toward women that gave him no peace; their very existence outraged him.

Emboldened in this small group of kindred women, I shared how Dad invented an imaginary ray gun capable of sterilizing the gonads of anyone at whom he pointed it. On his daily trip downtown in the subways, sur-rounded by what he assumed were the dregs of humanity, he protected himself by sliding his hand into his pants pocket and aiming the gun at their genitals. How he chuckled at his unique power to reduce the ranks of the less than human. And we laughed with him.

My tale sparked a story from T., one of the few victims in my group who'd reported satisfactory revenge. One day, armed with a sturdy spear, she dressed all in black, took the subway to her uncle's house, and rang the bell, catching him by surprise.

"This is how you hurt me," she yelled, driving him back into the living room, where she made him sit and listen to the details of his abuse, while he begged for understanding. "And I've told everyone in the family," she yelled, as she stormed out.

What amazed me was that she followed up with a letter outlining exactly how much her therapy cost, demanding he send her a check, and he did.

I could not do what T. had done. Not yet, anyway.

Chapter 13—The Facts of Life

"I LIKE THE WORK YOU DID," HARRY SAYS, when I tell him about stabbing the effigy and how, just last week, I bought a dozen hotdogs, took them into the garage, and bit, stomped, and cut them into shreds.

"I got the idea from group. Thing is, I'm not searching the house before going to bed or pushing the dresser against the door, like I used to after the kids went to college."

"You *what?*"

"I didn't tell you? I left a pan under the bed in case I had to pee. That way, I didn't have to move the dresser from in front of the door until morning. Before that, I had a boat siren rigged to the door."

I shrug. "Some of that's gone. I try to remember it was decades ago. It already happened."

Shaking his head, he leads the way to the bed.

"Draw your knees up," he says, standing at the foot, and when I do, he leans on my kneecaps, forcing my legs open.

Giving up has made him impatient. "Kick me away!"

He holds a pillow over his genitals. I kick a little, and soon rage takes over. I flip onto my knees and pound the mattress, seeing my father under me as I stab him.

"Die, you fucking son of a bitch!"

"On your back!" Harry orders. When I open my eyes, he's menacing me.

I curl in a fetal position. "I can't take it. I'm too little. I'm burning. I don't want you to do this. I'm sick to my stomach."

"On your back. Kick me!" And somehow I try.

When he sees that I can't, he sits beside me on the bed, one hand on my waist, then slips his fingers under my sweatshirt and rubs my ribs, sliding his large thumb up between my breasts, gently shaking my chest wall to open my heart energy. I've lost so much weight, I'm not wearing my bra under a thick sweatshirt.

"You said we could do hypnotherapy," I offer.

"We can start." Pulling his hand away, he sits back in his chair.

"Count down from twenty. Think of consciousness, trust, and experience. Let your mind down into your body. We're going to look at those places where your memories are locked away. Concentrate on your right hand. You can go into a light or a deep trance. Either one. Your hand will tell us by how light it becomes."

The index finger of my right hand feels bloated.

"Where are you?"

"In a house." My father is home. "I have no breasts. Where are my underpants? I want my underpants! I'm naked and I'm cold." I shiver, jaw shaking.

"Let it go through you, all the way down."

My knees are up, and suddenly my father, it seems, bends my right knee down onto the bed and spreads my legs. I can't tell Harry. I can't speak. I wait until it's over.

"He didn't hurt me, but it hurts here." I touch my twelve-year-old heart. "Mother said I wasn't supposed to do this until I got married."

Harry blows his nose and guides me back with long-breathed ahs, then "i" as in "hill," each sound expanding into a fragile comfort. I reach for him, eyes closed.

He leans far over the bed to hold me in his arms.

"But did it happen?" I ask.

"It doesn't make any difference. It's what you felt and that's real."

"I'm ruined. No decent man would want me. Can you love me, knowing what you do?"

"You know the answer to that. You weren't responsible for what happened to you. You had no choice. You didn't want that. You wanted love."

And then I hear him say quietly, as if to himself, "We've opened up a biggee here."

When I was a teenager and sang church solos, my father never went inside the building to hear me. Mother said he'd drive to church after services started and stand outside unseen under the high windows. Yet he took us to the New York concerts by Kirsten Flagstad, Marion Anderson, Fritz Kreisler, Yehudi Menuhin, and many others. He hunted Manhattan antique shops for seventy-eight-speed records of singers such as Galli-Curci, Rosa Ponselle, James Melton, Lawritz Melchior, and Caruso.

Night after night he played the old records, and also many new albums he'd bought. Before long, I recognized countless symphonies and concertos and could sing operatic arias along with the sopranos, especially if we had the score.

As teenagers, and later when Ann was home from college, we'd put on concerts, Ann accompanying flawlessly while harmonizing in a pure alto, Mother singing the middle parts, and I, the coloratura. We'd dive into German and Italian operas, hymns and ballads, and ham it up over "Iris, I'm kneeling at your feet, inhaling your sweet perfume."

Mother sang "I Dream of Jeannie with the Light Brown Hair" better than anyone I've ever heard, including, much later, Marilyn Horne, whom I heard perform it in Stamford. At home, Mother often sang "The Lord's Prayer" or "Elsa's Dream" from *Lohengrin*, while Dad sat on the couch, head back, enthralled. But also during that time he wouldn't turn the heat on in my bedroom, the very same bedroom he so lovingly decorated with new wallpaper, a powder-blue rug, and fresh paint to welcome me home from my first year at college—the college he wouldn't let me go back to, tuition $750 a year, my allowance, $15 a month.

"Come home and we'll talk about it," he'd snarled after I spent eight quarters to call home spring semester, begging for twenty-five dollars to reserve my place in the sophomore class.

If I took a shower in the icy bathroom next to my icy bedroom and he heard water splashing, he'd storm upstairs, pound on the door, and scream, "Turn it off, ya goddamn fool! You're wasting water and electricity." Being naked and trapped in the bathroom set my heart to banging. Sometimes during the day, when he was in New York, I'd go into the top of his closet and get down one of his pistols, turning it over in my hands, knowing the bullets were elsewhere, but where I could find them. Or I'd take his jockey underpants out of the drawer and turn them in my hands, as if I'd never seen them. Maybe I could wear them, was the half-hidden thought.

And so, after college, I moved home and went to work in a local factory.

Mother was ill. I didn't know that in four years she'd be gone. My brother was fourteen that year and kept to his room, reading a book a night. Although we were pals and I loved him, it seemed he was not really there. I don't think my mother saw him; if to love is to witness, I rarely saw her even acknowledge his existence.

I joined local concert and operetta groups, won solo parts, and often stayed out late at rehearsals. Back home, I'd pass through the living room on my way to the stairs to my room, and find my father skulking about in nothing by jockey underpants, having got out of bed to lay out my character flaws, beginning with the old refrain, "What's the matter with you, ya goddam fool?"

We'd stand face to face, trying to keep our voices down, Mother asleep on the other side of the wall, in the guest room with Sherry, four years old. I was selfish, self-involved, lazy. He'd keep at until I began to sob, then descend into a sputtering fury, disgusted at my self-absorption.

I had no way to let him know I wanted his help, his love, his reassurance, not his disgust.

I knew I couldn't bother Mother. I knew she never felt well and was injecting Pituitrin into her thighs for the diabetes insipidus, but I didn't know the rest of it. He did. Never one to tell us what we most needed to know, he kept it from us that Mayo Clinic had given her the diagnosis of Hand-Schüller-Christian disease, a rare, complex metabolic disorder, for her, a death sentence.

March was unseasonably mild, enabling Walter and me to spend long days walking the mud flats in front of his beach cottage or running through high tides and low with Friskie for the sheer joy of it.

But March also ushered in the end of my ten-week rape crisis group. I hadn't completed the work. All I could tell the others was that "something" happened in the basement and "something" happened on a walk in the woods. Nothing specific, except in body memories. Except in dreams. Except in flashbacks driving by houses in which we'd lived. Except when I exercised at the Lowens', and in hypnotherapy with Harry.

Infuriated, I could see and not see, know and not know.

"Why do you want to see it?" said Annie, the group coleader, somewhat unpleasantly.

"So I can live!"

"I'm not sure that seeing it will do all you hope."

"I want to know what, when, where. How long. That's my right!"

"Does your therapist know how to conduct hypnotherapy?"

Why did I find myself defending Harry and my right to know? I wasn't really angry with Annie. I was angry with myself.

For the second week in a row, I urge Harry to take me to the bed for hypnotherapy. I start counting while he places a large, warm hand on my waist. Suddenly a hot knife rips into my vagina.

"I'm burning!"

"I know. Breathe into it. Trust, sleep, and experience. Open the doors to experience."

I start again. "Twenty, nineteen—" I stop, start again, pause at twelve, go blank, then keep going, dropping into glee. I laugh.

"I'm ten and I'm *so* happy. I always wanted to be ten." I can see my own puffy, little girl's wee-wee with no hair, glad Harry can't see it.

I watch myself climbing trees, jumping off low-hanging garage roofs, exploring. Always exploring.

Harry chuckles.

Flick. A lightning bolt opens a room in my head.

"Where are you?" he asks.

"Mother takes me in her room to sleep in the other twin bed, and she pushes the dresser against the door. She's scared. Daddy goes to Washington three days a month, to the patent office, and she tells me secrets. I'll get the curse so I can have babies, she says, explaining menstrual cycles and what men and women do when they get married."

While Mother tells me the facts of life, an image forms in my ten-year-old mind. A young woman in a wedding dress walks upstairs right after the ceremony but stops midway so the groom can face her and insert his penis through an opening in the front of her dress. No emotion is connected to this woodenly enacted rite.

But it sounds like something I might want to do. I definitely want to menstruate so I can be a grown-up girl. It doesn't sound like a curse to me. It sounds wonderful, and it means I can have babies. I want babies.

Another flick. I stand in the bathroom door watching Mother, one leg up on the sink, shave off her genital hair. Daddy's coming home from a trip to Washington.

And another. I want to wear Ann's sweater to school. I want to be Ann. Ann only has one good sweater, and each night she dips the cuffs in cold water to tighten the wool where it stretches loose, and hangs it over the banister to dry.

"I'm not in a trance, Harry. I'm remembering stuff. Maybe I don't want to work. Maybe I just want to go into a light sleep and talk so you can know and I don't have to."

"It doesn't work that way."

I sigh, give up the resistance, breathe deeply, and drop into a well. As always, my father's there. Part of me is alarmed at what I'm putting Harry through.

"Cry into your abdomen," he says. "This is very deep."

"I have no breasts! I'm too little!" I draw up my knees. Harry lightly rubs my abdomen, breathing with me. And then it begins. My whole body tenses against the thrust. I cannot survive.

I curl into a ball and repel the past, willing my body to obey my command to come back, surface. And when I can, finally, I have no words, no sense of time passing, no wish to open my eyes.

Harry says, "Tell me what you're thinking. You didn't want it to happen. It's not your fault. You were too little. It was too much for you. You didn't want him to do that."

"Mother said it wouldn't happen until I got married, but I didn't know it would be my father."

"You couldn't handle it. You were too young to have this happen. Hold onto me. It's all right. You're going to be all right. He won't hurt you anymore."

"So much came up." I start—then stop—trying to figure out when or where that incident happened. "I'm OK."

"I know. I'm comforting the little girl in you. She wasn't OK."

Where was Mother? And then it flashes through my mind how I wept quietly in anguish when my gynecologist examined me just the week before, although I certainly trust him.

I'm not OK at all.

Harry stands and moves slowly away. When I finally open my eyes, I see the force and brutality of my experience in his face.

"Don't worry about *me*." He drives his fingertips into his chest. "I just feel empathy. How can I not?"

I glance at the electric clock near the bed. I've lost complete track of time.

While we worked, my large, framed portrait of Mother remained propped on his couch. As if sitting in a window, she fills a large canvas, hands lightly folded in her lap, body in profile, head turned to look out. A silent witness, beautiful and remote.

I used as my model her engagement picture, a small black-and-white photograph dated June 1929. She was twenty-three. Given free reign with color, I made her silk crepe dress and matching jacket a rich cerulean, the collar, cuffs, and pleated bodice creamy ivory satin. Her newly bobbed hair, once golden, is slowly darkening, her eyes, green-blue, are flecked with brown. Her smile is bland and uncommitted, eyes almost vacant, one slightly larger than the other, as in life. As are mine. The wish to die is not yet evident in her face, her destiny hidden by youthful ardor and illusions of the future.

I rise from the bed, cross the room, and slip into my sneakers. I look from Mother to Harry, aware that Dad dominates the room.

"I didn't want him. I hate him for what he did, but I will face this god-damn thing until I work it through. I will not spend the rest of my life half girl and half woman."

Taking Mother under my arm, I struggle out to the car and place her on the passenger seat facing forward.

It's ten minutes before I can drive.

Chapter 14—Confidence Game

IT'S UNNERVING WHEN I KNOW THE PATIENTS, AND I often do: Harry uses their full names, but I cannot and will not record them here. I know W. from the study group reading *The Course in Miracles*, to which I go one night a week. I sometimes meet W. for lunch.

Harry explains, "W. is not awake…He's very closed and asleep." Another day Harry tells me about a man named C. As it happens, I know C. from AA. "C.'s at Four Winds now…He's finally settling down…He took coke and got paranoid. He's a very psychic and very holy guy…He's also a little psychotic…so I told him, 'Look, there's two things: you're picking up forces around you, yes, but disturbance is also in you.'"

But it's the invitations that drive me to fury.

"I'm not going to meet you anywhere. I will get back to the trance work, but I can't just now. Besides, I have other issues I need to resolve."

He settles in his chair, face flaccid from compassion, and begins: "I think you and I, as we approach this and talk about all the subtleties of what makes one work, and wh—what one looks for, and how to sustain it, how to feel connected with it and comfortable with it. It—it has opened me to want to explore outside.

"I mean, it has given me permission, as I've tried to give you permission. The process of discussing and exchanging and evaluating and looking, this man, this woman, relationships. And suddenly it's a freeing, a—a choice available or an ex—chance to explore, well, find out. Our role is not for us to explore, I mean, get into the personal but to explore the aspect, wh—wh—what interferes with personal."

"Look, Harry, don't think I'm not grateful you want to bring me into your world, but I feel manipulated. I don't like that you've started inviting me to meet you here, there, and everywhere, and to some extent it makes me angry. It feels like seduction."

He points to a sturdy stool, leather padded on top, the Lowen stool with a pillow flopped over it. "Stand and bend backward over this, hands over your head, head hanging loose."

When I do, he straddles my legs, pressing his inner thighs tight against my outer ones, while leaning his hands hard onto my upper chest.

I explode: "I don't want you standing over me!"

"I know you don't. That's why I'm doin' it." He drives his knees between my legs, forcing them apart, brings his hands down and pokes hard at the muscles along the outside of my thighs.

I shriek. I scream.

But he puts his hands back on my chest and leans so hard I can't breathe at all. "Hold it. Hold it! Just a little more. Wait. Wait until you can't hold out on any longer."

I'll die!

When he releases my chest, energy rushes in, more than I've felt in weeks, months.

———❧———

It's an April morning, almost a year since my sister Ann and I last spoke. I miss her terribly. I grieve for her.

After we exchange greetings, I ask what I called to ask: "Ann, why can't we talk out our differences?"

"There is nothing to be gained by that." She explains that in relationships, not everything can be talked out. And she's right.

Even as children we couldn't cooperate—except for one game. In summer, when school was out and days seemed endless, Ann and I, and our girlfriend Birdie, perhaps at ages ten, eleven, and twelve, played prostitute in our attic bedroom in Manhasset. Mother would sometimes creep up the stairs to check on us through the banister, but we knew she wouldn't interfere. I'd put on the bra we stole from the ten-cent store, stuff it with socks, and lie on one of our twin beds, while Birdie brought in Ann, our customer, an ersatz man who straddled me, humping and grunting, her wooden reenacting of the sex act. We took turns in those roles.

Fanning the flames of our prurient fantasy were the headlines, in that year, on the *Journal-American* my father brought home: "Errol Flynn Intimate with Starlet." At dinner, I asked my father what "intimate" meant, and in fury, he answered, "Statutory rape with a thirteen-year-old girl."

———❧———

After my younger sister, Sherry, receives a letter from Dad with a newspaper clipping describing a rash of adolescent suicides in Wilton, she calls.

"He scrawled across the bottom, 'This is the result of greedy, selfish parents, even in good old Wilton.' Trudy, what do you make of it?"

"He identifies with the parent who sacrifices for his children to bring them safely through adolescence. And perhaps he did. None of us succeeded at suicide." We speak of how Dad hated our casually kept house, the shame of creditors calling him at work. He lived in trepidation that one of his law partners would stop by on a Sunday. They'd see we lived with shabby, ill-fitting slipcovers, too much bare floor framing worn Orientals, a grubby kitchen, smeared windows. We hadn't lived that way in Manhasset. In Connecticut, we moved six times in twelve years, before Mother died.

I've always thought he ought to have seen how sick she was and hired a maid. She loved to decorate with beautiful objects and collected Tiffany glass, Wedgewood, crystal, figurines, Limoges demitasse cups so thin you could almost see through them. I don't imagine she was thrilled with the rickety pine slabs of furniture with sharp corners he made for our living room, not a woman who sewed with batik and wool challis, bought water goblets for holiday meals, and collected fine linen.

Right after Sherry's phone call about the newspaper clippings, the familiar feeling of wanting to get rid of something comes back full force. My clothes and makeup are all wrong. Nothing about me looks right, especially my hair. I'll go to Jan Gage. He's the best. Somehow, I forget I hated the first haircut he gave me, no piece longer than two inches. Still, I'm compelled to make my third appointment in four months.

"Jan," I complain, settling into his chair, hair rubbery from a cool rinse, "the last haircut only looked good five days."

"You should have come back." Handsome in impeccable, gray flannels and a cashmere camel sports jacket, he is also emaciated, I notice.

Then, apropos of nothing, "And, of course, now AIDS," he says. "We'll pay for our high living—the cocaine, the overspending. *Whatever.*" He sniffs as he clips my hair shorter than ever.

"I don't see the world like that. Not everyone lives in a way where they have to pay for sins." Now we're enemies, backed into separate worlds.

Finished with another bad cut, he drops the scissors into his pocket and walks away, too disgusted to blow the hair off my neck. I struggle alone to removed the black silk drape, climb off the chair, and leave.

Humiliated and roiling with self-hatred, I am also painfully aware I've set myself up to be defeminized one more time. It isn't his fault. I started savagely cutting my hair when I was three.

This, I promise myself, will be the last butcher job.

We try starting the hour with hypnotherapy, but I'm unable to submit to a trance. Instead, I slide off the bed, kneel beside it, and pound the mattress. Within seconds it's my father. I grab a thick pillow. Not satisfied with beating him to death, I light an imaginary match and lean back to avoid being burned.

As the blaze dies, Harry walks away and flops on the floor to lean against the long blue couch. He pats the rug next to him. "Come sit with me."

I perch on the edge of the bed. "I don't trust you."

He doesn't support me. He never admits what happened.

"You feel you have to be alone. He not only hurt you; he wanted you to isolate."

"Yes, to be safe."

"He wanted you to isolate," Harry repeats softly, and when my eyes fill with tears, I rise, move toward him, and drop down to be held across his lap, head against his breast, as if a nursing child.

"I've been wandering around my house pulling books out of the bookcases looking for something," I say. "I'm not sure what."

"What're you reading?"

"Lowen's books. How it's the homosexual aspect of men that makes them want to service women, rather than make love out of their own healthy need for sexual expression. I reread parts of *The Body Has Its Reasons* and *Your Body Doesn't Lie*. Do you know Fisher's book on female orgasm? He says women who orgasm from vaginal penetration are less differentiated as people."

"Other studies show the opposite," counters Harry, stroking my hair back from my face.

I close my eyes. "Fisher says women who focus on clitoral stimulation are more determined and effective, more focused."

"No. Other studies say that response is younger, less developed."

Harry stands, pulls me to my feet, and draws me into his arms. I wait a beat and head for the door.

"What are you doing this weekend?"

Sneakers in hand, I freeze. "Unh."

"There's a workshop I want to go to. Maybe you'd like to come?"

I clench my teeth.

"Would you take notes for me?" He's watching my face. "I can't go, but it's something I'd like to know about. I'll pay for it, of course."

And then I remember I have a date with my friend Judy. "I can't."

Despite all, the thrill of his intense interest moves me lightly down the walk and into my car, over to the parkway, and home. I'm in love. More than that, caught. And then, rage. He set me up. First the tease, always an implication we'll be together, then the clarification that we won't be together. This clarification is not *with* him but *for* him—a detail divulged only after he witnesses me take the bait.

I hate him.

For hours, I'm bereft, immobilized. Finally, I decide I might feel better if I start another portrait. I set up my easel to paint from a small photograph of my new grandson-to-be, taken in Korea shortly after his birth,

January 31, 1987. An adoption angel will carry him in her arms all the way from Korea to the Midwest, where my daughter Laura and her husband will receive him and carry him home.

Two days later, the portrait done, I'm back in the swamp—trapped, furious, immobilized. And then…a shift. It isn't about Harry. I pick up the phone.

With each ring my resolve to tell my father everything sinks. After a dozen rings, I hang up. I sit staring at the kitchen wall. I don't have anything in the house to do it, but it won't take long to make arrangements. Knowing I have that option gives me energy to ask for help.

Harry calls right back. "What's up?"

"I can't shake the despair. It's isolating me."

"Say, what are you doing Saturday night? I have two tickets for a concert."

My neck snaps in astonishment. I spit the words out. "Are you saying you want to *give* me two tickets to a concert?"

"Yes. I can't make it. I'm going to the opera. I'll leave them in an envelope in the waiting room."

"It's useless talking to you. I'm sorry I called. There's no point."

"It isn't important what we talk about, Trudy, just that you make the connection, because I'm the one taking you through this."

He sounds reasonable, even happy.

But Friday when I drive to his house and check the waiting room, the tickets aren't there. I can't believe he would let me down this way. I just can't believe he'd pull another setup. It's enraging and unconscionable. Will he *never* stop?

I drive home, call the service, and wait.

He knows by my voice I'm disgusted. He's cheerful, friendly. "Come up Saturday, but call first. Make sure I'm here."

Saturday morning I hurry Walter through our ritual weekend breakfast. I must be home near the phone to call Harry and wait for him to call back.

Finally, he does. "Come at noon."

It's raining hard, but at twelve o'clock, freshly showered and perfumed, hair shining, I head up his walk, pulse slamming in my ears, stomach fluttery. My thank-you for the tickets is a box of a freshly made rugelach.

Before I can ring the bell, he's on the porch. I step back. Who is this man? Jeans, yes, but a gray herringbone jacket, button-down shirt, and tie. He stands still for a moment, makes eye contact, holds it, then bows deeply in mock courtliness to hand me the tickets.

Blushing like any fourteen-year-old, I fairly skip to the car.

Chapter 15—Chickenshit

"WOULD YOU JOIN ME FOR LUNCH?" I SAY. "I'll drive to your condo and pick you up in an hour."

For the second time, I'm going to practice being with my father while staying with the knowledge of what I'm beginning to know he's done. When I told Harry my plan a few days earlier, he started scripting how I might draw my father into a conversation, get him to speak about his life, then, hopefully, about my childhood, tips from books written for adult children reconnecting with difficult parents.

I snorted. "Irrelevant for incest, Harry."

———

I'm surprised to find my father somewhat different. He's more matter-of-fact; there are less of those barely contained, highly charged surges of anger, that archly flirtatious side. There's less self-absorption. He's not launching into stories and lectures about his superior prowess or knowledge of every subject. He listens, and that's new.

He admits he's having difficulty with many areas of his life. In fact, he doesn't want to live. "I hope I'll get hit by a truck."

Yet, at lunch, in the restaurant, he's inappropriately coy and flirtatious with our very young waitress. When I drive him back to his condo, I go in for a cup of tea. When I leave, finally, I'm hollowed out and frail, bleeding to death inside.

Late that night, the phone rings. It's B., the young woman having flash-backs of molestation. I still see her, from time to time, and comfort her, and Harry still asks me whether I think it was the boy baby-sitter or her father.

She tells me her sessions with Harry are usually on Saturday nights. She's nicknamed him Harold. They're "pals." I listen and soothe. What else can I do? I'm supposed to be the adult.

"I cry all the time," she says, "and I don't even know what happened, only that I can't stop remembering something I can't quite see. I think it was the boy next door who used to baby-sit me."

"It'll get clear for you."

"But I can't eat, and I'm sick to my stomach."

"It's the same for all of us. I'll come over and sit with you."

⁂

More draining is G., a patient my age.

"You can help this couple," Harry has told me. "You know a lot about alcoholism, and you can counsel him, set up appointments. She's a preppy Darien type, but very psychic. She's been working with a pendulum. When she brings it here, she's amazing."

His face lights up and he chuckles. "Tune into her, and let me know what you think."

What I think? She's the personification of the Darien woman: tall and thin with short, straight hair and a touch of pale lipstick. She looks unpleasantly pinched, as if she never had an orgasm in her life. The emblems of money are in full display: good-quality unisex clothing, an air of self-satisfaction and superiority, and the tight jaw squeezing words into an accent that in the Northeast is meant to suggest the upper classes.

She's a woman recognizable anywhere in the world as residing in the land of *Gentlemen's Agreement*.

I know. I lived twenty-four years in Darien.

I started seeing her in April. My most important directive was to spend long hours diving for her truth and mine using her pendulum. And we did.

When the pendulum swung back and forth, that meant yes. If it circled, undecided. If it stopped, then no.

One day in midsummer, Harry confided she'd suffered a psychotic break. He asked me to drive two hours to the psychiatric hospital where they took her. Or go with him—maybe.

"I'm afraid I wasn't paying attention," he admits. "She went too far with the pendulum. I'm sorry I encouraged her." His face lights up. "But she was really opening up spiritually."

I do not go. I believe from conversations with her that both her parents sexually abused her. When I talk with Harry, he is sure that is not an issue.

What I fail to ask is why I'm involved.

When she was committed, her husband brought her journal in for Harry to read, hoping it would shed light on why, after fifty years of fairly normal life, she cracked. The journal lies open half under the bed. It's there one week, another, and then another—until she gets out of the hospital and picks it up herself.

"Don't."

"Why not? If I tell him off, I won't ever have to see him again. Let him suffer."

"I have a suggestion," Harry says. "Something you might enjoy. I hesitate to bring it up, because you'll get mad."

"What is it?"

"You could do workshops." He means, as a career.

I shake my head and laugh through my nose. *Son of a bitch.*

But it is true: I need a job. I quit Cliggott in February, and now it's almost May. I don't know what I want to do. "What on?"

"Sexuality. You know a *lot* about it. You're an expert."

I hear the jibe but choose to answer seriously. "Actually, I used to lead group discussions for the divorced and widowed. The trouble with the widowed is they're holier-than-thou. The mates who die are elevated to sainthood. The survivors look down their noses at the divorced. Everybody knows *they* have problems."

Only driving home do I realize I was nasty to Harry. I call to apologize.

"You're tolerable," he comments, dryly.

So he is angry. I set out for a long walk around my neighborhood. Moving fast brings back a dream. An angel came to show me a wooden cradle. I like it very much. In it, I can sail away. It's cozy and safe.

Back home, I start cleaning the house. External order creates internal order. I've read that. To heal, one has to give up problems. Very well. I'll go back into hypnosis and face the rest of it. Get through it, get over it, get on with my life. Anything is better than wanting to die all the time.

———— ❧ ————

The first week in May, with Harry's approval, I go back to the bed. He pulls up a chair, and I close my eyes.

"Twenty, nineteen, eighteen—" I'm stopped by the image rising up and over me like a tornado.

"Oh, great," Harry says. "Why don't you just stop breathing while *I* count from twenty?"

He's right. Stop fighting it. Let it happen.

I give up and count down while Harry goes to the end of the bed to stand and press lightly on my bent kneecaps, opening and closing my legs.

And then, wham! The man drops from the black funnel—fully him. He leads me upstairs.

The attic...

I won't tell Harry, not a word. It isn't the worst time, and it isn't the first time. But I'm ravaged by the clarity of it.

How old was I? Always Harry's question. About eight. Yes, eight. But how can that be if I was happy at ten? Why was I ever happy? How did I manage to run, play, laugh, not only then, but my whole life?

Harry rounds the bed to sit beside me, a hand on my belly.

I have no way to get rid of it. I can't speak of it. I won't.

Harry strokes the back of my hand.

"You survived, Trudy. That was horrible, but I went with you. We went together and now you're back. That took courage. That was one of the worst things that happened to you." He bends to wrap his arms around me.

"No, it wasn't. The first time was the worst. But why am I seeing this? Did it really happen?"

"Emotionally it happened."

Emotionally? I jerk free.

He pulls back and spreads his hands in a gesture of helplessness. "Your feelings are valid, but I can't say what happened. I wasn't there. But I do know *something* happened."

Bloated with shame by his denial, I struggle to my chair. Am I constructing things that never happened? What sort of monster am I?

We sit. He pushes his chair back a foot.

"I have this patient," he begins. "It's sort of an unusual situation." He drops his head to stare intently from under eyebrows. "She's in love with her father."

My heart flops hard against my chest. My throat closes. "How old is she?"

"Oh, in her fifties."

"But—*how?* Does she live with him?"

"Oh, no."

"Then—why?"

He shrugs. "Oh, I guess he's seductive with her in certain ways."

I open my mouth to suck air.

"He doesn't want her," he adds, clamping his jaw shut. And then, eyes black with intention, "He doesn't want her."

My hand flies to my waist. The pain is sharp, hot. I must run.

He hates you. He doesn't want you. He never did. You love him and he knows it, and he resents it. Your father doesn't love you, and he never did. Get out, quick.

Keeping my face carefully arranged, I make my way to the door and down the steps, grateful for the intense heat of the car baking in the sun.

———

I am careful how I drive, sit, walk. I encapsulate his hatred of me, his rejection, in a bolus behind my ribs. I form a skin around it; otherwise I can't get through the afternoon. I must pack for a trip to the Midwest. My daughter's new baby has arrived.

I can't eat. I pack. I can't sleep all night. I make my way to the airport. I have to find a way to walk through the days of my visit without telling or crying. What I believed would be one of the most joyful weeks of my life is now ruined. But I'm not going to ruin it for my daughter.

I buckle myself into the window seat, drop my head back, and close my eyes, praying for strength to keep the pain walled off. I peer out the narrow aperture to my right into never-ending blue, from which comes the simplest solution. Whoa!

No need to struggle to see what, when, how often. No need. Stop remembering, reconstructing, reliving. Stop all of it. Get in the cradle and sail away. Yes, as soon as I get back. This way, I'll be free to nuzzle and laugh and play with that precious baby.

I smile. I enjoy my breakfast. I turn to the person next to me, and we chat quietly over coffee. After the trays are cleared, I pull out a pen and pad from my carry-on and let words define my purpose. My poem is for Harry.

Yesterday you held my hand
while I flew down the chute-the-chute.
"Just take a look around," you said,
as I slid back to childhood.

"He takes my hand
and leads me up the attic stairs—"
"Is it dark?"
"Oh, yes! Dimly lit, grimy windows,
old, dead spiders, scary stuff."

He kneels and offs his belt.
A whipping? Not today.
Oh, I know—he'll bounce me on his foot.
No. Not today. The other.
Thing. No thing. Place. No place.
Don't tell Harry.

"We'll fly," I tell her, happy, now.
"Away. Above. To safety.
You see how easy this is?
It's not going to hurt. I'm not.
She's not. It didn't. He wouldn't.
It never. Never. Never. Never."

But I didn't fly, couldn't fly,
not that time.
You held my hand.
"Are you lying down?" you asked.
"No. Standing." Rooted. Clearly me.

You held me down
while I died to will and rage,
while he imprinted me.

"I'm wet." I scream and claw my face.
Too pretty.
Am I the only one I can destroy?

Oh, angel from my dreams,
come away with me
to lead me back to me.
Because I can tell you, it did. She did.
He did. He did. He did. He did.

Oh, angel, cast away with me
to light so pure it heals the place.
Speed me through the mesh of gold,

the canopy of love, to covenant and grace,
to bells and birds and flutes,
to the God we knew once long ago.

Lift me now to safety that I might ride
on waves of long-remembered sound.

My first night at my daughter's, I dream I'm preparing for a journey.
I'm ill in a strange way and in a hurry to catch a plane for another planet.
And I'm happy, oh, so happy!

⸺◦◦◦◦⸺

"You don't back me up. You never say, 'I think it happened.'"

Into his long silence, I plead for mercy. "If it didn't happen, I'm not
going to go on living, because that means I'm totally nuts. Don't you realize
my life is on hold? I'm not working, not living."

He eyes me suspiciously.

"I'm going to go up there and have it out. I don't care what you think."

"That's arrogant."

"Why?"

*Why is it all right for my father to destroy me in every way but not all right
for me to lay it at his feet?*

"You don't know what happened, that's why."

"Then I'm going to go to *seven* hypnotists if I have to, to find out."

"Go ahead. What can they tell you? They weren't there."

"Therapy is *your* business. If you work with someone, you must have
an idea what's true."

"I do know something happened." He sighs and takes a sip of Long
Life tea.

"Great. Something is *nothing*."

"Look. Something major happened. Something huge. Something really horrible." He puts his mug down and offers fingertips.

I roll away. "Keep your fucking hands off me."

He glances at the clock and gestures to the door. "The guy waiting is a therapist who specializes in incest. I just heard him come in. I'll ask if he'll spend part of his hour with you. He'll do it. I know he will. All right?"

"Of course."

Harry ushers in a slender, gentle-looking man with a limp. "She's having a lot of denial."

What? I give him the fish eye. Why has he never said, "Of course it happened! You're suffering denial."

I tell this man, "Either it happened or I'm crazy. It's one or the other." And then I dissolve into tears. I'm up against two therapists.

The man waits for me to look up. "You know what happened."

And for just a moment, I do. For that moment, I've always known.

He speaks at length of his own father. "—and beat me every three days. He was an alcoholic." I know from his eyes, he's been sexually abused. Finally he admits it, offhandedly, as though, *There, that's settled.* He crosses a leg, his hands in his lap, a slight smile forming.

I jump to my feet. "My father wasn't an alcoholic. He was a rage-aholic who erupted every three days like clockwork, and he whipped me, too."

I shake my finger at him. "I'll tell you this! Whippings are *chickenshit* compared to what I'm seeing here." With that, I storm out.

Screw Harry. I slam my car door. *Screw them all!*

—⦅⦆—

"I just spoke to Dad," I tell Walter, on the phone. "He can see me this afternoon. I'm going to tell him." Walter knows what I mean.

"Will you come, Walter? I'll drop you in the village so he doesn't know you've ridden up with me. I'll drive to his house and pick you up after. Will you? Do you mind? I'll go alone if I have to, but I'd rather have you with me." A deep shudder makes its way from my back to my shoulders to my head. There's a low noise in my ears like gears grinding.

Dad has guns, countless guns of every size and description. Will he simply walk into his bedroom, load a pistol, and kill me? Or himself? Once, at Thanksgiving dinner, he spotted a massive turtle through the window. Without a word, he got a pistol from his bedroom, loaded it, stepped outside, leaned over, and shot it in the head.

I recall the neighbor's cat, when I was fifteen, and the cat hat he made. Gun or no gun, I'm going. If I let guns stop me, I'll be right where I've always been: knuckling under to a man's reality out of fear of his weapon.

Chapter 16—Confronting Dad

I PUT MY TEACUP ON A MAHOGANY SIDE table.

"I'm here because I want your help." I hope to sound reasonable, engage him as an ally. Maybe he'll admit something. If I attack, he never will.

My father is not a sweats-and-sneakers sort, rather a tweed-and-wool-tie gentleman. He's wearing well-tailored tan slacks and a white shirt open at the neck. It is, after all, May, and warm.

I noticed flowers as I walked the path to his unit in this condominium. That would be his doing.

"Here's what's been happening. About a year and a half ago, I was counseling with a woman therapist. My marriage wasn't working, and yet I couldn't seem to leave Walter, even though I knew I had to.

"She suggested I see Harry Brown. He's highly skilled in what she calls bodywork. She thought there was something wrong with me I had no words for, some sort of early trauma—and that's why she referred me."

I plunge into details of nightmares, hypnotherapy, flashbacks, how I'd said, "Why did you come into me?" I tell him that the same material surfaced in my sessions with Lowen and the other two psychiatrists at the Bioenergetic conference. I ask him if he will come to a session with Harry and me.

Wary and alert, tea untouched, he hunches on his couch, hands on bony knees. A moment later, he sits back and crosses a leg. His shoes are of finely cured, buttery-brown leather. I suffer a hot flash of anger at this man who set up a gentleman's farm with chickens, pigs, sheep, goats, and all necessary barns, shelters, smokehouses, and equipment, at his expensive deer-hunting trips, his collection of first-edition Ruger guns—while we were denied basic clothing.

Shorter, now, in his late eighties—probably no more than five eight and 140 pounds, but all muscle—his long, lean face is still relatively unlined. Those black-seeming eyes have faded to mustard. His sparse, sooty hair is gray only at the temples and in wisps curling around his collar. Seeing him alone, here, so much smaller and possibly friendless, I have a sharp pang of regret and empathy.

He is home, although he hasn't lived here long. Thus, I've come home. Being with him seems right in a way nothing else ever has. He is the closest connection I have to another human. He is, in a consanguine sense, me. We know each other all the way.

Here, a child with a parent, I'm instantly connected to all the years of my life and complete in ways I am not otherwise. No one else is mine in the way he is, not even my children, for I have let them be. In his presence I am most fully Gertrude. No amount of disgust can free me from kinship. Every glance, gesture, lick of the lips, shrug, or turning away is a known world. I am here and I am there, in all the years behind us.

He has listened conscientiously, intelligently. We exchange words. The language might seem ordinary to one listening, but the words are heavy with implications spelled out over decades of living together. Perhaps we speak in code, like twins. He can't surprise me.

He goes back to my remark that three Bioenergetic therapists believe he raped me.

"Well, of course you get the same answer each time. It's all coming from within you. You couldn't have been penetrated at five without being hospitalized."

"I don't know the age or the details. All I know is I feel raped and by you, and it blows me apart. In the reliving, I come close to being hospitalized. Walter takes care of me."

His eyes narrow. "Does Walter know?"

"Not too much," I lie, uncomfortable at thoughts of betraying my father to my husband.

"Wouldn't you have told your mother?"

"No."

"We were together at every meal. Wouldn't we have seen if your dress was torn or you were bloody?" He folds his fingers together in that odd way only he can do: he's missing a fourth finger—youthful carelessness with a rifle.

"I acted as if nothing happened. I think my soul left my body. I had amnesia." That feeling of shared heritage is taking leave of my body. I am his adversary.

He fishes in his pocket for a large, wrinkled handkerchief and dabs at his eyes, then blows his nose.

I think, for a moment, my heart will break, that I have done the cruelest thing a child can do.

When he can speak, he says, "You'll never know what you've done to me, accusing me of molesting you." He says it with such sorrow and distaste that I want to comfort him and take back everything.

Instead, I say, "What I've done to you? What about the anguish I've suffered these last fifteen months? I didn't drive up here at the first sign something happened. Don't you realize I'd give anything not to be here telling my own father he raped me? If nothing happened, why have I been terrified of you all my life?"

He is truly baffled.

"Why wasn't I able to sleep on my back until I was fifty, lying awake watching the door to see if you were coming in, keeping a loaded gun or mace under my mattress? Why have I always dreamed of being raped? Why, when you call and say you're coming to visit, do I shake for days? Why do I have to put on thick blouses and two sweaters? Why, when the boys and I visited you in New Hampshire, did I wake up screaming *every twenty minutes all night long*? I cut the visit short. I had to get out of there."

His tears vanish. "I told you I spanked you that time you ran outside to meet the bus naked, and you weren't even two."

"We're not talking about a spanking. I'm a woman who's raised four children. I've traveled the world and had varied experiences, many of them horrendous, and what I'm talking about is of entirely different dimensions. Not my fractured skull. That's *nothing*. Not spankings, punishments, whippings, operations, giving birth."

I glare at him. "What I'm remembering is so bad that my life is on hold."

"Wouldn't I have known if this happened to you?"

"I didn't show it. I split." As I say that, I know that I've moved from shared language and shared experience, that everything I'm uttering is as useless as if in a foreign language.

Yet I can't stop. "What about the walk? You said you never took me for a walk, but Ann remembers. You said I fell on a pointed rock and cut my genitals. I remember going to the doctor."

He hunches forward again, eyes darting and wary. He's a fox. "That never happened."

"Oh, yes it did. Ann remembers the incident vividly."

He straightens, as if to rise. "I'm going to call her right now."

"Go ahead!" I cross my arms, but my heart is beating so hard behind my breast, it flutters my blouse. If he gets up, will he go for a gun?

"Does she think this happened?" He sinks back onto the couch. "What've you told her?"

"She does. Or she did. I haven't spoken to her in over a year. Go ahead and call her. Look, you can decide this never happened and I'm crazy. I don't care."

He is silent.

Like a dog with a rat, I keep on. "It happened in the woods."

He shoots back, "There were no woods in Manhasset."

"Yes, there were. There was even a wood at the end of our street. I used to play there."

He frowns and clenches his teeth, lips a thin line.

"If nothing happened, why couldn't I go to school a full week until tenth grade?"

"Your mother kept you home to watch the baby."

"No. She kept me home because I couldn't make it through five days."

We argue I don't know how long, twenty minutes, half an hour, and he asks, "Wouldn't your gynecologist have seen the damage?"

And that stops me. *Do* I have proof? Actually, I sought it. "Not necessarily," I parry. "Other women in my group were molested at eight, nine, ten." I feel sick. "It heals."

"Maybe Kurt did it," he says, chin up.

At that, I just stare him down.

And then, quietly, with a smirk, he says, "Maybe it happened when you were a teenager."

I can't believe I heard correctly. My heart flip-flops. I don't know what to say.

He's looking out the sliders to where lawn ends at a bank of pines and deciduous trees clinging to the hill behind his condo. He seems lost in reverie. "I was never very sexy. That was one of the problems with your mother. I just wasn't interested in sex."

Not *interested?* When I was twenty and we commuted together to New York on the railroad, he never quit moving his penis around, never stopped touching it. It drove me *wild.* That was so much worse than his doing it at home. I couldn't get away.

At the same time—the early fifties, it was—Mother bought Van de Velde's book *Ideal Marriage.* Knowing I read it, he took an opportunity, when we were on the train, to lecture me about the good doctor. "He's depraved! That's junk. I don't know why Mid has that trash in the house. What he says is lascivious and licentious." He'd spit out the word, touching himself all the while.

And Van de Velde? According to his book, sex in marriage is an act of joy, his mission: teaching women to be orgasmic.

Why didn't I figure my father wasn't normally interested in my mother? I should have known. He was a virgin at thirty-two, when they married.

And then I don't care. I don't care what they did or didn't do. "Listen to me. This is life or death. I'm going to get to the bottom of it whatever else I do. If I'm wrong, if nothing happened, then I have to live with that."

I wait. My eyes sting. "If it didn't happen, I'm going to take my life. If I'm so insane and so destructive as to make this up, I don't want to live."

I look long and hard at him. I do not like him.

He asks me to leave.

I tell Walter on the drive home, holding tightly to his hand, "I don't have to love him, and that's very freeing. I don't have to ever see him again or pretend he's wonderful at my expense. I had the right to tell him what I remember. He took away my right to be and my right to speak. My right to my own body. I want my power back."

Why am I not surprised to receive a letter from him a week later?

> *I have been concerned about the proposed meeting with you and your doctor on May 28, and this is what I ask you to consider. 1) You have asserted that I raped you at some unknown time or place, and if the meeting confirms or suggest this, what does this do for you? 2) If the meeting shows that you are living under an illusion, a status devoid of reality, what will your doctor do for you?*

I write back saying I'm struggling with images shrouded in shadows, but I do not think I'm living under an illusion.

The next morning, I wake up with the birds remembering the many times Dad burned my warts off with acid. I always seemed to have a rash of them on my knees and shins. He'd take me to the backyard and apply petroleum jelly around the base of the warts, unstopper the brown bottle of acid crystals, and dab particles on the warts. I was soon stamping my feet and screaming from intense burning.

"Run!" he'd yell, laughing. "Outrun the pain." And off I'd go up to the new houses in Munsey Park, in one street and out the other, hoping to get lost.

I'm still waiting for Dad's confirmation of the appointment with Harry when I get another letter: I'm wrong in all my accusations. I'm weird. He and Ann (he claims) are worried about the direction my life is taking. He will not keep the appointment.

Harry's correction, his cure, is for me is to stay open to Good Father.

I try staying open and connected, try not to get angry or shut him out.

"I know you love me," he says at the end of a session. "I feel how deep that is." I move toward the door. He hugs me, then steps back, holding me by the tips of my fingers. "You're beginning to trust me, and I'm beginning to trust you. Now maybe you can begin to take me in."

Take him in? My skin crawls. I shudder. "Why do you refer to trust going in both directions?"

I flee before he can respond.

I'm defeated if I love him, defeated if I get angry, defeated by the disdain cycling through the sessions with regularity, stemming, it seems, from something within himself. Or is it my fault? The past few weeks, I've been nothing but trouble. He's given my hour to someone else. I have to ask him when he can fit me in. I understand why the early morning hours are for those who must get to work by nine. That still doesn't explain why I can't have a regular time. As always, Harry won't talk it through.

Ringing in my ears is the story ending with *He doesn't want her.*

He's shaking me loose; it's time to leave.

The anxiety is killing me. I bring up the subject several weeks in a row. He will not address the constant uncertainty of each next session or whether that means he wants me to leave. I beg for clarity; I leave without it.

All I know is that I need to get away. I'll go to Sherry's. I'll go for the weekend. New Hampshire is balmy in June. Just thinking about my sister brings a solid measure of peace and comfort.

The Friday morning I'm to leave, I arrive for my session with the car packed. Harry is sock footed, wearing blue jeans, the red seam binding tied around his neck, as always. When he sits I read the message in brown on his purple T-shirt: "Oh, Shit."

He is cool, distant, annoyed. I stay clear of saying anything to trigger more displeasure. At the hour's end, I realize once again that I do not have a next appointment.

"So, when?"

"Oh, come in Thursday or Friday at nine or at twelve."

"Thursday, then, at nine. But why are you doing this? It's one of your games, isn't it? Keeping me off balance."

"Not so. You're doing my thinking for me again."

I point to the "Oh, Shit" on his chest. "Is that for my benefit?" "Shit" is a word Harry never uses.

"Oh, no, no, no, no, no."

"I don't believe you."

"Listen, I put it on last night after I took a bath. I got up and put it on again. It was handy."

I start for New Hampshire. Driving fast on the highway releases tears. Before long, I'm heaving and hiccupping and sobbing the way children do. I start pounding my thighs, bruising them, beating every part of my body I can reach. It isn't long before I wanted to cut off my breasts, the constant plan of my adolescence.

Two hours, three, on toward four and a half, and still I cry. I approach the exit for Sherry's town, let it pass, and drive on to Canada. I'll find a motel and stay as long as it takes to obtain the means and courage to sail away.

The hell with Sherry. I won't go. I won't go to anyone. No one likes me. No one. I stop at a fast-food restaurant and call her from a pay phone. I want to hurt her—but also to alarm her, send her into action. I want her to be so thoroughly frightened at behavior so completely out of character for me that she calls the state police to have them pick me up. They'll take me to a hospital. I can feel the clean bed, nurses bending over, someone giving me a shot. I want to be wrapped and put to sleep. Forever.

"I'm not coming," I say. I hear her shocked uptake of breath.

What"

I'm going to Canada, and I'm not ever coming back."

Before she can muster a reply, I hang up, storm back into the car, and speed north

Hours later, hungry and exhausted, I realize no one is going to come for me—and the truth is, I don't want to die. Humbled, ashamed, and sorrowful, I call Sherry and try to explain the horribly cruel thing I've done. This time, I cry with her, for how deeply I've hurt her. And then I turn the car around and head south to New Hampshire.

But why Canada, I wonder, as the storm subsides. And then I know: Dad was not a Canadian, but he saw himself as one. He was, in fact, a member of the Canadian Club. He ate lunch there everyday, at the Waldorf.

———

We're on the double bed in Sherry's guest room rummaging through boxes of old photographs, looking for pictures or negatives of Mother. Over the years Ann and Teddy and I spilled our hatred for her onto anyone who'd listen, especially Little Sister, only six when Mother died. Now, with no time to lose, I begin sharing everything I know of her joyful, creative, loving, and expansive sides.

It's strange I want to do this. So much of what I suffer, particularly on my ill-conceived ride to Canada, is from her inability to contain him or stop him or report him or divorce him, or at least leave and take me and Teddy and Ann back to her mother and sisters in the state of Washington. She could have done anything. She did nothing.

Not only did she not protect us; she was also too often not home within herself when she was with us.

"It was like trying to hang onto a cloud," I told Melbourne in the sixties.

Now, and despite everything, I need her more than ever. I no longer care what she did or failed to do. I need her or I can't go on. If I can't take her in, there is no hope for me.

Because Sherry had Mother for only seven years, and because she lay dying all that time, and because my father despised her, my sister has no enhanced or balanced history of the tragic person who bore her.

I suggest we call this weekend together a Mother Festival. Mildred was a June baby, and this is June.

From a local garden center we buy a dozen salmon-colored poppy pips and plant them alongside the house. Mother loved poppies. Late in the afternoon, we giggle, mixing a mudpack from Mother's recipe: one-third each of egg yolk, Fuller's Earth, and olive oil. Faces coated, we try not to smile as it hardens.

While waiting twenty minutes, we whip up a batch of Mother's favorite candy. She taught me how to spin boiling sugar into brittle hairs, for divinity. Sherry and I take turns beating liquid into a thick pudding, hurrying to drop white dollops onto greased paper, then press a walnut into the heart of each.

All day, as we go about dedicating maternal sacraments, I stay busy bestowing on this motherless young sister as many memories of generosity, kindness, openness, courage, creative intelligence, and curiosity as I can recall, my antidote to the deeply maligned woman Sherry never had a chance to know.

As soon as I take the turn onto the southbound entrance to Interstate 91 south, I am a bug in a web, wild with frustration and wrath. The armistice is too quickly over. Knowing my destination is home, I'm already there in a sticky straitjacket, trapped in Harry's sweet talk of a spontaneous, vibrant life, the assurance of a self not yet possible, promises that only deepen my obsession with this creature who's made me his toy, this Harry James Brown, forever winding me up, then smashing me, until all I'm capable of is a tantrum red with madness. Or death.

Mile after mile I scream and yell obscenities. As the fury abates, I tell myself out loud that until I tangled with Harry—until fifty-three, -four, -five—the soloist, artist, senior editor, mother, lover, friend, and rational human being who never wanted to die, lost her temper, or flew into tantrums of horrendous scale, was never lost to herself.

Whatever internal resources I once had have been shredded. Hoarse and humbled, I finally make what I hope is a rational decision. I will take my power back the only way I know.

The minute I'm in the house, I call Harry's answering service and cancel my next appointment. I will never go back. Letting him go propels me through the house like a dervish. I destroy favorite dishes, potted plants, recent photographs of myself. Spent, finally, I pull out the vacuum.

The phone rings when I'm locked in my bedroom ready for bed.

Why am I canceling?

"I'm not coming back." I hang up on him. But hanging up leaves me feeling guilty. I must clear it. I call back. "Why do you torture me?"

"Look, *something* happened," he says, rolling out the old carpet.

I probe and argue and plead for validation.

His position? How could *he* know? He wasn't there.

I beg for a plan, any plan, to unlock the cage we're trapped in—we, because he's in here with me. After thirty minutes we hang up, exasperated, sour old lovers wanting only to be rid of each other. Where is the gentle bear who wooed me into and out of terror?

Two days later, I drive to the rape crisis center without an appointment and take my frustrations out on Mary Jane. She isn't thrilled.

"He won't admit my father raped me!" I yell. "He tells me a fucking story about a fifty-year-old woman who loves her father, and I know what he's saying. It's *my* shame. And we've never cleared it. He won't clear it up. *Ever*. He won't explain what he means. Then he jerks me around by changing appointments constantly. I never feel safe. And at the same time, he's taking me in hypnotherapy into the fucking attic, where I have to watch my father push my head down. And guess what? It didn't happen. He's driving me crazy."

"If he's driving you crazy, stop going."

Her counsel throws me into reverse.

I hate this self-satisfied, expensively coiffed and shod social worker. She's glib and remote, and she doesn't give a rat's ass about me.

As I drive away, I realize I must dope this out on my own; I know I'm incapable of not protecting him, and I hate myself for it. I'm unwilling to speak of the touching and hugging, kissing and fondling, the setups and titillations, the implications of getting together after therapy, the trips we'll take.

I remember that when I was driving home from Sherry's, I made a mental list of all the patients about whom he spewed details. It's over forty, many of them I know well: sponsors, my sponsee.

I must stop fighting him and accept him as he is. And then I see, like a white slip drooping beneath the hem of a dress, a scene from two weeks earlier when I told Harry I loved him.

He'd brightened. "You're beginning to trust me, and I'm beginning to trust you. Now maybe you can take me in."

Why did I let that terrify me? It's exactly what I need to do, take him in as a friend, a loved one. Stop reacting to his every utterance. Besides, he's right. I am unable to love, except children and animals. Too many women have let me down, and I know about men. Our arguments, Harry's and mine, aren't caused by what he's doing but by my reactions, just as he says.

As I pull into my garage, I realize it's not that simple. He doesn't tell the truth, so how can I continue to work with him? My will is broken. My spirit is broken. There is nothing I can do to change him or get him to help me. I must solve myself, and he is the only one who can help me.

Is it really possible my father is innocent, that I've created this myth, done all this damage to countless family members for nothing? First, I need to solve my relationship with Harry. I call and make a new appointment. He makes it clear I'm persona non grata.

July has always been a tough month. I always become ill, often with a bladder infection, sometimes a hapless injury, or worse. It heralds summer's turn into autumn. The grass is dry and the sun hot. Inchworms are decimating the trees sheltering my condo. I hate air-conditioning, but if I keep my slider open I hear the drone of my neighbor's TV or smell heavily perfumed softening sheets from their drier.

My doctor prescribes Elavil, but I soon go off it after a bad reaction. To keep head above water, I talk to my sponsor every day. I call Walter, my sister Sherry, my daughters, and sometimes my sons. Weekends I breakfast with Walter or friends from AA. Despite all the people in my life who wish me well and even love me, I anguish all the hours of the day and night. Whatever face I wear in the world is only discipline. Worse, although I may have implanted a mother in Sherry's psyche, the graft is largely failing in me.

Harry is cool, disinterested, and can barely tolerate me. He plays dead dog. I will send him a letter.

I have to know what happened, not every detail, but that what I keep seeing in dreams, hypnotherapy, and flashbacks did *happen. Last week I told you I had more intense and repeated dreams of being raped these last two months. You responded to that with a story about a woman who "also overreacts" to "minor" stuff her husband does to her. His "quirks," you called them. You said she acts as though he's trying to destroy her. But then you admitted he's sadistic. You then said it turned out it all happened in another lifetime. That he wasn't being cruel now, that he tried to destroy her in another lifetime, and that's why she was overreacting. And then you added, "He tries to hurt her and he can't stop."*

I want to write, *How would you like it if I said your wife died in another lifetime?*

I don't send it. I'm afraid to displease him. But writing serves a surprising purpose.

Not only mine, but his words and behaviors are recorded on paper; it's my compulsivity, my need to organize and understand my world, my training as a writer and editor that makes that easy. But I also need consensual validation, if I can get it.

I arrange to meet an acquaintance for coffee, a woman who was in therapy with Harry the year before.

For only the second time (the first was months ago in Pennsylvania), I share his cycles of seduction and rejection. She nods all the while.

"Then you *do* get it," I say. "Why did you stop seeing him?"

"He never gave me what I went in for, which was a simple written evaluation. He wouldn't get clear, and he wouldn't do the paperwork, which I had to have. I walked out after three months. And he *was* seductive."

"*How* was he seductive?"

She looks away.

I leave overjoyed—for a day. Before I know it, I've spiraled down in familiar ways: pain under the ribs, stiff shoulders, headaches, bladder pain, sadness akin to grief. Death promises lasting peace. I think of it constantly. I wish to be smaller and indeed have lost another fifteen pounds. If I could only hide, sleep, disappear.

I avoid everyone, even Walter, who telephones every day. One day, when I don't answer, he drives to my condo and lets himself in. He finds me on the third floor in the corner of my closet in the dark under a blanket. He telephones one of my children.

She calls the others, and they decide that my daughter-in-law, who knows Eileen and that she sent me to Harry, will call her and ask if he *is* reputable.

It's no surprise to me that Eileen gives him highest marks. "Definitely! She's in good hands."

The following Saturday I tell my daughter Elizabeth I can't go on. She and Walter get to my house at the same time and call Harry's service.

Elizabeth takes the phone. "Why don't you admit it happened? Why are you torturing my mother?" She listens and listens some more. Within ten minutes, she's smiling and nodding.

When they leave, I go to bed hanging on to their belief that he will take me through this. I have far too much shame to reveal all of what goes on there. I'm just like the woman who saw Harry for a written evaluation, who would not say how he was seductive. I barely understand that it's our shame that keeps us silent.

I refuse to believe he wittingly or unwittingly is deconstructing me, destroying me.

At midnight Walter calls. For once, I am asleep.

"I'm sorry to wake you," he says, "but I had to. Don't tell Lanny." His daughter, Lanny, is twenty and living in New Haven. "She made me promise not to tell, but I have to talk." He draws a rough, ragged breath. "Her roommate was raped in the apartment."

I sit up, dizzy, mouth dry. "And Lanny?"

Dear God, no.

"She was out. She's fine. It's Karen; she went out around nine to walk the ferret—God, those kids! She needed cigarettes. There's this strange man hanging around the store who kept trying to talk to her, and she was afraid, so she tried to be nice.

"Then she walked back. Only, she left the door unlocked. She was expecting her boyfriend any minute—stupid kid—and this guy walked right in. He followed her. She never moved, afraid to yell, afraid he'd kill her. He was only there ten minutes."

"But they're not safe! You have to get them out of there, now!"

"I know. It's done. They moved in with friends. They called the police and went to the hospital and all that. But here's the kicker—"

His voice is heavy with tears. "While they were packing, the guy called. He wants to see her again. He thought she liked it."

Chapter 17—Run for Your Life!

"LET'S HAVE A FEW EXPLORATORY SESSIONS. IF WE can talk out our differences, maybe we can continue the work." Harry's eyes are cold. "For now I want to tape every session, so there'll be no misunderstandings about what's said in here." His tape, his recorder.

He waits for me to digest that. "I want for you everything you have worked so hard for, and if that means you want to go on and work with someone else, then by all means do that. I want what's best for you."

At the end of the hour, he hands me the cassette. "I want you to listen to this with someone else."

I take it to Walter. "Tell me what you hear."

He eyes me warily.

"Listen, Walter, direct criticism is not as hurtful as a lot of other stuff."

After one of my legalistic attacks on Harry, Walter hits the pause button. "Trudy, I don't want to hurt you, but you're too passive. And he dances.

He doesn't answer you directly. He slips and slides all over the place. He's hiding something. He should have worked with me in network television."

Despite myself I laugh. "And?"

"You're critical and you're clear. In fact, you're precise beyond fucking belief. I think the problem is, you're extremely precise, and Harry is extremely imprecise. He ducks it. Harry seems to interpret your need for clarity as an attack. He won't own up to what he's doing, and when you try to get clear, he sees you as the enemy."

Over and over on the tape, I tried to trap Harry, as if he were on trial. At the same time, I could not ask for what I need, which is that he stop dodging everything.

We listen to the next sequence. Walter shakes his head. "You give him dead air. He asks you a question, and you're silent. You know, Trudy, that trait is maddening."

We listen to the end, and while it's rewinding, Walter takes my hand and says kindly, "What I hear is that you're terrified of being abandoned or rejected. Trudy, I see you as a fragile person looking for direction, looking for answers—and drowning."

We start at the beginning again. I hit the pause button after an impassioned speech in which Harry says: "I've told you over and over I'm not trying to stimulate reactions out of the past."

I know what he means: he isn't trying to hurt me by being tricky. But he *is* alternately seductive and sadistically rejecting. Why do the same things my father did and deny it?

Since Harry can't or won't answer that, I ask Walter.

"It's his game plan."

"But, Walter, he holds me and invites me places, all the time. He strokes my belly *under* my underpants! Slides his thumb up between my breasts. And that time he pushed his pants down."

"He's a doctor!" He looks me up and down. "He's not coming on to you—is he? I bet he thinks about you in the shower…No, it's got to be his master plan."

I start the tape in time to hear myself say, "I don't trust you."

Harry says, "Then we can't work together."

"Do you want me to leave?"

"No, you don't have to leave. I'll continue to work with you if it'll be good for you."

Later, alone, after twice through the tape, I'm no clearer than when I started listening. Humbled by Walter's responses, I turn the machine off. If Harry does have a master plan, and if this is the way I'll learn to stop "over-reacting" to every nuance of his behavior as though he were a sadistic psychopath like my father, then I have to take responsibility for that. I've stared long and hard at Harry's arrogance. I need to admit my own, and so I write to him.

> I can be very cold and distant, and that must be rough on other people. I'm watchful because I'm so fearful. From there I move to being highly critical of you, of the way you use words in some imprecise manner. I'm afraid of you because you're so intelligent, that you'll want to confuse and outwit me, instead of being glad that your intelligence goes to work in my behalf. So I strike out first and try to outmaneuver you. That must be horrible for you.
>
> It's not that I'm saying I'm all bad and you're just great. Not at all. I also see the great stuff I do, and I see your warts, too. But know this: anyone who underestimates me is not very sharp.

I mail the letter hoping that by my backing down, he'll continue to work with me. I have a dream, then, in which I'm looking at pages telling me about my life. The first page is blank but stained by clouds. The second page has more evidence and a few words. The third is full of information, and the fourth is detailed and specific. I understand what the dream means, and more than that, its implications.

———∞———

My letter softens Harry. He is once again full of hope for me. "When you stay with your truth, you will open in ways you never dreamed."

By truth, he means the truth about what Dad did. But how to get to it? I call a woman who was in the rape crisis group with me. We have each other's numbers, just in case.

"Maria, why can't I stay with knowing it happened?"

"It's easier if you imagine nothing happened. Then everything will be the way it always was, when something was the matter with you."

For that moment I understand her. More than that, I see the interior dynamics. "If I admit he did it and stand up for myself, I have to give up the dream of a resolution with my father and my older sister, give up what I've longed for all my life: finding my daddy."

———∞———

The next morning, I'm astounded when my daughter Elizabeth telephones to say my father called her at work. He alerted her to watch for papers he put in the mail. "He told me it's a nine-page document, a chronology about you. Things you don't know."

"Don't know about *myself?*"

"That's what he said. Apparently, he already mailed copies to your sisters and to Teddy. He asked me to make copies and mail them to Matt and Joseph and Laura. I told him I wouldn't.

"Mom, if he wants to do that, he can do it himself. When I get my copy, I'll mail it you, because you have a right to see it. I hope you'll burn it. He's insane." The wonder of it all is that he knew how to locate even one of my kids.

Sure enough, the document is a chronology of irrelevant incidents from childhood that supposedly triggered my angst and proves my father had nothing to do with it. He adds one detail I'd forgotten.

I came home after a college weekend with my high-school sweetheart feeling strangely disconnected from myself, especially arms and legs. I told my father this, and that I was frightened.

My handsome and brilliant boyfriend was the love of my life, but I had not been able to make love with him. I had not told my father anything about that, of course. In his letter to my siblings and my kids, Dad describes this seemingly dissociative episode to prove I've always been psychotic. He's failed to recognize classic markers for incest.

For evidence of his insanity, I want to keep the letter, but I can't bear thoughts of it being anywhere in my home. I burn it. Perhaps it's my children's confidence in me, and their unshakable conviction that I was raped, for now my dreams take on a quality more instructive than terrifying.

The old man hurt the little girl badly with a knife. Another man put her to bed to make her think he was taking care of her and that he wasn't connected to the one who injured her. I was watching from above and knew the real truth, that the second man fingered a knife and planned to sacrifice her. I watched for an opportunity to get her out of there. While his back was turned, I whispered, "Run, run! Run for your life!"

It's not the July heat but the humidity that drives Walter and me to walk the beach, grateful for offshore breezes. And here comes Don Alphonso from up the cove, Walter's friend from network television. Both were majorly successful vice presidents, Walter at the international level, Don as an attorney. We're cheered at the sight of him, and so is Friskie, who scampers to and fro as we tilt along the shoreline, gabbing.

In the past, we've enjoyed many heavy-drinking afternoons and evenings (even some mornings) with Don and his partner, Ellen. Since Don and I stopped drinking, our foursomes, usually in one another's homes now that the men are not working, consist of piles of organic veggies, seaweed, brown rice, and steamed fish. Don quit smoking, although neither Ellen nor Walter have, and I've at least quit buying them.

Walter stops to sit on a rock and light up, and waves us on. We head east to an old pier, wade to our knees in warm water to climb on splintery logs, and sit, bare legs swinging over the wavelets.

Don puts a hand on my arm. "I know you're still struggling with whether it happened, Trudy. Walter told me. I have a suggestion."

I shake my head, afraid he'll suggest I forgive my father, but he holds up a hand. "I've given it a lot of thought. Please hear me out."

When I finally nod, he says, "I want you to think of it as a court case."

"Naturally." I laugh.

"This is it: let's assume the question of whether your father did it or not is heard in a civil suit; to win you'd have to prove your case only by a preponderance of evidence. If it were a criminal case, you'd have to convince a jury beyond a reasonable doubt."

There is no sudden epiphany. I do not, like Saul, fall from my horse and kneel, blinded by the light of Truth. But a shaft has come through the stone wall of denial I've built to keep not only Dad but also Harry on the mountaintop, and the wall minus its keystone is crumbling.

A preponderance of evidence beyond a reasonable doubt. Dumfounded by the simplicity of the formula, it's clear even to me that my father is guilty. Harry may dissemble, my father lie, others pretend nothing happened, but the verdict is in.

More than that. I accept it.

Chapter 18—Ripe and Ready

THE FIRST OF AUGUST, HARRY PUTS ME ON an antidepressant at my request, one that worked in the past. I resolve to put all talk of incest behind me. The storms around my work with Harry between May and August nearly destroyed me. If I shelve incest and never refer to it again, I can heal. Besides, nothing happened beyond age eight. And I can live with that.

After only three days on the new drug, I'm calmer and able to sleep without waking up startled six or seven times a night. Harry and I are getting along better.

He is tender and supportive.

"When you're hurting, don't let it build, Trudy. Reach out to me, and ask for love and support."

We talk about inviting my children to a session. Ever since I told one of them I wished to die, they've been eager to come, only waiting for Laura and her husband to arrive in Connecticut the end of August.

Sitting in Harry's office with my four kids and their spouses gives me a tremendous sense of safety and courage. They'll stand by me no matter what. Their morning faces are scrubbed and alert, shining with goodwill and intelligence. I am so proud of who they are, I could weep. Their sober, clear-sighted views of the world, and their strong and effective places in it, give me a feeling of success and completion I have sorely missed since working with Harry. None of them has ever for a second doubted anything I suspect of my father. They know him. And they know me.

Harry deftly leads the session, explaining my stumbling blocks and reassuring me they can get better. He suggests the children and I meet for dinner at one of their homes every two weeks for a while, so that I am sure I know I have a family who believes in me. They leave the session charmed.

With their support, I concentrate on stabilizing myself. My dream is to finish college. Harry still wants me to become a therapist. It will be years before I'm prepared to make a living that way. In the meantime, I need to work. I can attend college outside working hours. I always have.

He insists I meet with his friend Dr. W., head of a local three-year training program offering certificates in Jungian analysis. Harry sits on the board. If I start this fall, I'll be done in three years. They do not require a college diploma.

"How do I earn a living with only a certificate?"

"People sign for you. I do it all the time. I train lots of these people. I train seventeen people a week. And they do good work. I already spoke to him. He's waiting for your call."

"Look, Harry, I have never, ever wanted to become a psychotherapist. I can't stand the idea. And I can't go to school full time."

Somehow my wishes fall away. Perhaps it's because I'm raw and physically weak from the storms I've endured over the summer. I still feel as though fresh from surgery. I tell him I'm frightened of entering a training analysis in which I must continually expose my history to colleagues and therapists. I will never heal.

"Just go," he says. "You don't know what it's like. They're good people. They all have a history. Go and find out."

Three afternoons later, I'm ushered into a dim room. I can barely meet Dr. W.'s eyes. I am so terrified of his divining my love for Harry, my obsession, that I can barely speak. I'm certain that Harry, so free with intimate details of patients' lives, has told this colleague stuff about me that I do not want known, or perhaps don't even know. I sit trembling—stripped, skewered, doomed.

I get out of there as fast as possible and am instantly amnesic about anything said, feeling only shame and humiliation.

I tell Harry I won't do it under any circumstances. I refuse. But Harry is not discouraged. I have a gift. I *must* become a therapist.

To appease him, I enroll in a school for certification in alcoholism counseling, no college degree required. Three thousand dollars and an investment of Thursday nights and half days on Saturdays for nine months, which means I can work part time. The savings I've carefully lived on since February, when I resigned from publishing, are nearly gone.

And maybe he's right. By counseling alcoholics I'll find out soon enough if therapy is my one true field.

Walter is encouraged by my even disposition and concrete plans for the future and speaks of retiring to the coast of Maine. He's wanted to forever. Seeing my life take shape and purpose, and knowing we will never get together again as man and wife, he begins the hunt for a place to live. I go with him. We find the perfect one-bedroom cottage on an inlet around the cove from Booth Bay Harbor. The tiny house is enchanting. I fantasize about moving in with him, and no, I won't do that, but I promise to visit often.

Neither of us can say the word "divorce." But it's time to make our separation legal. We make a firm decision we will not hire two lawyers. We will not fight. Before he moves, we find a woman willing to draw up the necessary documents and put us on the court calendar. I live on my husband's promise to come back and spend Christmas with me.

Harry tapes every session. The last thing I wish to do is replay them at home, so I throw the cassettes in a desk drawer, my mother's old secretary.

He tries to help me with my ambivalence about the future. I do not want to go back to editing. We talk about my inability to let go of Walter before now, how I'm afraid to let some others get too close. I start commuting to the alcoholism treatment school in Westchester.

Why did I not realize every lecture and class deals unrelentingly with the incest and childhood sexual abuse that pervades the alcoholic family? I knew that from meetings.

Since drinking is not an option, I get through classes and group-therapy sessions by eating bags of candy and drinking endless cups of coffee, which put me to sleep. I nod through class after class. I want to drop out. I don't care about the money. All I hear at school is how one handles rape and incest and terror and abandonment.

"No," Harry says. "Don't drop out. This is valuable for desensitizing you. Use it to that end." He also encourages me strongly to find work as a mental or physical health worker, preparation for a life of service as a psychotherapist.

"The home-health people took care of my wife," he explains. "I think it would be good for you to take care of other people. Or volunteer in the soup kitchen in Norwalk. Or see if you can join the counselors at the Norwalk Congregational Church. I know a woman who works there. Call her. Here's her name." He scribbles it down. "You'd be good at that. They do short-term counseling. You don't need credentials."

I call the woman but not the soup kitchen. Somehow I never quite follow up on the home-health-aid job. After years of playing the little mother at home, then raising four children of my own and rescuing Walter's, the last thing I want to do is change sheets, cook, and clean up shit. Besides, I can make fifty an hour as a medical editor.

It's a relief to find Harry intensely interested in getting my life on track. I'm to call him any time I start to lose the connection. Feeling supported by him and my children, I begin to look at the times I spiral down and isolate, when pain builds.

I'm paying attention to my instincts, instead of doubting most of them. I have dinner with a casual friend and leave battered from her self-serving instructions, provocative queries, and dogged attacks, mean and biting. I vow to stop seeing her.

My painting teacher always manages to touch me. After he pats my fanny one day, I cut the next class. But he's a superb teacher and portrait artist, and I have not finished an oil rendering of my son Matt. Can I go back and tell him he must never touch me again?

I do.

When I'm ten minutes late for a lunch date with my sponsor, a woman with a rigid sense of time, and she immediately scolds me for being late, I tell her, "You don't know who I am. All you know is my drinking and my wounds," and I leave.

Yes, she's been extremely kind, but she can't yell at me as if I'm a child. When I tell Harry there's still part of me anguishing over whether I've hurt her feelings, he says, "Trudy, you didn't attack. You leveled. You have the right to define yourself. You can say, 'Ouch! Stop kicking my shins.'"

Toward the end of September, my heart begins racing from the antidepressant. Before I can start on a new one, I slide into depression.

Harry warns: "You're going to want to get closer to me, and when that happens, the wish to hurt me will come up."

I don't believe him.

"You see, Trudy, you idealize me, and that allows you to defend against me. You're getting ripe and ready, and that brings up feelings of inadequacy. With Walter you didn't have to address your complex. Now you will as you move around in the world and meet other men. Don't run from the conflict. Let's see how little it is. Let's see how it comes up.

"All of us are inadequate to different degrees, no matter who we are, when it comes to intimacy and sexuality."

"I know," I say. "I set standards I can't meet—and for others." I'm about to admit this keeps me from getting close to a man, but Harry's eyes have turned inward.

"What are you thinking?"

"I saw scenes flashing of an encounter," he says, "the moment a man and a woman hope for. It reminds me of this couple who have to imagine humiliating fantasies in order to have sex, and they're preoccupied with orgasm."

He's a foot away, knees open, hands loose on his thighs.

"They have weird ideas of what's supposed to happen. Their inadequacies are fading now. She feels good about her body. Without shame. Her image of herself made her inadequate, not who she is. She's a phenomenally sensitive, sensual, in-shape person. You are, too."

He pauses to look down at his lap and lay his right ankle over his left knee. My cheeks burn at witnessing his sudden flow of sexual energy. It sets me on fire and freezes me simultaneously.

"So this is the crossroads. Can you allow yourself to continue to grow into the fullness?"

"I don't know."

"Who was there to teach you? Were you going to ask your father?" He chuckles.

"I certainly got more permission to *be* from my mother."

"I think that saved you, by the way."

⌾

It's the end of September; I come in holding a new red T-shirt. The health-food store is giving them away. He jumps up, strips, and puts it on.

Embarrassed and weary, I tell him the second antidepressant isn't working. I live waiting for life to begin, although I've taken his suggestion and begun working, not as a home-health aid but as a "nurse" in a chiropractic office. I order vitamins, do heat treatments, and give high colonics.

Harry's call to love him easily, openly, and without criticism puts me on the defensive.

Flat on my back on the bed, later, I tell him, "I see that seductive side of you." And before I can prevent it—"I know you've been unfaithful. And I know you've had sex with patients."

"Yes, I have. But I don't do that anymore. I commit very well in a relationship, very solidly, maybe too much. In one way I'm afraid of being hurt, and so I use that as a way to feel safe within intimacy—to avoid intimacy."

Uncomfortable by *his* intimacy, I turn the conversation to myself. "I've always been faithful, but I avoid intimacy in the selection process by choosing men who can't fulfill my needs in major ways. I need to feel safe, to know I can leave."

"I'd like a relationship, but it's difficult. I have no one to turn to now."

"I understand. I have you, but who do you have?"

"We can check back and forth to see how you feel, how I feel. How we react is a way of assessing how well we connect spiritually, sexually, bonding, intellectually. I'm looking. You're looking. By clearing all levels—spiritual, sexual, power, heart, and intellect with different patients—I know what areas I need to work on. Then I feel safer. By testing myself against patients, I know where I am, and I feel safer when I go out into the world."

I know the tape recorder is running. I want to listen to the words later, because I almost can't believe he's saying these things.

"You will experience me on all levels," he continues, "head, heart, genitals. Let the longing come up. See where you block. Your task is to try out this coming together on all levels so that you can go out there and be with a man of your own. There's a sense of frustration that it can't all be completed between us."

I know I should not wait for Harry. Or long for him. I know this is transference. Nothing changes around my heart, but I do know.

"I see a deep aloneness around you, Harry. Too busy as a way of feeling on top of things. Running to Hawaii to take part in the Harmonic Convergence. Going to workshops almost every weekend, all over the country. Lately, you seem very tired. You need to stop running and let come up what needs to come up."

He nods.

I watch him with tenderness. He has not, to my knowledge, tidied his office since his wife died a year ago. Personal letters and patients' personal effects have been on the floor for months, along with bank statements, canceled checks. I still occasionally find the previous patient's personal check face up on the table by my chair.

When I get up to leave, he points to the army blanket covering a deep hole in my chair. "What do you do to get things reupholstered? Know of anyone?"

He's asked me that before. It's a setup. I'm not his wife.

Determined to manage without an antidepressant, I set my alarm for five each morning to sit in meditation, pen in hand, hoping that by recording dreams and feelings I'll stay on an even keel. Two dreams offer a warning.

When I step outside, a werewolf approaches, a powerful, masculine animal with a dark side, one capable of great change. Although drawn to him, I'm afraid to be alone with him. I know he can become a man with me.

His lips and teeth are visible through shaggy, dark hair with gray in it. Energetic and self-assured, he paces around me. I'm on a path from Walter's house toward the open sea and new land, but the werewolf blocks my way. I'm afraid. Another wolf lopes into view, but he's old and not so active anymore.

The werewolf entices me to follow my path, yet blocks it at every turn. Finally I stop, a wolf on each side. I'm unable to move forward. When I whip around and bolt for home, they tear me to bits until I'm raw meat.

The second dream is more explicit.

Harry is to take me on tour with him so I can do the sexual part. I refuse. Instead, he walks outside the office with me and holds me hip to hip, becoming sexually stimulated. I know he's done this with many others, that he likes the long, slow seduction, likes stimulating himself at the expense of others. His wife went crazy with it. Now he wants a relationship with me, but I know he maintains sovereignty over his seductive nature by not letting any therapist work that through with him. I know he'll betray me if I keep seeing him, but I go ahead anyway.

I take the two dreams to Harry and read them aloud. He changes the subject. I bring it up later in the session. He does not address either one. Was he listening?

A year ago, when the flavor of the month in books were Indian master Mantak Chia's tomes on circulating male and female sexual energy throughout the body, I bought and read them. Now, it's November, and Master Chia is giving a New York workshop on those techniques. I'm to attend and take notes for Harry.

"I can see you training with him and giving workshops," he says. "You're a natural."

Chia espouses a system of ejaculatory containment. By not wasting sperm, man's life force remains intact into old age.

Women are to practice vaginal exercises with a small onyx egg inserted into the vagina. Not only will this help circulate the life force; with practice a woman can hold, squeeze, and actively stimulate different quadrants of that organ, producing a ripple effect that enables her partner to climax without thrusting.

Harry will join me, but in case he can't make it, I'm to bring his greetings to Chia. They're friends.

Highly stimulated by the workshop, I come home feeling joyful. I bought the small black egg and have taken notes on advanced Kegels and breast and clitoral stimulation, including sounds and exercises to enhance and move sexual energy throughout the body.

"Can I see your notes?" Harry asks.

I hand them over.

"Will you copy these for me?" he says, handing them back. "Say, what do you think about men not ejaculating?"

"It's not the same as ejaculatory reflux." I'm drawing on what little medical knowledge I recall. "I'm not sure it's healthy. Recent studies of prostate cancer indicate men who orgasm frequently are far less likely to have prostate trouble or cancer."

"I've heard that. I'm not sure I agree with the master, to hold back orgasm. There's that moment when you tense and it happens. I don't know if I want to give that up."

Chapter 19—Harry Gets a Girlfriend

"I've found someone," Harry confides. "And it's important I tell you. You'll pick it up anyway. This is new for me. I'm getting to know someone as a spiritual friend first, instead of sexually."

No shit, little Eva. The clues have been there for some time. He's slimmed down, trimmed his beard, hair, nails. He walks straighter, and light bounces off his cheekbones again.

He started the hour telling me he'd finally met one of the psychics he referred me to the year before.

"I like her energy. She has spiritual integrity."

"Pretty, isn't she?"

"Yeah, but she's not my type."

I laughed. "Not classy enough."

"Right. You're beginning to know me." He laughed heartily. "I'm *definitely* not turned on by her. Not at *all* physically attracted. Say, she reminds me of you!"

OK, I get it. I understand. If that's the way you want to play it, I'm going to see that you play it that way all the time and through to the end. No more setups.

At the end of the hour, when I stand to leave, he toys coyly with a loose button on his shirt. "How do you sew on a button?" He chuckles, then hugs me, his face in my hair. "You smell *wonderful.*"

Flip, flop, I think, pounding down the path to my car. Push, pull. I guess he forgot all the times he found me so exciting.

"How would you react if I got an erection in here?" he'd said, sitting next to me on the bed, looking at his crotch. "It *could* happen and you might notice. I'm not saying it's *going* to. You're *very* exciting. I have to be careful with you."

Before I could stop myself, I'd blurted, "It's real clear when you get sexually stimulated. You put your leg up and keep checking your lap, like maybe for a wet spot. I don't like it. I can't think or talk."

My remark was greeted with stony silence. But that was then, his worry about erections. Now I'm *definitely* not appealing.

At home, I yell, "Goddamn him to fucking hell!" I grab my sketchpad, draw a crude sketch of him, and burn it. "I'll never let you or any man in my heart again!" Even as I yell, I seem to see in the periphery of my vision the hulking spider who spilled hatred over my childhood. Keep the image there. This isn't about Harry.

True, he acts out all over the place. But I won't get anywhere as long as I fight him. It's Daddy who punished me for being a child, then punished me for not being a child.

If I focus on the old man, I won't need to start fights with Harry.

⁓

We have a saying in Connecticut: if you don't like the weather, wait ten minutes. Like an elemental drama queen, the forecast can swing dramatically from blizzards, hail, hurricanes, tornados, and floods to temperatures in the seventies.

We're heading into the Christmas holidays. The earth is bleak, stalked by stark trees and wounded bushes. It's hard to believe that in six months this state will explode with plant life. I once returned in spring from a trip abroad, astonished to find my state's verdancy rivaling that of England and France.

I've augmented a meager income free-lancing two days a week. I interview physicians from all over the world for a unique radio station that keeps doctors abreast of the medical news. I listen to the interview tapes, splice them for more concise reports, and write intros and closers for our broadcaster.

I rather enjoyed my varied tasks when I worked in that small chiropractic office. Here, it's the businessmen I can't tolerate. And I hate dressing up to sit cramped in front of a computer and the tape-editing device.

At school on Thursday nights and Saturdays, nothing is taught that does not spill into sexual and child abuse, but I've made a few friends with whom I share lunch or dinner, in the village. A lot of us are in middle age; most of the women are recovering alcoholics like me, and most were sexually abused. I cannot get away from it.

Walter's been gone three long months, and I am acutely lonely. I prepare for the holidays doggedly moving in and out of cycles of trying to love Harry on a spiritual plane and hating him for toying with my feelings.

My new life is not getting far off the ground.

"Say, 'I'm safe in here.'" Harry scoots forward in his chair, reaching for my fingertips.

"No." The hell with him. He's hurt me too many times. Besides, he's cozy with probably thirty women a week. "You're seductive, and it's all a game. You can't back it up."

"No, I can't."

"When I was seductive, I fucking backed it up! I didn't play a fucking *mind game*. A cock tease. That's you in reverse. You remind me of the minister where I used to sing in Westport: all tease but no action."

"That's power!" he shoots back, leaning forward to shake my hand too hard.

Three days later, I call him. "I need to connect. Something's come up. My father married. Months ago. No one told me."

Christmas is a week away. Harry is kind and supportive again. "You were the one in your family with that bright energy. You were tested in every possible way, repeatedly. You were in boot camp for the marines, only you never got out. You never felt safe."

Taking advantage of his largesse, I move to resolve our differences. "Harry, what makes it difficult is when you behave in ways that are not true for you, inviting me places when you know you're not going. You go as far as you can and then pull back and say, 'I'm not available.' I think it's a way of maintaining control over your own dark side. The part of you that wants to go to bed with the women patients you find exciting, and this is your way of draining it off. Right?"

Silence. I'm not surprised. He's always mute in the face of reality. I wait.

"If I'm projecting," he says, "I'm willing to own it. Rajneesh says that a woman with power can scare ten men. How many men do you know can coexist with a woman with real power?"

"None." Is that the right answer?

"But the man who is willing to support the woman will find in her the key to achieving the sexual-spiritual connection. She has to go out there and achieve it first, and then she can share it with him. He has to be careful to support her and not suppress her."

It sounds too much like the man's character and maturity depend entirely on hers. I say, "It's interesting that after I did the chanting in here a few weeks ago and symbolically let you enter my space, while I tested out not feeling broken and leaking and dying, that afterward you said three times, 'You sounded like an angel.' For me, the angel part was 5 percent and the 'e' sound was owning my power. I guess you're more comfortable with woman as angel than woman as power-ful self."

"No, you're doing my thinking for me again. You may have set me up a little bit."

At the end of the hour, he says, "This is very difficult work, to bring patients to this level. Not many people can do this, and not many patients want to go to this level. I attract the people who do." He stares out the front window as if knowledge is written there, then turns back.

"Sometimes I don't do enough work, allow myself enough time to clear all this, and when I think a patient is still over there, I find they're over *here*, and I'm not clear or in process with them. It's very hard. Sometime I'd like to share with you how it is for me."

I don't want to know. That scares me. I stand. After he hugs me, I lean back and hold his gaze. "Harry, I own the part of me that fears and projects shame and humiliation. It's OK for me to fantasize about you at times, to project down the line or to the future and see you there. As a patient, I have that right! But I also know where the boundaries are, and I feel humili-ated and embarrassed when you hit me with them. You don't need to do that. You don't need to tell me about your girlfriends. If you weren't too involved, you wouldn't have to pull back."

"I only do that to help you stay clear that I'm not available." He pulls me close, then lets me go. I stumble down the steps and out to my car, blinded by images of us dancing an elaborate roundelay, stiff as puppets, each move writ large and long ago.

The following week—the day before Christmas—I know without his telling me his relationship is not working. He's interested in me again.

"What are you doing tomorrow?" His voice is mossy.

"The kids are home. Walter's here."

"My kids are around, but she—I don't know—it's funny. I think I'll be alone Christmas." A small sound comes from his throat. He looks ragged and close to tears.

Wary of his swift change back to warm-and-confiding Harry, I don't rush in with comfort.

A few hours later, when I'm in the car with my daughter Laura and she asks how my therapy's going, I say, "I'm in another power struggle with him. He's determined to humiliate me, bring me to my knees."

We laugh at what she doesn't realize is not a joke.

When I see him the following week, I'm still on guard.

He scoots forward in his chair, determined to draw me out, pressing his knees against mine, rubbing sock feet over my toes, reaching for my fingers. He picks up my hands one by one and taps each fingertip playfully. "Tell me what's going on with you."

When he hugs me good-bye, it's "You smell wonderful. What're you wearing?"

"Peaches lotion," I murmur, mouth buried in his shoulder, silky beard caressing my cheek.

Back in the frigid reality of my automobile, I know I've taken the bait. I cancel my next appointment, write him five letters, do not mail them, and turn to my journal, hoping for sanity.

January 3. Feeling a great deal of grief and shame. I know I should go back and talk it out, and I can't. I don't understand him. Last Tuesday, he started the wooing again. I can't go through the cycle again. I can't take the bait knowing he doesn't mean any of it. I can't believe it's sadistic, but it feels sadistic. Why does it make sense to repeat all this in therapy—especially when Laura was here—spoiling Christmas?

It always feels I'm being brought down like a dog on a choke chain: "I don't want you." Like the cycles at home, my thinking I was in favor, that for the moment he didn't hate me, and then the hatred he would dump on me would be beyond my wildest imagining. It came from thinking I was OK. I thought that's what caused it. Then, wham!

I feel all the cutoffs. I never see Teddy anymore, or Ann, and we never talk. And Walter's gone back to Maine.

I cannot imagine healing. But I do know I will never let Harry see the agony he causes me. That is humiliation.

Maybe he says to himself: "What do I have to do to get rid of her? How many times do I have to set her up, shame her for loving me, before she leaves?"

When my marriage to Kurt was over, I was distraught with guilt. He kept saying he loved me. He didn't want our marriage to end. Then one day it was clear to me that his behavior would continue to escalate until I let go, that he was unhappy, too, and pushing me away. And that's exactly what happened. He finally pushed so hard, I ended our marriage, and I know it was a blessing for him. What he never wanted, though, was to wake up in the mornings without our children.

⸺⸺∞⸺⸺

Wanting only to die, yet afraid to take action, I cancel my next two appointments. Afraid of slipping beyond recall, I make an appointment with Eileen, his champion. Can she be mine?

I try telling her that Harry swings between seduction and rejection. She's unable to hear that. Her agenda is fixed. I'm a neurotic woman acting out an unrequited-love fantasy. Well, I am! But what about *him*?

Within a week I find the way. I'll borrow a pistol from Matt. I've done it before, when I stayed alone in the boys' Vermont ski lodge. I'll tell Matt I'm afraid.

Before I call him, though, I call Eileen to tell her I can't go on. She has to hear me. She has to.

"Do you have plans?" She means for suicide.

"Of course."

"Then go back to Harry and talk it out."

"I'll go back, Eileen, but please see me every week for a while. I'm terrified of him."

"If you want to see me, then that's your decision. I can't decide for you. Call if you want to come back."

Whoa! Call and ask for what I am at this moment calling for? I'm far too embarrassed to beg. I do know one thing very clearly, after I hang up: this is exactly the same double-bind dismissal Eileen put me through once before.

I'd been seeing her for a few months. Suddenly, I was surprised to find myself phased out, supposedly at my request: "See how things go and call me in six months, if you need to."

She was crisp and authoritative. Beaming, she told me that patients have the ability to "take a leap into health," if given the opportunity, meaning if dismissed. Believing she knew best, I waited six months, went back, and asked her why she'd discharged me. It was after that she referred me to Harry.

This time, I follow her suggestion. I go back to Harry carrying a letter I've prepared. I want him to know me, really know me. I want him to help me. I don't trust myself to get into a dialogue. I read the letter:

> I've got myself into a mess no one wants to hear about anymore. No one wants to work with me. And I also feel shame that after so many years, I'm still in despair and asking for help.
>
> The only way I have any dignity is to stay alone and keep quiet, and at least maintain the illusion of not needing you. I need you not to lie to me, to bullshit me about stuff you have no intention of doing.
>
> I can hear your disbelief that you have been there for me consistently for over two years, and why can't I see that's being true and caring?
>
> Maybe you think, "What do I have to do to get rid of her? This is turning into a nightmare. When I started working with her, I thought we could get somewhere, but I see now she doesn't have enough trust. I have an albatross around my neck."
>
> I'm not telling you how you think. I'm telling you that's my belief.
>
> I'm getting rid of myself a bit at a time. I don't think we can fix this. He despised me so much more than I ever dreamed. I lived in defense of that for so long, and I did achieve a lot. But I have no stomach for trying to make sense out of it anymore.
>
> I know my attitude is wrong. I know I'm failing at therapy. Last week, when I left, I thought, I have only a thread going out to Harry now, and maybe that's enough. I can do the bonding you want me to do, and I can take all the bait and feel OK for a bit, but then I know you will send a little test out to see if I hurt. And I don't have another test left in me.

You want to have it be something played out between you and me, and you set me up, therapeutically. Yet if we worked on what my dad did, and you were my ally, my friend, I think I could do that. But you don't want to work that way. When I get into a lot of rage, like last summer, you probably think, "I'll just let her cook with that, and maybe she'll wise up."

All I think is, maybe she'll destroy herself.

I no longer care about keeping up a pretense that I feel better than I do. I have so little self-love, you'd be ashamed anyone would choose to live like this.

I'm terrified of coming back to see you. I'm not better. I know I got better years ago. I had almost twenty years without wanting to die. I don't know why you do therapy this way. I can't understand half of what you do or say.

You can take this letter as one more stain on my character. I don't care anymore if you see that this is me, underneath the woman who looks the way I do.

This is me, what's under there. Inside. No hope. No will. No wish to spend any more time trying to understand why I got this way.

What is the core? Being real. Being real with you. Well, here it is, the inside part you were so anxious to see. Well, now you're here. Have a look around at what I live with.

How could anyone have hated me as much as he did? You won't even say he did it. You won't say, "It feels to me like he raped you. I feel it reverberating around the room. I hear it, see it, smell it, taste it. I feel you are right." You don't disbelieve I gave birth to my children, just because you weren't there, do you? I have not trusted you since last summer, when you wouldn't say he did it.

If you don't believe in me, there's no point in our working together.

To keep from wanting to die, I mean, to keep from wanting to kill myself, I'm careful to rise each morning at five o'clock and sit in meditation. I find enough peace to keep me from getting the pistol or driving to Canada or cutting off my breasts or tearing up the house.

To keep myself safe, I will lead him through this. I will prevail. I will survive. If he can't do it, I will.

In my journal, I write: *If I let myself open up and love him again, a new cycle will begin, and he will hurt me badly. It's better to withhold love, hate myself, and have it be my fault than risk loving.*

Within a few weeks, cycles of hopefulness and expansion gradually edge out the negative until they're limited, for the most part, to only part of the therapeutic hour. I catch myself getting angry or anxious and turn it around, saying, "I see what I'm doing."

With friends, I'm beginning to laugh.

It's March. Three months until my alcoholism training is completed. I hope to be through therapy. Maybe I'll have a life.

Harry's still inviting me to workshops. Instead of letting it bother me, I sidestep his invitations. My meditation is allowing me to see him from afar, accept his quicksilver nature, that he forever darts from person to person, devoted only to himself. My dreams and common sense warn me he'll stimulate me—or anyone else—and disappear.

Now that I'm working several days a week, I do three-hour meditations on Saturdays and Sundays.

"I almost called you," he says, referring to an earlier invitation to meet him in New York to hear David Hykes sing two notes at the same time. "I was hoping you'd go so I could introduce you. I was there and I looked for you. I didn't stay long, because—"

I cut him off. "I didn't go. And I don't want you to invite me anymore. I don't want to see you socially. It puts me at a terrible disadvantage."

He does not respond.

"Fine." I get up. "Let's work."

"I want you on the floor on your back." Striding across the floor, he picks up the largest red *bataka* and comes at me from the left with it stuck between his legs. As he approaches, he's lifting his legs, as if creeping, then looms over me.

I scream.

He drops the penis, kneels at my right, and wraps his arms around me. He gets up again to go back and forth between Bad Daddy coming from the left, as my father nearly always had, and Good Daddy. Then he stands between my legs and tells me to pound the stiff, red spongy mass. After throwing that down, he holds a pillow over his pelvis so I can kick his penis.

Driving to work afterward, thinking not only of that last enactment but also of all the mixed messages, no responses, and confusion, I suffer a sudden image of Harry without air, a rubber man, punctured, all the air phloofing out. The image stays with me all day until, by ten o'clock that night, I must call to apologize for standing up to him about his careless invitations.

"I'm glad you corrected that," he says. "I wasn't setting you up, you know."

His grudging forgiveness, instead of releasing me, leaves me bound and gagged in ways I cannot decipher. I cry myself to sleep. But—what is odd—I awaken renewed.

During the night my heart lifted and opened to Harry, while I shifted out of prison. In the dream, he reached out to me in a guarded, hopeful way that did not overstep professional boundaries. I saw much tenderness and fragility around him and understood he's endured much loss and cannot tolerate anger or coldness. That isn't all.

As though looking through clouds into sunlight, I comprehend that he is not playing games. He truly is not aware of what he does. As he himself says, "If it's a game, by definition it's unconscious."

Armed with new clarity, I vow to stay clear of his mess-ups.

What I don't know is what he has in mind for me.

⸺ ❧ ⸺

The invitations increase. I write a letter of protest.

> *In the most loving way possible, I want to ask you, please don't invite me, but not really, to do something that may or may not take place—to go with you, but not really, to this event or nonevent that you're not sure you're going to anyway, although all along you had other plans, but you did go, after all—For some strange reason I react badly to these invitations.*

It's amusing and it isn't. I don't dare mail it. Instead, I review journal entries, hoping for clarity:

> *Last week I saw much caring in his face, and it put me on the alert. Will he move in, use me, hurt me?*
>
> *I'm expanding and wearing bright colors. The mousy-brown era is over. I wore the red blouse in there feeling good. Then he called me "Carmen," and I started to feel wary.*
>
> *I know I talked nonstop until he interrupted to tell me about the woman with the dead pelvis. "I have this patient and she dresses up—she's attractive. All that fixing up is to hide her dead pelvis," he said, using his hand as if flipping water on me.*
>
> *I don't have a dead pelvis. I never did. I asked him, "Do you mean me?"*
>
> *"Oh, no, no, no, no. Not you."*
>
> *I'm hurt. Confused. Did I go in as woman again but without the vulnerability of a child? He doesn't like me to do that. But then, going out the door, why did he want me to go to New York with him again?*

Maybe it's because I challenged him by looking gorgeous, all woman in red and black, with earrings. He says I'm afraid of that baby within, of the dependency and the love, so I flip into Woman and leave Baby unsupported. Then why doesn't he talk it out with me or do bodywork?

I don't like being dependent. And feeling loved that way scares me. I feel sad letting the soft child come up. Children are dependent. But he loves that part of me. That's where I'm innocent and not on guard, he says, that I need to spend a lot more time with that little baby and let that softness be a part of me, not fear its being there.

He says I harden up. I still don't know why he talked about going into New York. Again. It feels like a game to me. Sadistic.

I won't go, if he calls. Because I'm not equal in this relationship. I'm exposed and he's not. He wants me to trust and do the bonding. If I do that, will I sidestep the humiliation and anger and all the other stuff that comes up when he talks about seeing me out of therapy?

This is all nuts because I am a full woman and feel like being that way in there. I have a right to that. Why should he take advantage by moving in too close?

He says I seek seduction and betrayal, and that I'm very angry about that, that I'm like an angry woman who has already been knocked off, and I'm mad as hell. And he hasn't even done anything yet. The whole end point of the projection comes up at the very same time I start longing for love, he says, that it's all over, in a sense, before it even has a chance to get started.

Then he says, "Stay with that baby who needs to nurse and suckle and see the love in my eyes and just let that flower, so it can come up and support your woman, who is then looking forward to sex as a completion, not as betrayal."

If I go back and be the baby, then I'm afraid and very sad. He says I can have that and not be hurt. I'm afraid another cycle will start. Downhill. The longing is there now, and that brings up shame. I don't know if I can back up to a feeling of a simpler kind of love toward Harry. I feel overwhelmed. I don't know what to do, what to work on, or how to stay open and honest and heal up those places.

"We're gonna try something new. I want your head at this end." The foot of the bed.

He sits behind my head, out of sight, hands on my hair. "A woman was kidnapped by two men who were going to violate her. 'Unless you enjoy it,' they said, 'we'll kill you.' She decided she'd rather live than die, so she pretended to go along with it. They kept her prisoner for days, molesting her often. Finally they released her. She enjoyed it, so they didn't worry.

"When she had them arrested, they were shocked."

I'm shaking. "I could have done that in order to live, but not with my *father*."

"Experience it, Trudy. I'll go with you. Let's pray to Jesus together."

Mouth in my ear, Harry starts. I close my eyes, breathe slowly down into childhood, and watch for the man to creep in from the left. He's thin, dark, stealthy, and his eyes have a steely glint. I almost hear the words: "If you don't enjoy this, I'll kill you!"

I cringe, but Harry holds my head between large, warm hands, all the while invoking God in my behalf; his whispered strands of semi-intelligible words are prayer beads on a string.

I will let it happen. And then it is. I writhe and whimper. And then a shift. I can stay with myself! He has no power over me. I'll expand into my own power and fill the experience with *myself*. I own the experience. I own it! It's mine. My own body, no matter what he does to me. My own body. *My own body.* He cannot stamp out my life.

And then it's over. The old man withdraws into the shadows like smoke flowing back into Aladdin's lamp.

"It's OK. I did it and I'm OK."

"Where do you want me, this side or that?"

My power vaporizes as he climbs into bed with me.

⌀

Another night of tears and no sleep. I begin writing:

> *It was healing to have him there and feel the male energy open and vulnerable.*
>
> *On the other hand, it was powerfully stimulating as he pressed me, full length, into his body, my face buried in his shoulder. He smells like soap. What soap I don't know, but it's a clean, not a perfumed, fragrance. He held me like a woman, not a child. Not wanting to get too stimulated, I sat up and knelt to lean over and hug him heart to heart, and that felt less man-woman and more of what I was used to. Finally he got up.*
>
> *I told him yesterday I didn't want him that close, that then I want him, and then I have to push that away, that I don't want the wide swings anymore from rejecting me vis-à-vis his insane invitations, to being too close physically, that I wasn't going to go through being hurt again, and that I didn't want to hear the I-am-not-available speech that follows shocking intimacy, considering this is therapy.*

I write, then, a prayer to whatever God resides within me:

> *I need You to tell me what You would have me do. My body is vibrating from a heavy, pounding pulse. Fear has washed up on the backs of waves of sexual energy, the old fear that the thief in the night creeps in to rob me of self, and I can't scream or cry out or let anyone know what is happening. I don't know who he is.*

Chapter 20—White Powder up His Nose

I'M TO ATTEND A TRAINING WORKSHOP ON PSYCHOTHERAPY on Saturday morning, in his office. He knows I'll have to skip classes and that it's only two months to final exams, in June.

"What time?"

"I'll call to confirm and tell you when to be here."

I wait. Then it's Saturday morning. I give up and go out to breakfast alone.

When I see him a few days later, I'm angry, but I'm not supposed to be. Anger is deemed an attack on him. It's seven in the morning as I settle in my chair trying not to show anger or that I'm hurt—I'm not supposed to let him hurt me.

The door to his family room closes with a solid thud. I hear three footfalls as he crosses the waiting room, three more up the stairs, and there he is, two cups of tea in one large hand.

"Here. It's a special Brazilian tea. It's a 'good morning.'" His voice is low and soft, eyes moist.

I stick my nose in the cup and inhale a licorice-smoky aroma, almost a Lapsang souchong. Despite the cheery greeting, his appearance signals torment. He's pale with dark circles under his eyes, and disheveled. He hasn't cut hair or beard since Christmas, and it's spring. His mustache completely covers his lips.

He could not possibly have a woman in his life.

It's the same blue jeans week in, week out, perhaps because he's gained so much. The pants gape at the waist because the top grommet is gone. I know the red suspenders are a gift from a patient, but they do not solve his expanding girth and the missing grommet. Even though he's pinned the zipper pull to his fly, every time he moves the zipper inches down. He has to watch his fly a lot, tugging at it repeatedly.

I shelve my planned confrontation about the Saturday bullshit. Because I suffer most days from a heavy pulse pounding in my ears, I bring that up, and that I'm desperate to move out of my house, a recurring theme when I'm anxious. "And I'm worried about money. I still can't work full time."

I wait.

His eyes are flat, alert to something inside, as if divorced from therapy and his role in it. His inward attentiveness gives him a vulnerable, wistful look. It's as if he's surprised to find himself here, as if his body doesn't fully occupy the chair and he's left himself somewhere else.

He's stopped touching me or taking me to the bed, except to hold me tenderly before I leave. There are other disturbing changes: my appointments run late, as he keeps others waiting; he seems bashful, deferential, unsure of himself, as though very young. He still insists on taping every session.

We talk, but I can't follow much of what he says, the odd arrangements of his words.

When I get home, I pop the tape into my cassette player. Sure enough, I cannot track what he's saying. I listen again, then again, and still can't. At one point, he sets a scene of us as lovers. He makes a proposal for life together in the future, yet it's shrouded in mystery.

With profound frustration and a twinge of disloyalty, I transcribe the entire tape and print it out. It takes hours. By the end of the first page, I see that he's incoherent. And then I remember odd behavior from a few weeks ago. He'd reached into the breast pocket of his shirt to delicately remove a small square of folded white paper. He unfolded it, pinched specks of white powder between thumb and forefinger, and sniffed it into his nostrils.

"Snuff," he explained, sneezing violently. "I love to sneeze."

But snuff is yellow.

And then I recall that he'd recommended ecstasy to a man I know well, a patient.

Profoundly upset, I head down to the kitchen to make a fresh pot of coffee, knees shaky on the stairs. Caffeine won't steady me, but the idea of it, its pungent smell, will give me courage. Somehow coffee connects me, as if an umbilical cord, to my mother, to those days I lay happily playing paper dolls at her feet, while she wrote letter after letter to her sisters in Tacoma, penning them on the drop-leaf secretary that is now mine, husbanding all of Harry's cassettes.

Wrapping icy fingers around my cup, I walk back upstairs to complete the transcript. One line amazes me. In the middle of a sentence about something else, I blurted: "I'm thinking of ending therapy."

I did not think for a moment I belonged out of therapy. The incest is not healed, or even adequately addressed; my income is less than minimal; and my life savings is dwindling. I said it because I had no other way to lobby against his constantly inviting me to meet him outside of therapy.

"Um," I had typed. His only response.

Then I said, "In AA, you're only as sick as your secrets."

"I'm gonna use that the next workshop I do."

I recall his enchantment with the phrase, that he instantly scrabbled for paper and a pencil in the mess on the table.

"What's that again?" he said, writing it down verbatim.

I meander back to the subject of leaving and wait.

"We could shoot sometime the end of June, or something, when you finish. Allow ourselves the freedom of working toward it. It would be a good focus."

Visibly upset, he was dropping nouns and prepositions. Nothing new, but seeing in print his inability to think scares me. He's talking his own special language.

"OK."

"That way we could kinda ease into this, rather than"—he claps hands three times to indicate smashing something (I typed *clap-clap-clap*)—"and talk about the connection and the taking in of the child—and being able to take in and at the same time confront. Have both available."

"Harry, in the last two or three months I've stayed very steady, very straight with you—" I drone on, not able to get to any point, either that I'm fed up with his invitations or that I am in no way ready to end therapy. Why can't he see that?

"Ahm." His only response.

"I don't like the way I'm being treated," I say. "You're seductive and covert. The only person who is swinging anymore is you, and I feel uncomfortable with all these setups and bullshitting invitations, and I'm not doing anything. They're not appropriate, and you're asleep, and the way you handle it is badly."

"Why'd you say that for?"

"—and I don't like it."

"Well, I heard you."

"But you don't do it."

"You don't know the problems."

"If you don't stop, I'm going to leave."

"OK. No, I'm not—You don't have to worry about that anymore."

"All right."

"We'll leave our work just here. I figured you're an intelligent lady, you'll know about those other activities—that there are invitations that don't work. It just didn't—the workshop didn't even come off, and so that was 'setup' if I invited you."

He sounded aggrieved, but I was pleased to then say what I wanted to at the top of my hour. "I arranged to skip school and make up the work so I could come on Saturday. It's a lousy way to treat somebody."

"I felt bad, too, Trudy, because I—shows you how messed up the whole thing was. I was here with two people, and someone else canceled the rest out."

"Did that have anything to do with your not being clear?"

I recall suppressing a wicked impulse to laugh.

"I tried to tell you what happ—maybe I didn't."

"No, Harry, I—"

"No, no, what got clear about this, was this a workshop or was this a training? That's where it got mixed up. That's what I was unclear about. Because half the people wanted it not as a workshop but as a training group."

Good God almighty. He has a thought disorder.

I put the transcript down and look out my third-floor window, bird level with the treetops. Soothed by fresh, green leaves sparkling in the sun, by a glimpse of blue sky, I take a deep breath and read on.

"Is this your Sunday-night group?"

I've typed in T or H to identify speakers.

H: Yeah, my Friday-morning group.

T: That you met with on Sunday night?

H: That was another group I met with.

T: Oh. That was another group?

H: But the Friday-morning group, we—they could not decide whether they wanted a training group, and then they wanted some open people. Then they all got mixed up. No—. [Pause] One was clear, and I—I'm unclear enough. So I apologize to—but when I reached the ah, ah, I told the people about you. And they were excited to have you. Someone want—Effie met you and talked.

T: *What?*

H: Not, I mean, not talked. *Met* you. She talked to you on the phone.

Effie, a rather slender, long-faced, homely woman, fifty or so, had called me the previous winter for a high colonic at the chiropractic office where I then worked.

When Effie arrived for her enema, she talked nonstop about Harry. I kept mostly silent during the two-hour procedure, disgusted with him for referring her, and more disgusted at meeting another woman longing for him. She was so enamored that she would do anything he asked. Actually, I knew from another social worker that Effie was in love with Harry.

After I finished the colonic and she got off the table, she immediately called Harry, from the office. Couldn't wait to tell him something. Had he instructed her to "tune in and tell me what you think of Trudy," as he so often did when he connected *me* with other patients?

She'd heard plenty about me, I was sure of it. And if she wasn't tuning in, why was she there?

Effie had been seeing him for about ten years; according to Harry, her "thirty-year marriage never quite worked." To illustrate, he had swirled fingers in a circular motion as though rubbing a child's scalp. She lost her mother when she was five and longed for nurturing. "Like you," he'd said. He was mothering both of us.

Around the time he sent Effie for the high colonic, he talked about coming in himself. "I should probably get that done."

"You'll have to get the other nurse to do that," I'd snapped.

His brief fascination with enemas didn't stop. He insisted his best friend, the reflexologist, book an appointment with me. Marilyn never showed. Relieved, I never charged her. But I remembered who she was. I'd met her at the spiritualist church right after his wife died. She seemed awkward and childlike.

On the transcript, Harry claims Effie was eager for me to join his therapy group for the training session.

"Effie? I gave her a colonic."

"Right, so Fr—yeah, Effie, I'm talking about you, but I'm just saying, people are—I explained who you were, and they were excited about having you."

When it comes to transcriptions, I'm a perfectionist. My pages are flawless, even to the ums, ohs, coughs, pauses, and so on. Here is Harry in black and white. I shake my head in dismay and disbelief.

> H: In that I let—I wasn't defined myself. Was this a training group? As is, we got closer and closer that it was gonna be therapeutic. The ambivalence and fear just rose. Rather than a training group, and that's where I didn't tend to that anxiety that people were frightened of exposing those secrets.

His sibilants, always juicy, sound wet.

> T: I had anxiety, but I was willing to do it.
> H: But no, half the group was—decided, see? Right. But half the group said no.

I repeated that I'd been willing to participate. But it wasn't true. I was frightened of being around a dozen of his cronies who no doubt knew far more about me than I ever would about them—and I knew plenty. I'd counted on his reneging. That is, after all, his style.

H: Right, but then, see, everything was moving along, and all of a sudden, we plan, we had, we rented the ah—conference room in the motel, and everything, and it bogged down. Instead of ten people in the group, only five decided they could make it.

T: And only two came?

I check back a few pages. Sure enough, I remembered that he said only two showed up.

H: That even got *more* mixed up, because, one, there were two people helping organize it, and I said, "We'll have a couple people—" No. You know what it is? I was going to have a meeting over this issue of this confusion. We weren't going to have the workshop, but I was going to explain to what I wanted to get people clear. And even trying to get people clear, one person called and canceled everybody. And myself and this other guy and one other person came. We were gonna have a group, a community type of, you know, a group, like a group therapy, a group-process meeting to find out what was going on with people.

T: And then the meeting never came off?

H: That meeting didn't come off. So, I lost all Saturday morning. Here, I'm sitting here—and I went out for breakfast. There must have been either me, them, us. The unconscious came blasting through on that one. So I—.

T: I know if that kind of thing happened to me a lot, I'd take a look at my role—.

H: Oh, I know very clear what my role was. I couldn't decide was I therapist or trainer? I think that's what happened in the last meeting. It was definitely a training experience, but by the end of the eve—afternoon, it was wide open and turned into a whole group-therapy process.

H: I think people were shocked at what came up. They didn't want that. They wanted training. It just regressed so many people, and ahm, shoo.

"Shoo" accompanied an airplane gesture with his hand.

H: The work will do that. When we talk about it, you just touch somebody, and you open it. It will bring it up. I had other people touching each other, other than me, and many people felt unsafe. Weren't quite ready for that level. And that's my mistake. I thought people were way beyond that; that would not be an issue. So it got clouded.

After about five more minutes of rambling, he said, "It falls back on me! People were angry with me. 'Why didn't you take more charge?'" He thumped the arm of his chair angrily. "I never said I *would*." Thump.

H: It would have been a lovely group. I don't know why they panicked. It could have been a very easy system.

T: To get back to what I was saying, it seems to me you've opened up a lot of doors, and it's a no-win situation for me. I don't like it.

H: I heard you last week. You're a hundred percent right.

T: I don't like you getting so close physically. It's too seductive. There's lots of ways I can be soft and open and receptive, and there's a lot of feeling and caring and love—of a kind—that can go on without your lying on the bed next to me, without being so stimulating, because I'm here now [I gestured toward my heart] and not over there [I pointed to the bed]. It doesn't feel appropriate, and I've asked you that before when everything blew apart in December and January. You're a lot like an ocean liner. I come along in my little sloop, and say, "Hey! You're swamping my boat!" And you just keep going. You have an agenda. You have a fixed—.

H: Port of call.

T: You have your compass set.

H: I thought I heard you whistle once more.

T: I have whistled a few times. This is only a sailboat. I am not an ocean liner.

H: I do want you—please feel free—and do it often.

T: I do it every *time*.

H: The messages that you've given, I've tried to respond to.

T: I don't want you to stimulate the hell out of me, then sit back and say, "Hold it—I'm not available." It feels like a game, the swing back and forth between "I'm Harry the therapist, but I'm gonna lie in bed with you." The person that gets hurt is *me*. I want to try to stay clear about what I'm doing in here and where I'm going. I've brought it up again and again and *again*. [I can hear my fist pounding my chair.] Every time, *Harry* has not been hurt, *I've* been hurt. And if it happens again, I have to leave, on the spot. I'm not sure that it's been necessary for the therapy. Maybe a year or two years from now I'll know, because in some ways the work is brilliant.

H: It's so tricky. I guarantee you on that one. It is like that. Shoo, shoo, shoo. [Airplane hand flying each time.]

T: No, that isn't what I mean.

I have to stop and breathe, look out the window, get a grip. As I calm down, I have two thoughts. One is that I'm so like a fucking dog on the end of a rag. I just won't give up, ever. The other is, I ought to quit reading and find someone to take this transcript to, a professional, someone who does not know either of us, someone objective who can help me.

I can't imagine who that could be and read on.

H: I do have that tendency, as you get close. That closeness has to arouse sensuality or warmth or man-woman feelings. You're not a little girl and I'm not a little—I'm not a daddy, although I could play Daddy and you can play Little Girl.

I remember that with that, I had started to shake. Reading it sets my body and teeth on edge.

T: I'm afraid of loving you, and I do love you in certain ways, ah, in the gut. If I open to loving—not only you—I get scared. I think, "I shouldn't love Harry. Watch out. You'll feel too sexual, too scary."

And then I abruptly changed the subject to gems, *his* interest. I skim a lengthy discussion of where to buy stones in the city, and stop where I say, "So let's get back."

His response: "I went through a period when I was involved with somebody on a more active basis. It was both very pleasurable and very disruptive. I learned a lot, but it was destructive. Maybe I was the ocean liner. Maybe this person was saying, 'Am I a little boat?' It was OK in certain ways; in other ways it was not. I think it had fallout for me. I think it began in November, and I think it ended in February. I'm just letting you know where I was, and I'm getting clearer and clearer and clearer."

H: I was on a roller coaster, and the people that I am in contact with—the average person I'm sitting here counseling, I don't think it has any impact.

T: I know.

That I agreed with him pisses me off.

H: That's why I'm sharing you, because it doesn't affect me.

Dropping prepositions again.

H: They don't notice that, and I'm not allowing it to get on that level. It's much more cerebral and confrontive, and it's very little contact. I only work with ten people on this level, a couple men and about seven or eight women. And it's no question there's a seductive part of it, a love part of it, a progressive part of it. There's a healing part of it.

Sitting across from him, eyes locked, I had thought his protocol brilliant. But *are* therapeutic levels separate compartments? Is that how I will learn, suffering during the seductive part, blossoming during the love part? What does "progressive" mean? And where *is* the healing part?

H: Part of it that I have found for me, and I don't know why, is that if either the man or the woman has a fairly satisfying relationship somewhere else, I don't get into this. I try to share you with—.
T: How much easier it is with Paulette?

Despite his garbled language, I know what he means. I'd referred Paulette, an incest survivor from my group, to him. Young, he'd said, telling me about her, and juicy.

H: With Paulette, she brought her boyfriend in.
T: It's much easier.

I said that only to make him feel better. That wasn't what I thought, which is that because I don't have a lover, is it *my* fault we're so enmeshed?

H: I was scratching my head. I saw her Saturday and did all the same things I do everybody else, but she takes it—. [Pause] When she leaves here, there's a man out there waiting for her.

Was he doing all the same things with everybody else? How many didn't stop him? How many sat up when he got in bed with them?

And—wait a minute! He saw her *Saturday*—in addition to all the craziness of planned and unplanned group meetings? Where was truth here?

H: And whether I get suddenly caught up in feeling—and I know I have—It's interesting, Trudy, I think I probably ought to go to some Al-Anon meetings. I have a slight tendency to rescue. [Pause] I'm *not* available. It's like participating in some sort of—it *does* happen. There's something in me. I *want* to do it. There's no question it's my own little addiction. Look at my own family. And to get into—I learned a lot with this relationship, that I was trying to rescue this person.

He meant his girlfriend from last winter.

T: It's not going to nurture you very much.
H: But I get caught. It gets sloppy and then I invite, "Come on along." I want you to feel good.

He talked on about his girlfriend, adding, "I was definitely betrayed. She set me up, but I should have known better. You have a right to be pissed at me. I do know better. When we touch"—at that, he scooted forward in his chair, reaching for me—"it's a two-way street. I'm affected as much as you. I am not some blank screen or some sort of robot. Things happen."

Then I'm right about all the times he checks his lap and lays his leg across his knee, looking spaced out.

T: I have trouble not wanting you, when you do that.

H: And I will do that if I am not careful. I will slip into that.

T: I'm the one that gets hurt.

H: Because there's no follow-up.

T: Right.

H: It's all titillation. You blow the horn. I'll blow the horn. We're in boats. [Laughter]

T: Nobody's home here.

I put the transcript down to gaze at my budding trees, their embryonic leaves fluffy as duck down. My third April with Harry. Spring has always been the happiest of times for me; even my body knows: I'm not allergic to new growth or pollen or anything to do with spring. I come alive, pregnant with new life. Or used to.

I read my final remark: "I'm laughing, Harry, but I don't like it. It's like the dream I had of the minister at church slyly telling me, 'Pretend you're four years old and sit on my lap,' so he can get an erection."

Surely we are only pretending therapy, pretending love, pretending to be Harry and Trudy.

Chapter 21—Home Visit

MAY ALWAYS SEEMS TO ARRIVE FROM UNDERGROUND, PUSHING up primrose, daffodils, crocuses. People shed coats, wear bright colors, shake out their hair; men sweeten their lawns with lime.

Every lunch hour, in Stamford, where I'm still working three days a week as an editor for the physician radio station, I drive a mile to Shippan Point and walk along the sea. I suppose I trespass, but no one has ankles in the water yet or is barefoot in the sand—except me. Happy there, I'm reminded of Walter's oft-repeated ditty: *Hurray, hurray, the first of May, outdoor fucking starts today!* If only. I wish I felt more alive, had a man around. I've had a few dates—regrettably.

To graduate, I must pass exams and finish a term paper on nutrition and alcoholism, a subject that fascinates me. Good nutrition is a lifelong habit and hobby. As a medical editor, I'm still in the unique position of having access to medical journals, which enables me to weigh biochemistry against cries from the natural-foods industries.

Therapy is ending, willy-nilly, the end of June. I expect Harry to prepare me for closure.

Instead, he uses the next six weeks to talk about problems he faced in his marriage and with his three children. He speaks with longing about an ideal life. He wants to get to know me "without our roles." He can't imagine not seeing me frequently or having a friendship with me. Like him, I am on a spiritual path. I am not only unique; I am special.

He "cherishes" me, yet "that can never be." He sends me to see a movie in which I'm to listen for the "right" phrase. I'll know it when I hear it.

In the film, a guardian angel spends years hovering over and around a certain woman and falls in love with her. Yet he cannot touch her unless he agrees to reincarnate. Finally he does, that she might see him, know him, love him. And she does, saying, "You are the one."

So what does that mean? I demand to know what I was supposed to glean from the movie. He can't really say. More innuendo. I'm furious. "What about this dream of impending disaster?" I pull a paper scrap from my pocket, wave it at him, and read: *I'm traveling a rocky road and come upon a washed-out area, beyond which lies disaster. A sandbagged red sign reads: 'Go no farther!'*

No comment. Now, I'm really angry. "Harry, you said, 'Would you take me to the cemetery with you?' Why did you say that?"

"Only because of, I guess, I've been up in that area. I just sensed something special was there. I just wanted to feel it."

"There are a lot of things you say that enter my space."

"Hmm."

"At first, I think, 'Oh, that's wonderful!' And then I get angry because I know you're tricking me. You're calling me closer, and then you're going to hurt me. And, of course, you do. Over and over. I think, are you sadistic? You don't seem caring of me. It's crazy."

"I understand," he says. "Maybe what I had left was like an unclear, 'Let's have a session there,' or something, to show me that side, let me experience Wilton. It's probably crazy, because it invites you. You have a big invitation side."

He laughs and continues, "What I do, and I do it with other people, is just set a scene, and then the person says, 'Let's go.'"

I shake my head. "You didn't expect me to invite you to go for a walk?"

"Well, expect me—but you were saying, I guess it's a meaningful place for you." He waits. "I'm available."

I shake my head again. "See, we're not getting clear. You're entering my space, setting up fantasies, so that I go through the transference. Right? You sort of worm your way in; why else would you do it except as a therapeutic tool?"

"I could see how that could do that, but I still like doing home visits."

Home visits? "Look, I acted crazy last summer because of this. I end up wanting to take my life, and then you say you're not doing anything."

"I may have been playing an unconscious game. There's a part when you get into this deep work that it must trigger something off in me, as well as trigger off in that person. There's a piece of craziness that gets activated, and it has to get worked out."

He spreads arms and legs wide, as he says, "When you confront me, it arouses two parts in me: a deep, healthy part and a part that's not. What I do with you, I don't do with anybody else—promising you, inviting you, arousing you. There's a set of behaviors between us that is unique."

My jaw starts its rat-a-tat-tat. "I'm afraid."

"There's a part of me that'll just go with the flow. That's one of my weaknesses. I avoid certain levels of responsibility by saying, 'That didn't happen.'"

My whole body is quivering. "I feel *I* have to control the situation."

"We're working towards practicing, sustaining—to both get clear. Practice is important. I'm not going to lie"—he laughs—"but thinking about the past year, I had a lot of longing sitting around, and even some confusion and impulsiveness. I try to live a spontaneous life. What I did on Mother's Day—"

From there he veers abruptly into a tale of a chaotic day with his kids, in New York City, trying to outrun loneliness. His eyes are bright as he shifts into a description of an ideal love relationship.

"What's really exciting is when both people know they're responsible and interested in taking care of themselves, and they're willing to share that joy. So if I'm doing it and I'm in joy, and I'm clear about it, and you're doing it and you're sure clear, there's like *boom*. It just goes."

"Yes, yes, now see, that makes my jaw shake. I'm afraid, I'm afraid—"

"You know where I used to see this? At Peabody Conservatory. My friends who were musicians, if they were a couple, they would each have their own inner truth."

Harry and I are both musicians.

"And I, you, someone—The best relationships were two fine musicians who were also in love because they were on their own path, and they were alone out there practicing or writing."

Even as I see us together—him practicing therapy while I write novels—I know the cruelty will never stop. My vision of a future with him is a pipe dream. He can't mean what he's implying.

I have to stop it, and I have to stop right now. I lean forward, as if lecturing a child. "Listen. I'm obsessed about wanting you, to know you as a man, not as a friend. I don't want to be obsessed. You're calling me to love you, and it isn't fair. It activates a death wish. See? I'm shaking."

"The infant," he replies. "The infant is not fully here yet. I'm not, not—" And then, he starts to cry. Shocked, then concerned, I get up, wrap an arm around him, and lean over his chair, pressing his head into my shoulder.

"It's a very deep feeling you activated," he whispers into my breast.

He seems to be an infant. I know his mother beat him with a nightstick. "You lay in the crib and your mother—"

He cuts in. "My wife was despondent when [first son] was born."

Terrified by this intimacy and frantic from yearning for the promise of a love I can never have, I pull away and sit to wait for whatever is to come.

"I got caught in one of those weird traps," he says, going on to describe disappointment early in his marriage, and years later, when "her therapy failed" and he was left with "a depressed, abandoned, slightly disturbed person. It never worked after that. She changed the rules on me."

I can't breathe or speak.

"What I was rehearsing in my mind," he says, squirming, "which you heard, was—I was having a conversation outside this room with you."

I know what he means by "which you heard"; it's his fixed belief that I'm psychic enough to read his thoughts from any distance.

"OK, what is it?" *Do I want to know?*

"Talking to you in another setting." His words come out in a whoosh of anxiety.

"That would be odd for both of us, wouldn't it?" I make a supreme effort to speak evenly and not move, but my heart races, then abruptly stops as if forever, before plunging on in a rush of hard bubbles that strain and burst. I press my hand over my breastbone to ease the ache spreading from under my ribs.

When I don't reply, he adds, "It's important to count that experience."

My jaw has gone loose again. Teeth chattering, I'm quivering all over. I can't feel the chair under me. I know he wants encouragement. I wet my lips, and say. "I would like to do that. Let's do that—it brings up fear, doesn't it?"

Head to one side, he seems to study me. Or is he looking beyond me into his own world?

I swallow hard. "It doesn't?"

"No. I was thinking where this might take place."

"Come to my house." He knows I must say that. I have to keep our seeing each other secret, for his sake.

"That's exactly what I was thinking! I've always felt, every time I do a home visit or I visit somebody, the whole scene is different. Not only am I a guest and a friend—"

I take a deep breath. Reality crowds in. Knowing we'll meet in my home is grounding me, and I would not have believed that. But which is it, a home visit or visiting someone as a *doctor?*

Oddly, I settle down, my mind clears: *You don't know who I am. You don't know my competent side. You've never seen it. Perhaps I wish to warn him:* "There's a side of me I can't bring in here."

"I'd like to experience that with you."

"When?"

"Let's plan it for next week, or the following."

"Not next week?" This is our last session! Why doesn't he remember? Or perhaps he does and now he'll begin to court me. He has to come right away. I can't bear the anxiety of waiting.

"Oh, no, no, I'm pretty well filled." He brightens. "The following week I have some spaces."

This is June 22. I have no choice but to agree to the Friday night after July 4.

"That's an interesting—that's a good idea," I say. "I have my—" I'm embarrassed to mention baby-sitting because it will remind him I'm a grandmother. I've been keeping Joseph's new baby overnight nearly every weekend. As much as I want to see Harry, I don't want to break my promise to my kids, and I adore my first grandchild.

He shifts, stretches, expanding into himself again. "Show me around the area. We'll take a walk, then we'll have tea. You can show me your place."

Somehow, we're able to converse superficially another twenty minutes, as if strangers intent on not disturbing a loaded atmosphere. I tell him they fixed my back deck. He thanks me for the referral of my boss's troubled daughter, adding the girl is odd, then glances at the clock behind me, stands, and opens his arms.

"When I come over, you'll have to show me what you got in there."

Harry sends me home with the cassette. I listen, but sit more on the side of longing for the time we can be together than on the side of the clear-eyed editor or the stubborn patient who will not cross the biggest boundary of all, under any circumstances.

The doorbell on my townhouse rings at nine thirty. It is a Friday night. Joseph and his wife dropped the baby off earlier and went out to dinner. I told them I needed to be free for something else at nine.

I fly downstairs and open the door. I'm five pounds lighter than five days earlier. His old, red Volvo is parked across from my door under a flickering gas lantern.

We hug awkwardly. I step back for a closer look, distressed by a long, thick, damp-looking clump of dark-brown hair flopped over the wrong side of his head, a bungled attempt to cover a balding crown. Why the comb-over? Who *is* this man?

He follows me upstairs. As we walk through the dining room, I catch him eyeing himself in the gilded pier glass over my mahogany sideboard. He stops, bends down, peers in. "My hair looks terrible."

It does.

We sit at opposite ends of the couch. I tuck tanned, bare feet—also for this meeting, freshly manicured red toenails—under me. I look good in snug, white cotton slacks and a loose-knit, peach-colored top. My hair is freshly washed and curls softly around my face. Still pretty, very pretty. I'm trim and curvy. Here, in my own home, I know exactly who I am.

Bit by bit, without seeming to stare, I take in his outfit: a salmon-and-beige-patterned sports jacket, more than one shirt showing at the neck. Why? It's a hot night. His shoes are a combination of two light colors. His socks are black.

I don't judge people by what they wear, but this is bizarre. In my narcissism, I can't help wondering if the getup is to discourage me, a hidden signal, like so many. Like his stories.

He tells me he's just left a housewarming party at the home of a patient newly married. He went to help celebrate. I tell him my back deck is newly buttressed. Carpenters were there all day. He asks about my writing. He wants to see where I work. I lead him upstairs to my office. At the top is a rose-colored room with a king-sized bed. If this peculiar alliance is ever to go anywhere, he ought to know where we'll end up.

"My bedroom," I tell him, as I head down the hall to my office.

Within minutes we're back on the couch, two feet apart, sharing a pot of tea. He gulps his down, gets up, and heads down to the door. I follow. After a delicate hug, he calls cheerfully over his shoulder, "See you Wednesday!"

Wednesday? Good grief! He's halfway to his car, but I yell, "I told you I'm *never* coming back."

I pace from the living room to the kitchen and back. Why did he come here? Was that a date? He said nothing about getting together again, except at various upcoming workshops.

I'm astonished by how socially inept and ill at ease he is. Is it my fault? Should I have reached out to him, touched him, helped him connect with me, held him, as he so often held me? Was I distant and subtly rejecting, sending out waves of fear? *Keep away!*

Two days earlier, the date for the home visit reconfirmed, I had to know whether he was coming professionally as a therapist or as a man, so I called him. I wanted it clear, very clear.

"Are you coming as my therapist?"

"No. As a *friend.*"

Now, wishing for a stiff drink, I turn the lights off and go upstairs to get ready for bed. *What does he want from me?*

It's well after eleven. I crouch in a pool of yellow light on the floor next to my bed, pull the phone into my lap, and dial his office, the only number I have.

Unless it's an emergency, he can't be disturbed.

"It *is* an emergency!" I shoot back. Within seconds he calls back.

"Harry, what is it you want? Why did you come over here?"

"We talked about it! I told you, a home visit."

"No, I asked *specific* why you were coming. You said, 'As a *friend*.'"

"Well, yes, but you were through therapy, and I wanted to socially welcome you to the world."

Through therapy? Jesus God almighty. Fuck! Then why the "I'll see you Wednesday"?

I'm enraged. "You can't come in my home to socially welcome me to the world. What is it you *want?* If you're dating me, then *say* it. I can handle that. I know what to do if I date someone. I don't know where I am with you. Do you want a man-woman relationship, or not?"

"I never, *ever* wanted a man-woman relationship with you."

"Then I'm *fucked*, aren't I? You're not my therapist. I can't tell you things anymore. I need treatment, but it's over, and I can't get it. You're all over the place. Who are you? You're not my friend. That's bullshit. Back and forth, back and forth, a fucking swinging door. You want me, you don't. I don't have a therapist, and I don't have a man. I'm left with *nothing*."

I'm crying. "Why did you do this to me?"

"I never said...you assumed," he begins, but I hang up.

Toward dawn, I call an old friend whom I know is always up by four thirty. Within minutes he's at my door.

<hr />

The absurdity of ending therapy this way, followed by the home visit late on a Friday night, has left me stranded with regret.

Harry often says, "Don't walk out. You need to close things up. Those are cutoffs and they hurt."

I stand it as long as I can, a few weeks, and call. "We need closure. I'm in agony."

As a child, I lived constantly with a raw, burning pain in my solar plexus—that hollow just under my ribs—a fire I could not extinguish. The simmering coals were an extra organ, as if heart or liver, throbbing, always throbbing. As I got older, the sharpness of it faded, unless someone hurt my feeling. In my thirties, doctors called it gastritis. Drugs helped. Liquor helped. Liquor stopped everything in all directions.

The hot coals are exhausting me. Night after night I awaken from sleep to find my face wet with tears.

I creep back to my torturer, humiliating myself for having set him up, having false expectations, bungling our work. Complete abasement softens him. He can't be more solicitous. And then he says, "I'm leaving for India, for a month, with Shyam."

He scoots over and takes my fingers in warm, fleshy hands. "A group of us. I'll call you before I go; then I'll see you early September."

He calls the next day to make sure I'm all right. "When I come back from India, I have two days here, then the workshop over Labor Day. It's four days, or five, the workshop. Marilyn's making the arrangements. Call her. I want you to go with me."

"What? Where?"

"Pennsylvania! It's a lodge. You'll like it. Call her. Will you do that?"

He wants me after all.

Chapter 22—After Meeting in Pennsylvania

THE MONTH PASSES, AND I HAVE NO RECOLLECTION of how. I am hollow without him, absent, on hold. And then, it's Labor Day. Although fearful and trembling, I drive to Pennsylvania, and check in at the lodge.

I visit with a few of the participants, then sit on the floor in the midst of maybe a hundred persons gathering at the feet of a famous Indian master who is about to give a talk. Harry arrives late, sits alone in back, and is dressed all in black, wearing black sunglasses.

We break for lunch. Harry sits at a round table with his best friend Marilyn, the reflexologist, and a few others. I sit nearby, wary and observant.

After lunch, he invites me on a walk. He speaks in obtuse sentence fragments that imply we'll be together after this. We sit on a bench, and he drapes his arm around me. My hand rests on his thigh. When he gets up to drive back to Connecticut, I walk alone far into the woods, crying, praying, longing, singing, hoping to ground myself.

If this is my one true love, why is it so painful?

I complete the workshop in a dream state, frightened, sad, and hyper-sexual. My few minutes alone with the guru are spent trying to get him to see into my future. Will *he* be there?

Driving home, I start out knowing Harry wants me, with heart and genitals connected.

What am I doing? He'll reject me. He always does, after the tease.

Even before he sits, I take aim and fire.

"This isn't about my father. It's what's going on in here now. If you think you're going to wrap me in a blanket, so I can rage like a two-year-old, while you stand there as Mr. Cool Adult, you're full of shit."

He pushes his chair back. "You said you were afraid of your rage. I offered that as a safe way to work."

"But why did you have to get closer in May and June? I wanted to get out."

"But was that bad?"

"Here it is the end of September, and we're still caught up in all this, 'I want you, I don't.' How do I separate from someone who's getting closer?"

"Wait a minute. I was not coming closer as a lover. I was coming closer as an available human being."

"You did confusing things."

"I'll own that. My plan was to say good-bye and socially welcome you to the world."

"You're kidding yourself. When I saw you in Pennsylvania, Labor Day weekend, I tried to stay in a very pure place, open to you on all levels: mind, heart, body. But because you're my therapist, we're not *equals*. Your friends were all around. You held me in your arms, yet you don't want a relationship with me. I can't tolerate this. I can't function. Two months now."

I look down. His tape recorder is running.

"And when you came into my home—you can come in my home if therapy's over. Then we're on equal ground. But you can't go in there as my therapist, because I have no place to go with that.

"I can't go into a social relationship with you. In social relationships I have enough control to monitor what's going on. And you're not offering a love relationship where I could be open. With Walter, I could be belly-up. But I don't have that with you. So where am I? I'm nowhere. That's so unfair."

"I never, ever, suggested anything to you." He sits back, Buddha-like.

"You suggested it energetically and with your affect."

"That's your interpretation."

"Then I'm fucked, aren't I, no matter how I interpret it."

"You're labeling things for which I have no reference point. 'You did this; you did that.' What am I left with? It did occur, or it wasn't my intention, or it was a fuck-up. I made the mistake of following through on an invitation. I was trying to make up for all the times I invited you places and hadn't followed through."

"The trouble was not that you didn't follow through, but that you invited me places *at all*."

"If anything, it was the opposite. I was trying *not* to set you up. It's as if whatever I do is called a setup. I explained real clear to you why I was coming to your house."

"Harry, the way that you did it was saying things softly, like, 'I wonder what it would be like to talk to you in another setting without our roles.'"

"Not with that kind of tone. You just threw seduction in there."

"You did it like that."

I have the tape. I transcribed that one, and I have others, maybe two dozen.

"Look," he says, "you started the hour by asking me how I feel about you. Let me restate it. I never—past, present, or future—have thoughts about a relationship with you."

"Don't you think in the middle of transference you could have been more clear, before you came over to my house nine thirty on a Friday night?"

"I'm sorry; that's where I was not clear. That was a mistake on my part."

"I don't want to be in a guessing game with you."

"I thought you were beyond that and you weren't. You were dating; you were finished therapy; and I agreed with you. My mistake was, you weren't finished."

"I couldn't get hold of why you were coming over, Harry. You don't have to come into my home to celebrate that I'm a woman. I have no way to deal with that. You didn't say, 'It's for one hour and I want you to pay for it.' So I called you before you came and said, 'Are you coming as a friend or as a therapist?' and you said, 'No, as a friend.'

"That's terribly confusing. Everything in therapy is larger than life; it's not like a relationship out there where if somebody fucks up, I can handle it. I feel like I'm caught in a sticky web. I can't get done and I can't get out. You're too involved with me. I try to get clear, and I can *never* get clear.

"Three times in April and May you invited me to things. You had no business doing that. You must be able to control your mouth in some way. I'm belly-up. I'm naked and you're clothed. It's so incredibly unfair."

Venting softens me. I glance to the left. He always came at me from the left, in the car, in all the bedrooms of my childhood, always the left. Harry's bed is on my left. "I've told you again and again, there's a part of me that loves you. It's something that's happened to me in this lifetime. And it's made me *more* vulnerable. You've always discounted it, as far as I can see. It meant you had to be more distant and *more* careful. And you never were. You just kept flowing into me.

"Finally one day I said, 'I'm straight with you, and you're all over the place.' *You're* the one. Lying in bed with me. I was the one who moved away. Putting your hand on my breast for five minutes to heal it.

"When you do that meditation to have me imagine you flowing in and out of me, it's certainly as intimate as any intercourse I've ever had."

I feel myself collapse, my spine crumbling. "Maybe it's OK, because you're going in there to heal. My father had no business being in there, so I guess you had to heal that. And you did it with my full cooperation."

"And I told you, that's all I'm willing to do."

"You're all over me. I said I was leaving, and you're saying things like, 'I wonder what it would be like to get to know you in another context.' But you never said the next thing"—I scream it—"which is that you didn't *want* me. That you never, ever want a man-woman relationship with me. You never said it until I called you at eleven thirty at night after you left my house, and I was frantic.

"And if you weren't dating me, why were you there? When I called after you left, the answering service says I can't disturb the doctor. You're dating me, and I don't have your phone number? Why did you put me through this? If you didn't want me—you knew I loved you. Why the hell didn't you help me?"

"I'll accept that I somehow messed that one up."

"Well, then, what do I have to do? Get another therapist to go through the transference and get out?"

"Let's just phase it out."

"Every time I come in here I get caught in the web again."

"Well, then, let's just end it. Stay away from the ending. I mean, stay away from the web."

"I've been belly-up with you. I want you to be clear with me."

He sits up. "I want to end clearly with you, without any false expectations or stimuli, to help undo that sticky side. I don't want to set you up in any way, so that you walk away taking all the hard work you've done, and you feel strong and clear."

"I earned that."

His eyes go dark as his cheekbones flush dark red. "I'll tell you what bugs me about you," he yells. "I'll tell you. Out of my humanness, I share you. You ask me things. I don't say, 'Get away!' I tell you. Then you twist it. If I sat here long enough listening to you attack me, I'd end up believing I'm the most seductive psychopath alive!"

His anger cows me. Then it *is* his master plan, has to be. He is doing brilliant work, and it will heal me, eventually. "Maybe I've had a fixed belief that you'd be there for me after therapy." Admitting that shames me.

"I picked that up. I tried working with it, to bring it to a higher elevation."

"Yes, you did."

"I thought, if you saw me someplace, you might see me in reality and cut through the transference. I shared you what happened in my own transference, how I spent time with that person on a trip and lost the transference. I don't have that special feeling for him anymore.

"You don't know who I am. Here, I'm acting in an idealized way."

Idealized? Good God almighty. And dropping prepositions again. "I'm aware of that."

"What was here was our *work* relationship. And this is always special. And this is intimate, or you can't get through those levels. You and I talked how hard it is for both people. I only have a handful of people I can go to these levels with. And every one of these people struggle. One of the ladies—She's getting married now. But it was like pulling teeth and nails. She never saw me as her *lover*. She saw me as her mother.

"This is the oddest thing. I'm a mother letting go of this little girl. How the hell did I get into that role?" He leans forward. "Trudy, I want you to get clear."

So he wasn't struggling with whether to love me as a woman. He was toreador, red flashing between his legs to tease out my complex. "In May and June you got closer as a therapeutic tool—"

"Let's say it happened."

"You should have stayed clear with me, and I'll tell you why. I have always blamed myself for loving and for opening my heart. And if I blame myself for the last two months, then I live with shame again."

"Oh, no, no, no, no, no, no, no."

"Yes. It's like my father. It's shameful."

"No. You've been radiant and clear. You're getting where you need to get to. You seemed grounded."

"If you blame me, then it's what I've done to you, Harry. It's like I've done it to my father. I was beautiful. I was exciting. I was loving. I opened my heart. It's my shame."

"No, no. You have nothing to be ashamed of. I haven't been clear enough with you. I made a false assumption, and I'm truly sorry."

"You had to set me up again and again, didn't you." It isn't a question. Hasn't he told me I have to go through cycles of exquisite pain ten or twenty times, until I no longer react to the setups?

"Let's stop the setups," he says.

"I thought we stopped in May. I told you, 'Don't ever do it to me again or I'll walk out,' and what you did was set me up in the biggest way possible."

"It was my attempt *not* to set you up. There's the mistake."

"See, I think that's the therapeutic technique but that you won't own it."

"I have no technique somewhere that I plan that. But I will admit that it did set you up. And I don't want to do that, now or ever. Let's let it heal. Let's close that off."

"It's like you're a surgeon, and I'm looking into a wound. Most of it's shame."

"That's where forgiveness comes in." He scoots forward, reaching for my fingers, but I push away.

I'm to call him in a few weeks to phase out. But it's autumn, my season of woods and wounds, of furnaces and tiny, green-plaid dresses.

Within days I'm pregnant with old memories, heavy from scene fragments of beds and doorways on the left, too many nights in too many houses, seeing for the first time what my father intimated so mysteriously, when I confronted him the year before.

"Maybe it happened when you were a teenager."

Chapter 23—Sexual Peccadilloes, Addictions, and Anomie

THIS AUTUMN, MY THIRD WITH HARRY, I'M STILL working three days a week, still interviewing physicians all over the world by telephone and summarizing their clinical trials for our news service. Our offices are in a warehouse loft next to a filthy railroad terminal, home to drunks and drug addicts. Hip to shoulder with our building is a huge electrical power substation. High-tension wires hum overhead.

Frequently the elevator jams. I dash up six flights through a concrete, soundproof stairwell, stepping over urine from those who presumably spend the night. I rush past locked offices and, at the top, bang on our door, hoping a coworker hears me. If not, I run back six flights for the on-again, off-again elevator.

That isn't why I hate my job. Some of the men I work for remind of my father—financially successful, arrogant, and a little cruel. My tolerance is gone.

I'm a lumbering mammal with swollen teats and a dripping birth canal, compelled to circle and recircle a huge, dead fetus.

But also, it's September, and the world is full of promise, Harry's latest promise: "Let's wait six months, then see what we have together."

Can I get well—return to what I once was, only better—in six months?

Reluctant to ask him for hypnotherapy, I brush aside dreams and flash-backs of adolescence. Being molested as a child is one thing. Being an adolescent implies consent. How can I ask a man waiting for me to look at an unforgivable past?

Besides, Harry is treating me as an adult, friend, and confidant, and spends most of my hour now discussing patients. The admonition to support others is not remotely new, but the number increases dramatically over the next six or eight weeks, until I'm attending to as many as six to eight needy women on the telephone or over lunch or dinner. My role is to comfort and counsel, encourage and probe, and report back to Harry.

Clearly, I'm being groomed.

He is sympathetic. He's also devoted to planning my future. If I go back to college for two years, graduate, then get a master's degree in social work, I can relocate to Vershon, Vermont. He's planning to set up a therapy outpost and supervise his social workers on weekends. He'd like me to part of that system.

For now, I'm to study Shiatsu. At his urging, I'm to spend six months learning pressure points from a woman who is his "friend," whatever that means. He still talks about my making a living giving workshops on esoteric sexual and holistic systems. Or I can leave. That's what I think when, apropos of nothing, he tells me about his being in line at an airport terminal.

"This stewardess wouldn't let us leave on time, and here I needed to catch my plane. She kept us waiting and waiting. She was feeling sorry for herself and screwing up. All she had to do was ask for help. Instead she got into helpless and hopeless. It kept us hung up." He waits a beat. "I wasn't going to punish her." He stares intently at me.

Where am I going wrong? If I can get my life back—if I can keep his interest—there's a chance we *can* be together. Then perhaps the things he says won't be so confusing, wounding, infuriating. After all, we're both musicians, both single parents. And aren't I helping with his patients?

The five who call me most often have what I see as massive confusion and low self-esteem. All cling to one or another of Harry's ever-vaporizing New Age cures. One, Nancy, a married therapist in her fifties, is losing her job because of a crippling addiction to alcohol. Yet, Harry is arranging for her to have sex with one of his much-younger male patients, Larry, one who indulges in homosexual "flare-ups." Larry likes older women. They've both told Harry they're "horny." Why not put them together? Sex with Nancy, he tells me, might help Larry give up the gay life.

Another patient—Harry's good friend—is a gifted voice teacher who once soloed all over Europe. She has a magnificent operatic instrument. I knew her years back when I was studying voice. I like her immensely. She's bright, warm, forthright, and giving.

I ought to study voice with Lorna. I tell Harry that after twelve years of voice lessons, I'm done, done with church solo jobs, done with performing in operettas and concerts. But singing with her will "open and heal" me and "enhance our work." He urges me to join Lorna's inner circle. After a number of lessons, she welcomes me to an evening meditation gathering.

Harry shows up, and I leave.

This woman—still in therapy with Harry after ten years—has married and divorced the same man numerous times. I stop the lessons I don't want and can ill afford, and drop out of her circle.

What am I to do with details of his patients' sexual peccadilloes, drug addictions, career aspirations, marital problems, and anomie except "tune in" and report back to the hub of the wheel, spinning ever faster?

Chapter 24—He Dogs It

FOR ALL THE MONTHS I WORKED IN MEDICAL broadcasting with other writers and editors on the sixth floor of the warehouse in which it was located, I spent most of my time alone, unlike my ten years in publishing in Greenwich.

In Greenwich, teamwork was everything. We consulted one another all day long, happily. My top boss, the owner for whom the company is named, as well as the underbosses, were beneficent beyond anything one sees today, or in any office that I have worked in or heard of.

We celebrated one another's lives, whether editor in chief or secretary. On May 9, I'd find my office filled with birthday cards and handwritten poems, unique artwork taped to windows, balloons on the ceiling, chocolate and flowers on my desk, knowing we'd all go out to lunch early, have a drink or two, and pass around enough tongue-burning Chinese concoctions for the twelve or fourteen who partook.

In this warehouse by the power station and the railroad, when my lunch hour comes, I flee. It's a few blocks to the Sound. I sit on a blanket or a dry spot of sand. I walk the beach (barefoot, if I can) or the wide, clean sidewalks shaded by huge, well-tended trees gracing the lawns of expensively groomed shorefront properties. If it's rainy, I eat my sandwich and drink my Thermos of coffee in the car.

An hour's reprieve. I must walk. Not only does walking restore me, but I also pray, or I can't get through the day. I pray for guidance, for peace, and for Harry.

I love him, not from joy but from a wound deep inside, believing that if we connect, finally, I will be healed. I try ever harder to please. Sometimes I try to make him jealous by telling him of men I meet here or there and occasionally date.

At the same time, I'm having intrusive new flashbacks. Like jagged lightning, they flicker nervously in the periphery of my vision, long enough to expose the thirteen-year-old lying awake in the dark in the Bigelow house in Wilton, the fifteen-year-old staying up all hours in the Belden Hill house, hoping he'll fall asleep before I turn in.

I can't bring myself to tell Harry what I'm seeing. Rage simmers under the surface of my every thought and interaction with him. I tell him again and again, "I want to do anger work."

He won't.

Chapter 25—Waking Up

As I listen to tapes from earlier that fall, I hear myself implore him to help resolve another of his sadistic and wounding machinations. What I begin to see is that I stubbornly refuse to believe he can't.

He's missing a part.

I lived compartmentalized as a child—maybe I still do. I enjoy some aspects of editing and some of my colleagues, and dislike and even fear some of the men here in this new job. I'm hopeful and uplifted during lunch at the water's edge and terrified in my own house at night. I actively seek Mr. Right on dates and am desperately, sickeningly in love with Harry. I attend concerts but no longer sing. I cherish cozy dinners, lunches, or breakfasts with old pals from Cliggott Publishing, new ones from AA, and long-time friends from way back—yet far too often eat alone, longing for Mother. I drive often into Manhattan to the Metropolitan Museum of Art, but I no longer paint portraits in oil.

The big, beautiful, happy boy in the Midwest is too far for weekly baby-sitting, but I enjoy him vicariously through my daughter. My other grandbaby is fifteen minutes away. With her, I am utterly at peace. I work hard arranging to see her weekly, often more.

Because Harry lets me know he's enchanted and stimulated by the residual joy shining in my face after I've been with her, his pleasure somehow cheapens one of the greatest gifts of my life.

Dan, former lover and before that close friend, calls frequently. When his relationship with the love of his life is on the fritz, which it often is, he visits me, understanding sex is out. We order Chinese takeout, cuddle on the couch, watch a movie on the VCR, and laugh at everything and nothing. Sleepy, we snuggle in my bed, hold hands, and talk quietly for an hour or more, sharing secrets and dreams.

Soon, I tell Dan everything that's happening with Harry. It isn't only feedback I need; it's to hear myself. I know too well the great secret of AA: You're only as sick as your secrets.

Toward the end of November, I begin opening to a few other friends. Everyone suggests I get out. Some are angry. "He's abusing you!" Another puts it more succinctly: "He tortures you."

I begin confiding in a writing group I organized the winter before. We three women meet faithfully one night a week at my house to read and critique each others' novels. My book is this book, my journey through incest. Harry loves it that I write about him.

When I began this memoir, I wrote that he guided me gently through hypnotherapy, suggested workshops and seminars, opened me to spirituality, that he comforted and healed me. My starry-eyed beginning was a tapestry woven from obsession, each strand, in the early sections, carefully selected to create an overall pattern reflecting Harry's image of himself and my idealization of him.

Nowhere, as I began it, did I mention his looking into his crotch when he got stimulated, cupping my breast, kissing me on the lips at his wife's wake and funeral, rubbing sock feet sensuously over mine, lying bare belly to bare belly on me on the floor, playing with my fingertips, holding me in his arms in every session. There's nothing of his staring in meditation into my eyes, asking me to "suck" his sexual energy. I left out that he slid his hand under my underpants to stroke my abdomen, took his trousers down, shirt off, admitted to erections because I was so exciting.

Nowhere did I mention his shaming me with weird stories, telling me intimate details of dozens of others' lives, including those of his wife and children. Nowhere did I complain of his connecting me with a dozen or more infantile, alcoholic, borderline, and schizoid patients, to caretake them at my expense.

Nowhere did I lay out the volume and extent of his invitations, lies, mental derangements, thought disorders, and decompensations, or his inability to cut his hair and beard for a full year, and for long stretches at other times. I glossed over the psychopathology of a chaotic office. And what about the highly erotic, seductive, manipulative, gamey, destructive, dishonest language?

Nowhere in my first draft of this memoir did I mention what was really happening in therapy with Harry James Brown.

Chapter 26—Authentic Hypnosis

THE NAME FOR THE FINAL PHASE OF MY therapy is erotic work. He lies on top of me on the floor until I weep. He stays there until I stop crying and let sexual feelings build.

"When you move it up," he says, "it's spiritual. It's no longer sexual. Then you have something to celebrate."

"You're making me sick. I have bladder pain all the time."

"The work'll do that," he explains, cheerfully. "I warned you. It'll bring it up. Let's watch it, see where it goes."

But I don't want to.

Years ago, I met a man named James Mapes, real name. He's a hypnotist (and far, *far* more) who one day gave demonstrations at a theater on Candlewood Lake. I was enchanted. For some reason, his name pops into my mind. I know—I'm absolutely certain—that Mapes has integrity. I will be safe with him.

I tell Harry I want to consult this man, see if I can look all the way into my past.

Harry is confused about whether he'll go with me or not, whether I should see a different hypnotist, whether Mapes is qualified, and whether I ought to go at all.

I immediately book an appointment.

―∞∞―

With Mapes at the helm, I drop down through the years, revisiting the crib, the furnace, the attic. At ten, I'm reasonably happy; at eleven, in shreds.

We stop at the end of two and a half hours. His head throbs, and mine is light and clear. I not only saw the years sequentially spread out before me, the different beds and woods and attics, but also when it stopped. And why.

I'm sixteen. It's a Saturday morning in the Belden Hill house. I'm cleaning my room. Mother is ill, as always, and in bed with her new baby swaddled under her arm. My father's across the hall from my room, repairing pipes under the sink in the bathroom—or he was, until he moved into the hall in front of the stairs, swearing at me for something I failed to do.

When I see his face twisted from fury and hear the first "goddamn you," I walk straight to him, pull my arm back, and slap his face with all my might, saying, "If you ever bother me again, I will kill you."

Astonished, he falls back, arms up. And then rage. Lunging, he shoves me down the stairs, but I twist in midair, take the treads by twos, land safely at the bottom, flee out the kitchen door, and fly across two fields to the Perkins', where I know I will find succor in "Jim," Mother's best friend.

Was I in a dream state? Yes, to the extent that consciously I was simply warning my father to quit yelling at me for not doing enough around the house, or not doing it perfectly. Unconsciously, I delivered a powerful ultimatum. And that's when it stopped. The poor, sick bastard never knew I was totally amnesic. I can't wait to tell Harry.

But—his reaction is boredom. And I don't care because now I'm going to talk about my adolescence, those last years at home with my father. I need to acknowledge it and let it go. Harry doesn't want to hear it. And that's just too bad.

Chapter 27—Enough!

WE SIT FARTHER APART THAN USUAL, MAYBE THREE feet, sipping herb tea. I hug my mug because it's very cold outside, and I'm layered under my thick sweatshirt.

Sixth grade, I tell Harry, in Wilton, then New Canaan, my father butchering chickens every weekend, Ann and I, sometimes Mother, plucking and cleaning them for the freezer Dad rented downtown at the Village Market, our lone grocery store in what was Ralph Petersen's white colonial. Because we've burned the bottom out of at least two huge aluminum vats, we're keeping eyes on this one as we boil down into syrup the thin fluid drawn from our maple trees. When I can, I hang on the fence my father built to keep our pig enclosed, watching her girth to see if she's about to release the piglets for which she was bred.

Cleaning the house, because Mother can't, vacuuming, then playing hooky outside in the woods with my brother, trekking as far east as the river, making fires to keep warm while baking potatoes in hot ashes—and sometimes getting poison ivy so severely my eyes are slits.

Listening to my father lambaste Mother in the library at night in front of the Franklin stove, furious at her for buying what I know now were necessities.

Harry does not move or respond.

Fuck him and his sour mood. I look away and talk on about my fear of the bus driver, an older man who seemed smitten with me, how I'd "miss" the bus so Mother had to drive me, or, last resort, wave the thermometer under hot water to earn another day home with her.

Harry's face? Still impassive.

Since seeing Mapes, I know what happened at age twelve in that first Wilton house; at thirteen in New Canaan; at fourteen, fifteen, sixteen in the second Wilton house, on Belden Hill. It's odd, I think, that by chance the arrangement of doors and my beds meant my father came at me from the left.

I take a deep breath and wrap my arms around my midsection.

In junior high I changed my name to Ginny, I tell Harry. I stood in the schoolyard, not in my body at all. If someone had looked inside me, they'd have put me in a hospital.

"The trouble with living in New Canaan…It was sophisticated, especially our neighborhood. My parents bought and could afford but didn't know how to live in a house with front and back stairs, nine bedrooms, five baths." I'm ashamed to tell Harry Dad kept pigs hidden in a pen out back.

"Our neighbors had gardeners and full-time help. They wore evening clothes to their country clubs. The wives had fur coats and their hair done every week."

"They were not good times." Surprised by his response, I look up. "Not good times at all," he adds.

Harry knows I've been driving over to the Belden Hill house, almost two years now, to park and walk a two-mile trek on country lanes. The land is beautiful and high.

For a moment, my mind goes empty. I close my eyes, then see Dad angrily roaming our property Saturdays and Sundays, hoeing, butchering a pig, a lamb, chickens, all the while seething from inner storms. I'm afraid of him. He refuses to let me date, except for proms.

And then I smile. "We had two goats, Marmaduke and Wellington."

Harry is not amused.

"And a smokehouse Dad constructed to cure bacon. He'd call this old Italian, Christi, to help him slit the throats of the pigs or the sheep, and oh, the screams as they were noosed and led to slaughter! He wanted Mother to make him a jacket from sheep hides, and set me up outside kneading sheared-sheep leather on a washboard in a bucket of cold water. Mother refused to touch it, so he sewed it himself on her Singer.

"Well, and the cat hat he made and wore, but I told you that—" How he shot our neighbor's pet. How he tried to make me drown our cat's kittens, and when I couldn't, told me to spray them with Flit to get rid of their fleas, knowing the chemical causes a slow, painful death.

I'm beginning to regret my litany, but now Harry wants to continue.

In tenth grade, I was taken to Miss Tacke's office one day because I couldn't stop crying. Still crying after three hours, Mr. Kenney called Mother and told her to take me to a psychiatrist. My father put a stop to it.

Enough!

The morning sun spills gold between our chairs and warms my toes. A slice of it bleaches the end of the long, blue couch. In back, the double bed, with its patterned sheets, pillows, and folded blanket, waits.

"Let's work," I say.

He pads after me and pulls up a chair, a chaste hand on my waist.

"Let those feelings…Breathe into them. Follow them as they move somewhere inside of you. Follow them as they move into that experience, that part of your body. Allow your inner eye—"

"I'm very cold."

He covers me with the blanket and moves closer.

"Let that sadness circulate down from your gut into your pelvis, see where it goes. Your chest, belly, heart. Allow that sadness to move around."

I start coughing, then choke, gasping for air. Harry moves his hand to my belly. "Let it open. *Easy.*"

The back of my neck feels electrically wired. I grit my teeth. There's a huge bubble in my solar plexus. Although never bulimic, I want to vomit.

Breathe, I tell myself. The longer I keep away from what is there, the longer I will suffer. I give a soft shake to my shoulders and let myself nail a year, and move up. Eleven. Fifteen. Sixteen.

Always from the left.

He did. She did. It did. No use pretending.

My time is up. I sit and drop my legs over the edge of the bed, too weak and shaky to rise. Harry stands, lifts his arms in a gesture of supplication, and gets ready to say something.

I slam a hand through the air. "*Don't say anything.* You like to tell your Ericksonian stories, and if you do that now, you're going to do tremendous damage. *Do not do it.* This is not the time to do your toreador number to tease out the complex. You like to play your little games. Not now. You do it now, and you'll create incredible damage. *Do not say anything.*"

I disappear into the bathroom. When I come out, he's in the doorway of his room, head hanging.

"But, Trudy, I was trying to help." He offers a hand palm up, then slaps it down with the other to show I rejected him.

I step into his arms and bury my wet face in his neck.

At home, I do not feel as lost; I'm more productive, outgoing—but a few nights later, my knee is stuck fast to Harry's blue jeans in a dream. It's a sticky, wet spot over his sticky, wet penis.

I tell him clearly, the next time I see him: "It means I'm warning you. Stay away!"

———⚬✥⚬———

Confident he heard me, I'm relaxed the next time I sit waiting in my chair. And then he's there, saying, "I'm all wet," as he plops down, spreading heavy legs far apart. Watching me, he briskly rubs his hands up and down inside his thighs, saying, "I'm still wet."

Without warning he scoots forward in his chair, jamming my knees into his genitals. Before I can push away, he grabs me in a bear hug, trapping me between his arms and thighs.

It's ten minutes before I dare move.

I cancel my next appointment, and two weeks later, Christmas Eve, I go in only to say good-bye.

Chapter 28—Breaking Free

I TELEPHONE MY CHILDREN'S FATHER, AN ATTORNEY. HE gets it, the whole story, very quickly, one of his great gifts, and wants to help.

"Call Koskoff, Koskoff & Bieder. And do it now," he cautions, "before the statute of limitations runs out."

Within a week, Karen Koskoff is having all my cassettes transcribed, faces Harry's attorney in Stamford Superior Court to get the ball rolling (front-page story in the *Stamford Advocate*), and has me making notes for the civil suit and a malpractice report to the State's medical board in Hartford.

I *know* I'm in good hands, the best, but I do not believe Karen when she says Harry sexually abused me. For me, sexual abuse still means rape.

<hr/>

Within six months, after two useless attempts on my part to effect closure with Harry, I find a woman therapist who does not work with him, think he's wonderful, or fudge a commitment to testify in my behalf, if needs be.

In August, despite my new therapist's misgivings, I make one more appointment with Harry. This time, he's in the room waiting for me.

"I have to have closure," I say as I sit.

He looks away and begins to share that he sometimes encounters patients with *holes*. He tries to fill them with himself, as mother or father. Rescuing is his failing. Some patients are too needy, and he has to back off to protect himself.

Now I'm the one not responding.

He stares at me as he leans into my space. "This guy had a vortex of negative energy in the solar plexus." Raising an arm, he swirls his fingers, as if laying something into my chest and waist.

"I could see it!" he says. "It made me ill! David met him. *He* saw it, this swirling vortex of black energy. A therapist can't deal with that. He'll get sick and die. It's dangerous when you see that. You can't even be *around* it. We could get sucked in. 'Stay away!' we said."

He flips his hand again, throwing the curse on me like water off his fingertips. "You know the person."

Well…once again, I do know to whom he's referring, a man who, when he married a girlfriend of mine (another Harry lover) a few years ago, died within six weeks; no one quite knew why.

(Harry's psychic friend David, to whom Harry once sent me for a "meditation workshop," is a self-styled therapist and high-school dropout. I know from Harry's incestuous grapevine that David gave patients sex and drugs, torturing one man to the brink of suicide, and was reported to the State for unethical practices. Still, Harry supervises David, recommends him, and signs off on David's insurance claims.)

Midsummer, and Harry calls, all warm and friendly. The spiritual workshop we went to in Pennsylvania the year before will be in the same lodge Labor Day weekend. He uses the words "invitation, sharing." Will I be going? He's going.

"No," I say, and hang up—too late. Rattled and afraid, I know he has entered me, and frantically start telephoning supportive friends. Despite good counsel, I spend the next few days weeping, raging, and dreaming of death.

Just when the poison's draining away, the telephone rings early, waking me.

The workshop is over, he tells me. The guru was different. Since Harry uses "he" to refer to himself and also the guru, it's impossible to know the antecedent for who is now "a very wise and gentle man."

I don't have to grab my lined paper pad to transcribe verbatim—although I do—because I'm on to Harry's messy invasions.

"Last year, he didn't know what to say; he just sat there," Harry says.

Actually, it was Harry who sat in back dressed in black, dark sunglasses instead of eyes. After lunch, we walked to a bench overlooking the lake, his arm around my shoulder, mine around his waist.

But socially inept and ill at ease, he wasn't able to say anything except about the topography.

"This year he had a speech prepared," Harry says. "He was ready. He'd been through it before and knew what to say."

Cat and mouse. It's all I can do not to laugh. Still, I write furiously in the shorthand I learned to use covering medical conventions.

Warm, inviting, personable, he blathers on for a half hour, and I hang up amused at his pathetic insinuations, amused, that is, until the next morning when I realize he's entered me again, poison words from a hypodermic while I slept.

I hurry downstairs, fix strong coffee, and put water on for poached eggs, anxious to read my scribbles, praying they will save me.

Bottom line? *He's different, now. He'll know what to say. This year, he's different.*

Well, how nice. My therapist would not approve of what I'm going to do, but after all, it's my life.

I place the call, and when he calls back, I'm warm, inviting, personable. "Come on over, Harry; we can be friends!" *That's what you want, isn't it?*

"Yes, Trudy! It's important we maintain that friendship. I'm glad you called. I want to come over. It's very important for us to see each other. We had a very deep bond. We can't just cut this off. It's too deep…be together…can't come this weekend…taking my daughter to school. I'll call you Monday. *I'll call you Monday.*"

Right.

I'd like to say I never saw him again, but I had to push for three meetings that spring, looking for closure, or maybe because I was still in love.

That fall, I follow through on my alcoholism training and win a job as a counselor for adolescents at a treatment facility, Arms Acres, Westchester. Within three months, I'm conducting group therapy twice a day, structuring and leading family interventions, in addition to seeing patients individually. They are fiercely protective of their boundaries and exhibit signs of extreme vulnerability, engulfing adolescent sexuality, and incest—which we find in *every* girl and some boys. I'm beginning to view my work with Harry from the other side.

By the following summer, I'm off the antidepressant; but as an incest survivor, I cannot heal as long as I'm caretaking other incest survivors, and I begin looking for another job.

In late August, June surprises me by inviting me for lunch. June and I were close friends for thirty years, until she began see Harry and I began my civil action with a report to the State for medical malpractice. Feeling I'd betrayed them both, she dropped me. I understood. Hadn't I been far more enamored with Harry than she ever dreamed of being?

As soon as we order, she says, "He realizes he made mistakes with you. He wants to help you. He knows you're struggling. Call him, please."

Outraged at his discussing me with her and using her as messenger, I try telling her how his words and actions caused so much suffering. Heart pounding and with icy hands, I ask her why she can't hear that he has no boundaries, that he shouldn't have invited me to over thirty places. Thirty! He broke anonymity on over fifty people, put white powder up his nose, took his pants down, lay on me, jammed my knees into genitals, insisted on meeting me outside of therapy.

Her eyes glaze over.

I signal the waitress to bring the check and a box for my uneaten Rueben.

Why do so many give this man a pass? I shake my head, and then I know. I did. Sad and furious, I drive away knowing June and I will never get together again.

Still, back home, in my kitchen, my safe place, I begin to feel the seepage, the poison, this time from even the mention of his name. *Fuck! Face* it!

Trembling and determined, I pick up the phone.

"June tells me you want to talk," I say when he calls back.

I stand at the glass door in my kitchen, washed by the gold and hot pink of a setting sun, and face the hill across the valley, only a mile or two as the crow flies from where we lived on Belden Hill, in the old farmhouse my father rebuilt and added on to, a house with no secrets anymore.

"You're having a tough time, Trudy, and I feel bad. I talk to June, you know. I want to help you with this. We could meet, have coffee, talk about it. It isn't finished."

"Let's cut through the bullshit, Harry. You're calling because you're afraid of my lawsuit, and that the medical board knows."

"No, you're wrong. I'll handle that just like I handle any other lawsuit. No. I'm hearing from people. People at Norwalk Hospital, Fordham, in the social-work program, things about me. You're doing a lot of talking. Twisting things."

His voice drops. "I can help you move through this."

"You can't help me! Each time I went back I got caught in the web, and I went back May, July, then August. You didn't help me with it in December when I walked out. Nothing."

Silence.

I wait. When he doesn't respond, I say, "You asked me to meet you at the Gurdjieff lecture last spring, so we could go out to dinner afterwards with David and his girlfriend, even though I'd already sued you in court. In the parking lot after dinner, I asked you to come by and get the book I was writing about you, because you said you wanted to read it. And you staged a coughing fit and walked away without a word. The message was, 'I'm choking on what you said.' But who knows? And why did you invite me if all you wanted was to run?"

Silence.

"Remember when you said you were going to California, for three weeks; 'I'll call you when I get back,' you said. 'I want to take you to din-ner.' *I loved you. I still love you.* I don't want to, but it's a curse. I bought a new dress, and you never called.

"That was May. So, I went to Eileen demanding answers, and finally she leveled. Effie was caught in your seductive web, like I was, but for ten years!

"'Go see her,' she said, 'and maybe it'll set you *both* free.' You were pissed when you got wind of it, because I spilled the beans, everything you did, and Effie went running to you, of course. I'm sick of your stories, the vortex of death or whatever."

"You see, Trudy, you twist things. Then you start talking. It gets back to me. I don't like what you're doing. You're doing me a lot of damage."

"The only one who can ruin your reputation is you. Don't you *dare* lay that on me. *You're* ruining you. A few months ago, this stranger calls, Bev, and says, 'Harry told me to call you.' How *dare* you?

"We met at the diner and I find out she's an incest victim, and she's telling me how she wants to fix you up with her sister because you're lonely. She worries 'cause you're despondent. You sent her to that foot reflexologist, that Marilyn, your best friend. And Marilyn told Bev all about your sex affair, how the woman was used up when you were through with her. The word was 'devoured.' They're saying you *devoured* her."

"Yeah, she talks too much. She tells things. I have to talk to her about that. What do you think of Bev? She picks up a lot, right? She's working on herself. She's doing good work."

"What kind of therapy is it when this poor woman is doing incest work and the whole thing is contaminated by your sexuality, your needs, your friends? Why should she have to picture you *devouring* a woman? That's not therapy. No way are you doing therapy."

Furious, now, I hurry to spill it all before he hangs up.

"Remember when you set me up for voice lessons with Lorna and I told you I don't want to study voice? The longer you work with her, the more confused she gets. Eighteen years ago she was not like this. She wants to die.

"Remember when you set me up to take care of Nancy, get her into AA, and I did, except you arranged for her to have sex with Larry? And she's married. Do you have any idea how she felt knowing he's telling *you* how *she* is in bed? She got sick over it. He's twenty years younger and homosexual. You knew that. Nancy told me you set him up to have sex with five of your women patients. *Five.* And he's impotent. *Shit.* What about HIV? What do you think the health department might say about that?

"What do you think happens when these people go somewhere else and find someone to help them after they leave you? Do you think therapists who hear these stories are referring you?"

"That gets twisted," he says. "Nancy met him to talk, and they had things in common. I connect patients. That's your interpretation. You twist things. That's where you get off track. See, I want to meet with you. Clear it. I can help you with that."

"*No*, goddamn it. She said she was horny and her husband was in Germany, and you laughed, 'You oughtta meet Larry. You're horny for young men; he's horny for older women.' *That's* what happened. She told me. And I heard from down at the social-work program at Fordham that a former patient was still trying to get over sex with you. She's warning others. That doesn't come from me. That's *your* stuff.

"Even June, who likes you, told me she went to a party and heard a woman, your daughter's teacher, say, 'Oh, yeah, Harry, he's a womanizer.' I hear things all over, and they're not coming from me."

"Well, I've always said I listen to you, Trudy, and I learn from you. Everything you say, I listen. When you confront me, I listen. And I'm doing it."

"I wish you were hearing me, but you're just like that ocean liner going along. Your own agenda."

"Who're you working now?" No preposition. I stifle a laugh.

"I worked with Mrs. S., and she wasn't trained, not for this problem. You know her?"

"At Norwalk Hospital?"

"Yes. So I went to this really good psychiatrist in Norwalk, and I said, 'OK, I want an evaluation and a referral. I want to know what's wrong with me and what I have to do to get better.'

"Harry, I couldn't even look at him and huddled in the chair. I never was like that. You know what he said right off? 'I've heard he's had sex with patients.'

"You know what else he said? 'Trudy, what's wrong with you is Brown. You went for treatment for being in Vietnam, and this guy took you *back* into Vietnam.'"

I didn't tell Harry that the psychiatrist also said, "I hope when you feel better you take civil action. Somebody should shut him down."

Harry is silent. I wait, but he doesn't hang up, so I tell him, "I'm working with another woman, now, and I'm getting better, but what you did—" For a moment, I can't speak. "You shredded my soul. I don't know if I'll ever heal."

"See, I want to help you with that. Heal that. Close that off." His voice is low, soft, inviting.

"No. You can't help me."

Epilogue

MY CASE WAS TAKEN BY THE MEDICAL MALPRACTICE law firm, Koskoff, Koskoff & Bieder. While one of the firm's typists began transcribing twenty-six-hour-long cassettes, Karen Koskoff arranged for me to be interviewed by other psychiatrists and set me to work gathering evidence. As I began making lists, I was appalled to discover that Harry had betrayed the confidences of at least fifty-four persons, mostly patients, many of whom I knew. After exhausting memory on that score, I tallied what Harry had caused me to spend on esoteric, spiritual, psychic, educational, New Age, and wacked-out conferences, sessions, consultations, lessons, classes, exercises, weird treatments, and healers over three years: seventeen thousand dollars.

Faced with so much evidence of malfeasance, I was forced, finally, to acknowledge the depth and breadth of his derangement—to say nothing of my own! What I could not believe was my attorney's insistence I was *legally* a victim of sexual abuse. My only *real* criterion was rape, and that never occurred.

On a parallel track, I was directed to submit evidence for censoring to the medical board in Hartford. Actually, their office "lost" some of our documents, much later "found" behind a file cabinet. To my surprise, we were not the first complainants but the second and third. I also went before the local board, in Norwalk, with another Harry victim, a man. Those physicians (one, I noticed, had been my family doctor) made us testify at the end of their monthly dinner meeting, and we did, weeping, while they enjoyed coffee, ice cream, and cake.

That I was able to enter therapy again—indeed to dress, drive, eat, sleep, and look for employment—is testimony to the person I *was* for fifty years. My new psychotherapist was a woman, of course, but when at times

I had to consult a male physician, my fear of submitting to an examination was so great, I wept.

My children always and in every way believed in me, in everything I said and did, and had such faith that I clung to them, for quite a while. They generously allowed for my lapses and ineptitude, for unrelenting grief and rage and spotty employment. I'm especially grateful for the times they quietly counseled against some occasional quick fix—moving to England, or to an island off the coast of Seattle, are examples.

Others who also knew me well were—and are—unable to accept reality. Countless stigmata are diagnostic of incest and full-blown PTSD, including flashbacks, nightmares, and the trembling terror occurring with any number of triggers, all of which I exhibited. To the deniers, I'm telling "lies" or I'm "psychotic." Given I was the queen of denial, I can hardly find it in myself to blame them.

Although I soon achieved full employment, attended and gave many parties, sang solos, went to weddings and funerals, wrote stories and books, painted portraits, made new friends, traveled abroad and across America, and even dated, I daily for fifteen years grieved the loss of the self I thought I knew—until I moved away, away from constant triggers.

After trekking to villages from Westchester to southern Vermont, I chose Bethel. Although only twenty miles from where I grew up, married, raised the kids, and worked, this hamlet might be among the bogs of Ireland, for all it reminds me of the past. Nestled in rolling hills, away from major arteries to Manhattan, Bethel remains unspoiled and unsophisticated. Thankfully it's only an hour north to one daughter, where I often see her twin, and an hour south to my sons.

By the time I moved to Bethel, I'd shed my resentments toward Harry and his coterie of women therapists and patients who thought so highly of him and not of me. But I needed more healing and soon engaged in another therapy, eye movement desensitization response (EMDR), which began dissolving the remaining stigmata at a much faster rate. With EMDR, one need not recall the worst—dig at it, relive it, or *prove* it—but instead visualize mildly disturbing, loosely related events while moving eyes right to left and back, crossing the midline of the brain. This powerful technique uncouples and releases those damnable depths of memory for which we have no words. I call it Roto-Rooter, because healing continued for years after EMDR therapy ended.

This is a sketchy description of what is often a series of rigorous two-hour sessions (following careful evaluation and preparation) devised originally for Vietnam vets with PTSD. Information is easily located on the web.

I cannot know, chapter and verse, exactly what happened to me, although I am aware my father came close to killing me three times. I do know he was certain he had the right to play out shockingly cruel notions, inflict pain and unnecessary punishment, and humiliate and express irrational hatred toward me as well as countless other innocents.

Odd as it may seem, I'm profoundly grateful to him for his many personal and financial sacrifices while I was growing up, and for preparing me for an intelligent and multifaceted adulthood by introducing countless worldly disciplines: ways to understand and assess politics and international events, familiarity with the world's greatest literature, close and detailed knowledge of classical music, and not least, the value of hard work in school, at home, and on our small farm, where we produced an abundance of the purist comestibles, from honey to lamb shanks, applesauce to bacon, pickles to pot roast.

As for Harry, I appreciate his efforts to reparent and heal me, as he so often claimed he was doing; his frustration at my inability to recover and depart. He must have hated my obsession, my dogged attacks on his methods, recommendations, and overtures, and to his credit, he rarely got angry. He suffered, unfortunately, from seemingly untreatable massive confusion and a need to seduce, then inflict pain.

On a much happier note, a follow-up on two important others: "Kurt," our children's loving and extremely dedicated father, passed away after a long and excellent life, and left me an amazing gift, for which I will always be grateful. "Walter" passed away in a VA hospital in New Hampshire, but not before I thanked him for loving me before, during, and long after our marriage.

You may think it strange that I don't regret life with my father or therapy with Harry Brown. Perhaps it's faith in God as well as faith in myself. I feel compassion for adults losing faith after terrible events. I never lost mine. Also, I've had good teachers: my books.

William Faulkner, on the last page of his novel *The Sound and the Fury*, lists those who came through—TP, Frony, Luster, Dilsey—and the reason: "They endured." Faulkner's final words. Sometimes simply enduring is enough.

He doesn't talk about forgiveness. I also do not like the word "forgive." It's often tossed like cheap candy at sufferers. Too many persons battered me with that word when I was too thin to work, seeing no way out except through death. Better, I think now, to know I come from God and, like everyone else, have been given tasks to overcome, one of which is letting go of wanting others to behave as I think they should—or should have. Perhaps I learned this from another teacher.

Viktor Frankl tells us in *Man's Search for Meaning* that while interred in a concentration camp, he decided not only to endure but also survive. He knew he did not have ultimate control over that, but he saw many around him give up, fall in on themselves. Instead he fought, often only interiorly, because for him life had to be larger than grieving for his wife and family, nobler than submitting to starvation and humiliation. He recognized that his task—his God-given human assignment—was to survive that he might write, teach, and love.

That he might tell.

NOTES

Incidence of Female Sexual Abuse in General

- Forty million women—one in four—are sexually abused in childhood and by definition have post-traumatic stress disorder (PTSD). Such persons have difficulty setting limits and boundaries in protection of their own egos or against those who wish to harm them or injure their interpersonal space, particularly persons in authority. These women are the fish in a barrel, as one survivor aptly named her book.

- Close to 100 percent of females in an inpatient program for drug and alcohol abuse have been sexually abused as children, a large, vulnerable subset that in recovery seeks therapy.

The Potential for Psychiatric Sexual Abuse

- Forty-six thousand psychiatrists have been board certified since the thirties. Assuming many died or don't practice, of the remainder, 70 percent have had at least one patient reporting a forbidden-zone relationship with a former therapist; 70 percent of, let's say, even thirty thousand, is a large number—and does not include licensed and unlicensed counselors.

- Eight percent of therapists do not report abuse to authorities.

- Abusers know that 96 percent of victims will not expose them.

About Books by and for Psychiatrists and Psychotherapists

Often not found in public libraries or their search engines, books on psychiatric sexual abuse of patients are available on interlibrary loan, *if* you know they exist (see references). Most are also available online.

Unlike incidences of reported clergy abuse, still receiving massive publicity, therapist abuse, when reported, remains largely hidden. Unfortunately, many psychiatrists, as well as Catholic priests, are repeat abusers, some in stunning numbers.[1] Although psychiatrists lobby against colleagues' unethical behavior, as recently as thirty years ago, some therapists were still suggesting sex with patients is therapeutic.

A 1975 American Psychiatric Association (APA) study states that "many" therapists treat women patients as sex objects.[2] Harvard psychiatrist Nanette Gartrell left the APA in protest of her colleagues' failure to report knowledge of sexual abuse of female patients. When Judith Herman, also of Harvard, attempted to get the Psychoanalytic Society to impose sanctions on a psychiatrist who exploited a female patient, she was told: "Doctor, we are not a consumer organization."[3] In 1990, she protested again: "[T]he see-no-evil, hear-no-evil stance on therapists' misconduct just won't do anymore."[4]

---

1   R. Z. Folman, "Therapist-Patient Sex: Attraction and Boundary Problems," *Psychotherapy* 28 (1991): 168–73; J. Herman et al, "Psychiatrist-Patient Sexual Contact. Results of a National Survey, I: Prevalence," *American Journal of Psychiatry* 144 (1987): 164–9; C. Bohmer, *The Wages of Seeking Help: Sexual Exploitation by Professionals* (Westport, CT: Praeger, 2000).

2   The American Psychiatric Association (APA) Task Force on Sex Bias and Sex Role Stereotyping in Psychotherapy, 1975.

3   A. Bass, "Sexual Abuse—The Tide Is Turning," *The Boston Globe,* (18 June 1990): 30.

4   Ibid., 29.

The psychiatrist Judd Marmor dryly observed that his colleagues write a great deal about the seductive patient but nothing about the seductive therapist.[5] Hays, in "Sexual Contact between Psychotherapist and Patient: Legal Remedies," laments: "It is doubtful that the unethical sexual contact will decrease."[6] In 2000, Carol Bohmer wrote: "I do not believe that the professional sexual misconduct movement will ever be widely recognized and well-financed…or that those professionals will 'come to be shunned by their colleagues, instead of supported.'"[7]

Unfortunately, the works of psychotherapists and psychiatrists such as the above as well as Carolyn Bates, Peter Rutter, Susan Penfold, and Kenneth Pope, among others, rarely reach the public. Victim's exposés are rare.

More than thirty years ago, Lucy Freeman and Julie Roy revealed an incestuous psychiatrist in *Betrayal: The True Story of the First Woman to Successfully Sue Her Psychiatrist for Using Sex in the Guise of Therapy*, followed by its TV special.[8]

Not until fifteen years later did another memoir appear, *You Must Be Dreaming*. Barbara Noël, with Kathryn Watterson, exposed the honorary life president of the World Association for Social Psychiatry, Jules Masserman, MD, as Ms. Noël's "sodium amytal therapist," a man who drugged and raped her during her sessions.[9]

After that widely publicized book and its television redaction, virtually everyone in the United States knew what Masserman had done to Ms.

5   J. Marmor, *Psychiatry in Transition: Selected Papers* (New York: Brunner/Mazel, 1974).

6   J. R. Hays, "Sexual Contact between Psychotherapist and Patient: Legal Remedies," *Psychological Reports* 47 (1980): 1247–54.

7   C. Bohmer, *The Wages of Seeking Help*, 59.

8   L. Freeman and J. Roy, *Betrayal: The True Story of the First Woman to Successfully Sue Her Psychiatrist for Using Sex in the Guise of Therapy* (New York: Stein and Day, 1976).

9   B. Noël with K. Watterson, *You Must Be Dreaming* (New York: Poseidon Press, 1992).

Noël and a number of other patients. Yet no peer testified against him. Furthermore, he was then honored at the eleventh World Congress for Social Psychiatry, where he received an outpouring of affection and praise. His license was suspended for five years. He and his wife, Charlotte Masserman, authored a book rebuttal, *Sexual Accusations and Social Turmoil*, in which "a world-famous psychiatrist falsely accused by a former patient, describes his ordeal…"[10]

Christopher Hyde, in his 1991 *Abuse of Trust: The Career of Dr. James Tyhurst*, divulges Tyhurst's disturbing habits: sexual abuse, master-slave rituals, and flogging. That same year, on the twelfth of November, PBS's Frontline ran a TV profile, "My Doctor, My Lover," revealing three years of sexual exploitation of psychiatrist Melissa Roberts-Henry by Denver psychiatrist Jason Richter. Although he confessed, he retained his license, his colleagues continued to refer, and his practice did not suffer. The victim's practice did, however, and that of her subsequent psychiatrist; both were forced to relocate.[11]

Exposing the high incidence of psychotherapist abuse is hampered by patients' vulnerability and, understandably, their unwillingness to expose everything about themselves. A look at patient populations explains the first.

The sitting ducks—or the fish in a barrel[12]—are a large patient subgroup, usually women who've endured early sexual and emotional abuse and thus doubt their own rights, particularly sexual. These are the very persons likely to seek relief in therapy. They have difficulty with boundaries and limits in protection of their own egos, and difficulty setting realistic

---

10   J. H. Masserman and C. M. Masserman, *Sexual Accusations and Social Turmoil: What Can Be Done* (Regent Press. 1994).

11   M. Beck, K. Springen, and D. Foote, "Sex and Psychotherapy," *Newsweek*, (April 13, 1992): 52–57.

12   G. Tower, *Fish in a Barrel: A True Story of Sexual Abuse in Therapy* (Salt Lake City: American Book Publishing, 2005).

limitations on persons who wish to injure their interpersonal space. In short, they are vulnerable to persons who wish to harm them.[13]

Memoirs of Psychiatric Sexual Abuse

2005: Grace Tower's *Fish in a Barrel*

1997: Paulette Trumpi's *Doctors Who Rape: Malpractice and Misogyny*

1992: Barbara Noël with Kathryn Watterson's *You Must Be Dreaming*

1991: Christopher Hyde's *Abuse of Trust*

1986: Evelyn Walker and Perry Deane Young's *A Killing Cure*

1986: Ellen Plasil's *Therapist*

1976: Lucy Freeman and Julie Roy's *Betrayal: The True Story of the First Woman to Successfully Sue Her Psychiatrist for Using Sex in the Guise of Therapy.*

Help for the Sexually Abused

- Aching Heart—a website resource for women survivors of sexual abuse and incest

- After Silence—a message board for survivors of rape and sexual abuse

- Angels in the Night—a support site for children of sexual abuse

- Angels of a Golden Sky—a support board for adults who were sexually abused in childhood

---

13   K. S. Pope and J. Bouhoutsos, *Sexual Intimacies between Therapists and Patients* (New York: Praeger, 1986).

- Becoming Gold—a virtual support network for survivors of childhood sexual abuse that encourages balance in the healing process through creativity, education, and support

- Butterfly Gardens—a site dedicated to victims/survivors of sexual abuse and incest

- Covenant of Light—a site designed for rape or sexual abuse survivors who are raising children conceived by rape or sexual abuse

- Dancing in the Darkness—a site offering help and support for survivors of rape and sexual abuse, a safe place to share stories, hope, and courage

- Gentle Touch's Web—a site that offers a comprehensive list of references and resources for survivors of all forms of abuse

- Healing from Abuse—a site that seeks to address the unique issues of the emotionally, physically, and sexually abused via a chat room, helpful links, book recommendations, support groups, Healing Steps, and more

- Healing Minds—a site dedicated to survivors of abuse and sexual assault

- The Hope of Survivors—a site that provides support, hope, and encouragement for victims of clergy sexual abuse and misconduct

- Journey to Freedom—a site offering hope and healing for victims and survivors of child sexual abuse and sexual assault

- Journey to Healing—a site that offers help and healing for sexual abuse, incest, and rape victims

- Kingdom Abuse Survivors Project—a resource for survivors of childhood sexual abuse in the form of forums, chat rooms, help, and advice

- The Linkup—a site offering support and recovery for victims of clergy sexual abuse

- Miss Kitty's Place—a site offering useful information for victims, abusers, and survivors

- My Twisted Sukha—a site that deals with the affects of sexual abuse by a female perpetrator

- Nana's Nook—a sanctuary for abused children of any age, creed, or color

- Safe Haven—a site for survivors of sexual abuse and rape, including personal stories, poetry, tips, advice on coping day to day, and an interactive message forum

- Secrets No More—a site that gives survivors of sexual abuse the information they need to recover, cope, and move forward with their lives

- Survivors—stories, writings, links, and resources for survivors of sexual assault

- Survivors Chat—a support site with chat rooms, and resources for survivors of rape, incest, and sexual abuse

- The Survivors Forum—a site that offers chat rooms, forums, and other resources for survivors of sexual abuse

- Survivors of Abuse in Religion (SOAR)—an online support group for survivors of sexual abuse in any religion

- Survivors of Green—dedicated to survivors of Dr. Green, guilty of multiple counts of indecent assault against male patients, Loughborough, Leicestershire

- Survivors Sanctuary—a safe place of support and resources for survivors of sexual, mental, or physical abuse, regardless of gender

- True Perspective of Sexual Trauma—information on blame, therapy, dissociation, and anger, including resources, predator types, and behavior patterns

- Whitedoves' Nest—a site dedicated to sexual abuse survivors and their supporters where you can share your story, poetry, art, books, and tips on recovery

Plus these websites:

- http://www.helpabusedwomen.org

- Betty Griffin House: http://www.bettygriffinhouse.org

- Loudoun Abused Women's Shelter, Naples, Florida: http://www.loudoun-net.com/laws

Bibliography

Bates, C. M., and A. M. Brodsky. *Sex in the Therapy Hour: A Case of Professional Incest*. New York: Guilford Press, 1989. These authors name the victim yet protect the name of the abuser, Dr. X, despite his rampant and repeated offenses.

Bisbing, S. B., L. M. Jorgenson, and P. K. Sutherland. *Sexual Abuse by Professionals: A Legal Guide*. Charlottesville, Virginia: The Michie Co., 2000. This comprehensive guide for attorneys handling therapist sexual exploitation cases is written by a PsyD and two attorneys.

Bloom, J. D., C. C. Nadelson, and M. T. Notman. *Physician Sexual Misconduct*. Washington, DC: American Psychiatric Press, 1999. These essays by therapists and patients shed light on the ethical, legal, educational, and therapeutic problems that arise when boundaries are crossed.

Bohmer, C. *The Wages of Seeking Help: Sexual Exploitation by Professionals*. Westport, Connecticut: Praeger, 2000. The author addresses the effects that the male dominated field of psychiatry has had on professional and lay women's ability to address and redress the problem.

Bridges, N. A. *Moving Beyond the Comfort Zone in Psychotherapy*. Lanham, Maryland: Jason Aronson, 2005. This more fluid approach to therapeutic boundaries suggests that maintaining patient safety is possible.

Burgess, A. W., and C. R. Hartman, eds. *Sexual Exploitation of Patients by Health Professionals*. New York: Praeger, 1986.

Dorpat, T. L. *Gaslighting, the Double Whammy, Interrogation, and Other Methods of Covert Control in Psychotherapy and Analysis.* Lanham, Maryland: Jason Aronson, 1996. The author shows how control and manipulation of patients can lead to intentional and unintentional abuse, from lack of respect to gross malpractice.

Freeman, L., and J. Roy. *Betrayal: The True Story of the First Woman to Successfully Sue Her Psychiatrist for Using Sex in the Guise of Therapy.* New York: Stein and Day, 1976. Therapist Hartog's cure for patient Roy's worry that she might be homosexual was a sexual relationship with him.

Freidman, J., and M. M. Boumil. *Betrayal of Trust: Sex and Power in Professional Relationships.* New York: Praeger, 1995. Also, Kindle Edition. The authors provide insight into why vulnerable women are subject to sexual exploitation by psychiatrists, doctors, lawyers, clergy, and educators.

Gabbard, G. O., and E. P. Lester. *Boundaries and Boundary Violations in Psychoanalysis.* Washington, DC: American Psychiatric Press, 1989. This series of essays by leading professionals explores all aspects of boundary violations.

Gartrell, N. *Bringing Ethics Alive: Feminist Ethics in Psychotherapy Practice.* Philadelphia: Haworth Press, 1997. Gartrell addresses many boundary issues, including those of women who having difficulty learning to say no.

Giovacchini, P. *The Impact of Narcissism: The Errant Therapist on a Chaotic Quest.* Lanham, Maryland: Jason Aronson, 2000. The risks of transference and counter-transference with the narcissistic patient are explored.

Herman, J. L. *Trauma and Recovery: The Aftermath of Violence—From Domestic Abuse to Political Power.* New York: Basic Books, 1992.

Hyde, C. *Abuse of Trust: The Destructive Career of Dr. James Tyhurst.* Vancouver: Douglas and McIntyre, 1991. Hyde exposes Tyhurst's sexual abuse, master-slave rituals, and flogging.

Jehu, D. *Patients as Victims: Sexual Abuse in Psychotherapy and Counseling.* New Jersey: John Wiley & Sons, 1994. Discussions of risk factors for abused patients and abusing therapists in North America and Britain include the preconditions necessary for such abuse.

Kelley, J. L. *Psychiatric Malpractice: Stories of Patients, Psychiatrists, and the Law.* New Jersey: Rutgers University Press, 1996. Attorney Kelly writes as one who defended malpractice cases and who also brought his own.

Lott, D. A. *In Session: The Bond between Women and Their Therapists.* New York: WH Freeman & Co., 1999. For the woman asking, "How can I have been so stupid?" here are some definitive answers.

Lowen, A. *Bioenergetics: The Revolutionary Therapy That Uses the Language of the Body to Heal the Problems of the Mind.* New York: Penguin Books, 1976.

McNamara, E. *Breakdown: Sex, Suicide, and the Harvard Psychiatrist.* New York: Pocket Books, 1994. Although the Boston psychiatric establishment ran to Dr. Bean-Bayog's defense, she paid one million to the family of her victim (he committed suicide) and surrendered her license rather than face trial.

Myers, W. A. *Shrink Dreams: The Secret Longings, Fantasies, and Prejudices of Therapists and How They Affect Their Patients.* New York: Simon & Schuster, 1992. A daring look at the all-too-human therapist—with a warning for therapists and patients alike.

Noël, B., with K. Watterson. *You Must Be Dreaming*. New York: Poseidon Press, 1992. This gifted musician, drugged into near oblivion, fought the psychiatric establishment long and hard to expose her abuser, Jules Masserman, MD, past president of the Illinois Psychiatric Society.

Penfold, P. S. *Sexual Abuse by Health Professionals: A Personal Search for Meaning and Healing*. Canada: University of Toronto Press, 1998. Herself a victim, Dr. Penfold is in the unique position of combining personal experience with her professional life and her scholarship.

Peterson, M. R. *At Personal Risk: Boundary Violations in Professional-Client Relationships*. Westport, Connecticut: Praeger, 1995. The author and her clients share insights and stories concerning four subtle boundary violations: role reversals, secrets, double binds, and giving privileges.

Plasil, E. *Therapist: The Shocking Autobiography of a Woman Sexually Exploited by Her Analyst*. New York: St. Martin's/Marek, 1985. This beautifully written personal account describes how cult abuse, for that's how many will see it, rendered Dr. Lonnie Leonard's control over his patients nearly complete.

Pope, K. S. *Sexual Involvement with Therapists: Patient Assessment, Subsequent Therapy, Forensics*. Washington, DC: American Psychological Association, 1994. This lucid, detailed, and humane treatment includes resources for attorneys and witnesses.

Pope, K. S., and J. Bouhoutsos. *Sexual Intimacy between Therapists and Patients*. New York: Praeger, 1986. These profiles of therapists and patients at risk for boundary violations are instructive for professionals and patients.

Russell, J. *Out of Bounds: Sexual Exploitation in Counseling and Therapy*. Thousand Oaks, California: Sage Publications, 1993. Because the potential for patient sexual abuse ought never to be ignored, this author, after interviewing 40 patients thus abused, offers suggestions for changes in how therapy is conducted.

Rutter, P. *Sex in the Forbidden Zone*. Los Angeles: Jeremy P. Tarcher, 1989. Drawing on one thousand case histories, Dr. Rutter reveals the hidden epidemic of abuses of power in male-female relationships and explores what drives professionals to risk all and patients to succumb.

Schoener, G. R., et al. *Psychotherapists' Sexual Involvement with Clients: Intervention and Prevention*. University of Michigan, 1989. At 837 pages, this tome is the gold standard for understanding and dealing with boundary violations, their sequelae, and remedies.

Shepard, M. *The Love Treatment: Sexual Intimacy between Patients and Psychotherapists*. New York: Peter Wyden, 1971.

Tower, G. *Fish in a Barrel: A True Story of Sexual Abuse in Therapy*. Salt Lake City: American Book Publishing, 2005. This is a profoundly moving account of power lost and regained.

Trumpi, P. *Doctors Who Rape: Malpractice and Misogyny*. Rochester, Vermont: Schenkman Books, 1997. Drugged, raped, and inseminated by her trusted psychiatrist, Pauline Trumpi endured farcical legal trauma resulting in surrendering her child for adoption.

Walker, E., and T. D. Young. *A Killing Cure*. New York: Henry Holt, 1986. The author reveals drug and sexual abuse at the hands of Dr. Zane Parzen.

About the Author

Trudy Seagraves was a medical editor, writer, and copywriter for over two decades, a soprano soloist for many more, and is a portrait artist. Her stories have appeared in many literary journals, including *Aethlon*, *MacGuffin* (first prize), and *So To Speak*.

In 1993 Ms. Seagraves participated in a research project, *Sexual Involvement between Health and Mental Health Care Providers and Their Clients*, sponsored by the UMass Department of Sociology. Responding to Estelle Disch, PhD, principal investigator, Ms. Seagraves sent a synopsis of her treatment with Harry Brown. She also named Brown when she spoke at a Connecticut Governor's Conference on Victims of Crime.

In 1992, after Ms. Seagraves and one of the other complainants against Brown went before the Fairfield County Medical Board to no effect, she agreed to an interview by a Fairfield County weekly.[14] Its front page, "Prescribing Sex: *Did* Psychiatrist Harry Brown Sexually Abuse a Female Patient—in the Name of 'Bioenergetics'?" refers to a two-page spread.

---

14   S. Elan, "Prescribing Sex: *Did* Psychiatrist Harry Brown Sexually Abuse a Female Patient—in the Name of 'Bioenergetics'?," *Fairfield County Advocate*, April 23—April 29, 1992.